Media, Markets & Public Spheres

The European Science Foundation (ESF) is an independent, non-governmental organisation, the members of which are 80 national funding agencies, research-performing agencies, academies and learned societies from 30 countries.

The strength of ESF lies in the influential membership and in its ability to bring together the different domains of European science in order to meet the challenges of the future.

Since its establishment in 1974, ESF, which has its headquarters in Strasbourg with offices in Brussels and Ostend, has assembled a host of organisations that span all disciplines of science, to create a common platform for cross-border cooperation in Europe.

ESF is dedicated to promote collaboration in scientific research, funding of research and science policy across Europe. Through its activities and instruments ESF has made major contributions to science in a global context. The ESF covers the following scientific domains:

- Humanities
- Life, Earth and Environmental Sciences
- Medical Sciences
- Physical and Engineering Sciences
- Social Sciences
- Marine Sciences
- Nuclear Physics
- Polar Sciences
- Radio Astronomy Frequencies
- Space Sciences

Media, Markets & Public Spheres
European Media at the Crossroads

Edited by Jostein Gripsrud and Lennart Weibull

intellect Bristol, UK / Chicago, USA

First published in the UK in 2010 by
Intellect, The Mill, Parnall Road, Fishponds, Bristol, BS16 3JG, UK

First published in the USA in 2010 by
Intellect, The University of Chicago Press, 1427 E. 60th Street,
Chicago, IL 60637, USA

A catalogue record for this book is available from the
British Library.

Cover designer: Holly Rose
Copy-editor: Heather Owen
Typesetting: Mac Style, Beverley, E. Yorkshire

ISBN 978-1-84150-305-9

Printed and bound by Gutenberg Press, Malta.

Contents

Foreword

This volume is the product of a major programme under the title Changing Media – Changing Europe supported by the European Science Foundation (ESF). This programme was the first to be sponsored by both the Social Sciences and the Humanities Standing Committees of the ESF, and this unique cross-disciplinary organization reflects the very broad and central concerns which shaped the Programme's work. As co-chairpersons of the Programme it was our great delight to bring together many of the very best scholars from across the continent, but also across the disciplinary divides which so often fragment our work, to enable stimulating, innovative, and profoundly important debates addressed to understanding some of the most fundamental and critical aspects of contemporary social and cultural life.

The study of the media in Europe forces us to try to understand the major institutions which foster understanding and participation in modern societies. At the same time we have to recognize that these societies themselves are undergoing vital changes, as political associations and alliances, demographic structures, the worlds of work, leisure, domestic life, mobility, education, politics and communications themselves are all undergoing important transformations. Part of that understanding, of course, requires us not to be too readily seduced by the magnitude and brilliance of technological changes into assuming that social changes must comprehensively follow. A study of the changing media in Europe, therefore, is indeed a study of changing Europe. Research on media is closely linked to questions of economic and technological growth and expansion, but also to questions of public policy and the state, and more broadly to social, economic and cultural issues.

To investigate these very large debates the Programme was organised around four key questions. The first, the major focus of this present volume, dealt with the tension between citizenship and consumerism, that is the relation between media, the public sphere and the market; the challenges facing the media, cultural policy and the public service media in Europe. The second area of work focused on the dichotomy and relation between culture and commerce, and the conflict in media policy caught between cultural aspirations and commercial imperatives. The third question addressed the problems of convergence and fragmentation in relation to the development of media technology on a global and European level. This led to questions about the concepts of the information society, the network society etc., and to a focus on 'new' media such as the internet and multimedia, and the impact of these on society, culture, and our work, education and everyday life. The fourth field of inquiry was concerned with media and cultural identities and the relationship between processes of homogenization and diversity. This explored the role of media in everyday life, questions of gender, ethnicity, lifestyle, social differences, and cultural identities in relation to both media audiences and media content.

In each of the books arising from this exciting Programme we expect readers to learn something new, but above all to be provoked into fresh thinking, understanding and inquiry, about how the media and Europe are both changing in novel, profound, and far reaching ways that bring us to the heart of research and discussion about society and culture in the twenty-first century.

Ib Bondebjerg
Peter Golding

Preface

As arenas and agents in the public sphere, the media are central to political and cultural life, thereby decisively influencing most social areas – from the socialization of children to the workings of the economy. This is why the media are also the focus of so much attention and debate – in the media themselves and in day-to-day conversation among people. This book is about the development of European mass media and the public sphere that they form a constitutive part of. It has a rare comparative perspective, both across nation states and across decades of European history.

Work on the book started from the idea that it is both useful and possible to establish a degree of empirical overview of both major general trends and some of the national differences in European media developments over the last 40–50 years. Using a sample of so-called popular and 'quality' European newspapers and their TV listings as a stepping stone, a team of leading media researchers from 10 countries here present overviews of structural changes in press and broadcasting as well as in-depth analyses of a number of specific areas – within a non-dogmatic theoretical framework inspired by the historical and analytical category of 'the public sphere'.

The book is thus a report on a unique collaborative research effort. It also provides a highly useful concretization in relation to the theory of the public sphere, the most central approach to the question of media and democracy. It is furthermore, and perhaps most of all, a contribution to the charting of the plurality of histories and socio-cultural forms that is commonly referred to as 'Europe'. It will thus be suitable course literature for a variety of courses in media and communication studies, European studies of different sorts as well as courses in social sciences such as sociology and political science.

Peter Dahlgren's introductory chapter, 'Public spheres, societal shifts and media modulations', presents a theoretical framework for the book. Its point of departure is the development of European democracies since around 1960. It focuses on power drifts and cultural shifts before it goes in-depth into media development trends, e.g. deregulation, globalization, concentration and digitalization. Changes in European public spheres are analysed against this background. Three dimensions are especially discussed – the structural, the representational and the interactional – mostly in line with a Habermasian tradition. The conclusion is that on the one hand the media criticism formulated by Habermas is still valid, on the other hand postmodern media give more people access to media contents. However, the author concludes, what this means for European democracy is an open question.

The section on 'structures' opens with Lennart Weibull & Åsa Nilsson's 'Four Decades of European Newspapers: Structure and Content', a chapter which presents the development of the contents of the leading European newspapers since 1960. The point of departure is the roots of the European press and its structural changes until the late 1960s. The basic dimensions – political, cultural and geographical – of the European newspaper markets are analysed. Against this background the changes in newspaper content are presented. The study covers the leading quality as well as the leading popular papers and includes volume, e.g. number of pages; form, e.g. sections or supplements; and traditional contents, e.g. business, culture and sports. The chapter argues that there is an ongoing tabloidization within the European press, and that the traditional distinction between quality and popular is blurred.

In the following chapter, '50 years of European television: an essay', Jostein Gripsrud attempts to provide an overview of key developments in television from its pioneering phase in the 30s, 40s and 50s, over its classical phase in the 60s and 70s to its third phase, one of commercialization but also of diversification. The chapter ends with a discussion of the role of television in the twenty-first century, where the medium exists in a sort of symbiosis with the Internet.

The last part of Gripsrud's chapter points toward the theme of the following section, which has been called *Intermedia* since it is about the relations between different media – in the life of individuals and societies. The first piece here, entitled 'The public reception of early television: When television was new in the Nordic countries', is co-authored by Taisto Hujanen and Lennart Weibull. The aim of the chapter is to provide an understanding of how newspapers treated the new medium of television in the 1960s and 1970s. It is based on close reading of both quality and popular newspapers in Denmark, Finland and Sweden for one week in October 1960 and one week in 1970. All types of content are studied, including advertising. On the basis of the results it is argued that in the 1960s especially the popular press strongly interacted with television, making journalism out of TV-programming, whereas the quality press treated TV more as a political phenomenon. A decade later there was little difference, mainly because of the social integration of the medium.

Juha Herkman takes as his point of departure in his 'Televisualization of the popular press: An eye-catching trend of the late twentieth century's media' the discussion on the so-called visualization of culture since the late twentieth century. The focus is on what is called televisualization, which means the specific kind of visualization that was realized largely in European popular newspapers during the 1990s. In short, televisualization refers mainly to television's impact on the 1990s' popular press. The chapter analyses various implications of televisualization for the popular press, using mainly the Finnish popular press from 1960 to 2000 as an example. Further, the scope is widened and linked to the development of tabloidization and commercialization of the media. The conclusion is that televisualization must be understood as a cultural phenomenon closely related to deregulation policies and technological convergence in late twentieth-century Europe.

Herkman's concluding remarks provide a good lead-in to the following section, which is about (media) policies. In the first chapter here, John Corner's 'British media and regulatory change: The antinomies of policy', the aim is to examine some of the significant changes to the organization of the media as public institutions that have occurred in Britain over the last four to five decades. The focus is on the interplay between what is called the 'public frame' and the 'market frame' occurring in the organization and practice of the media. The focus is on the development of British media policy in the area of broadcasting, but newspaper concentration is also discussed. It is concluded that British media are now much more firmly located in the 'market frame' than was the case in the 1960s. Largely, this is due to the gradual weakening of the 'public frame' for broadcasting over the same period, a trend accelerating during the 1990s when programmes shifted towards a stronger commodity status despite the initially quite robust public regulation.

Josiane Jouët follows with the chapter 'French media, policy regulation and public sphere'. It aims to provide a synthetic overview of the major changes that have affected the French media and public sphere over the last four decades. It argues that today's mediatized public sphere results from fundamental changes since 1960. It describes the very rapid differentiation of the French radio and television channels since the 1970s as well as the declining popularity of daily newspapers and the stability of the fragmented magazine market. The chapter discusses the role of political decisions behind the break-up of the state monopoly in broadcasting, which was paralleled by the emergence of a neo-liberal economy that facilitated media concentration and the development of marketing techniques. It concludes that the withdrawal of the state from the control of media has been encouraged by a number of public policies which have varied depending on the makeup of the government. Finally there is a discussion of the role of the media in French public debate.

Turkey is on the margins of the European continent but also part of it and tied to it in a myriad of ways. Mine Gencel Bek contributes a chapter entitled 'Changing media and public sphere in Turkey: The role of the state, market and the EU candidacy'. She maps the media scene, considering the concentration and conglomeration of the media, a developing advertising industry, and increasing competition. She also examines the ways in which big media groups cooperate to increase profits, and the ways in which they influence national politics. The pluralism and democracy claims of the 1980s are seen in light of the emergence of private television channels. The state and market dichotomy is considered here in terms of how the commercial media positioned themselves as multiple and diverse alternatives to state uniformity. The chapter concludes by evaluating the changes in legal regulations and the effects of the EU candidacy in the 2000s on the changing public sphere in Turkey.

In the following section, called *Contents: records of cultural change*, several contributions take a closer look at the actual contents of European media over a period of 40–50 years. The article co-authored by Daniel Bilereyst and Lieve Desmet, 'Reconsidering the paradox of parochialism and the shrinking news agenda', deals with the increasing concern and debate about a growing parochialism or a shrinking news agenda in Western news media. It points to an interesting paradox between, on the one hand, a pervasive discourse on globalization and, on the other hand, an often-feared decline in foreign and international news in the major news media. The chapter describes some central issues in the study of foreign/international news research before discussing the paradox of parochialism/globalization. In the second part it presents some comparative research projects on the issue. Results concerning the foreign news contents of a so-called quality paper as well as a so-called popular paper are presented, showing among other things that the popular paper decreased its output of harder political-economic foreign news both in quantitative and qualitative terms. The chapter ends with a discussion of some ideas about the threat of a growing information divide along the lines of differences in education and cultural capital.

We then turn to Eastern Europe, where Wieslaw Godzic, in 'Fakty vs. Wiadomości: On competition and confusion in Polish TV news', tells the story of the introduction of competition between television channels and, specifically, TV news programmes. The radical transformation of the media systems and public spheres of Eastern European countries since 1989 has many consequences, central among which is the introduction of commercial television competing with reformed versions of old state broadcasters. This chapter is a thoroughgoing analysis of the relations between the main newscasts of Polish public and commercial television respectively. It thus provides highly interesting insights into the past and, in particular, the present Eastern European mediascape and usefully challenges some of the traditional preconceptions of Western European media and communication research.

Dominique Pasquier's contribution, 'When the elite press meets the rise of commercial culture', asks if press coverage of culture can be a good indicator of changes in cultural hierarchies and the recognition or status of art. The analysis is based on a study on the evolution of the designated cultural pages in a sample of European popular and elite dailies selected from 1960, 1980 and 2000. The focus is less on the quantitative changes than on qualitative evolutions. The results, based on analyses of French, Italian and British quality newspapers, show that the ways in which the press deals with culture has gone through obvious transformations in the topics covered, in the ways of tackling them, and in the modes of presentation. These transformations relate to general changes in the press that are not necessarily specific to culture, such as the systematization of specialized headings or the rise of visuals. Yet they also express and refer to new approaches to culture in Western societies, less reverent toward the high-brow humanist tradition and more concerned with media-linked cultural forms.

Klaus Bruhn Jensen and Peter Larsen follows Pasquier's analysis with their co-authored chapter: 'The sounds of change: representations of music in European newspapers 1960–2000'. If any one field may be said to articulate and symbolize the reconfiguration of 'culture' in Europe during the post-1945 period, it is music. Rock and roll became an integral resource of citizenship as understood by anti-authoritarian movements from the 1960s onwards; it also served as an object and a vehicle in the intensified commercialization of culture. Simultaneously, the place of other musical forms in society at large was in for re-examination as part of public and political debate across the high-low divide. Jensen and Larsen explore the representation and redefinition of music as a set of cultural forms, as reflected in the newspapers of major European countries since 1960. Focusing on the years 1960, 1980, and 2000, the analysis identifies key political issues and cultural themes which have been associated variously with 'classical', jazz, and rock music. Following an overview of coverage with reference to its placement either in separate sections or as a constituent of other news coverage, as well as a comparison of countries in this respect, the chapter gives special attention to conceptions of music as art, as a political practice, and as a communicative phenomenon that traverses all media. In this light, music remains a challenge still to be met by media and communication research, also in view of the emergence of new soundscapes in digital settings. Hence, the chapter concludes by outlining a research agenda on music and sound generally for the media field.

This section, and the book as well, is then rounded off by Graham Murdock's diagnostic analysis, 'Celebrity culture and the public sphere: The tabloidization of power'. He explores the shifts in what is called the visibility culture by looking in more detail at the portrayal of stars, celebrities, politicians and corporate leaders in popular photo journalism since about 1960. The point of departure is the development of photo journalism at the beginning of twentieth century. The analysis is based on a close reading of the two major British daily tabloid titles, the *Daily Mirror*, the first paper in the world to base its appeal primarily around its use of photographs, and the *Sun*, owned for most of the period in question by one of the leading media moguls, Rupert Murdoch, and the most successful daily tabloid in the world. It concludes that the rise of celebrity culture provides a powerful counter-force to this revivification of the public sphere, and, as the market in voter loyalties has become increasingly volatile, politicians have had to devote more and more time to building and marketing brand identities.

We sincerely hope readers will appreciate the book's moving back and forth between big theoretical issues and more or less colourful, detailed, concrete renditions of the highly complex, interlaced set of histories we refer to as European media history. As we move further into the digital era, knowledge of our past will only become more useful – and even necessary.

Paris and Gothenburg on 4 April 2009
Jostein Gripsrud and Lennart Weibull

Part I

A Theoretical Perspective

Chapter 1

Public Spheres, Societal Shifts and Media Modulations

Peter Dahlgren
Lund University

W orking with a wide brush and broad strokes, this chapter aims to sketch a few key themes in the evolution of mediated public spheres in Europe in the period between 1960 and 2000. The perspective taken will set these changes against the background of structural alterations within European society, with an emphasis on the health of democracy. The period 1960–2000 incorporates many different national narratives within Europe, and here I will only be able at best to make reference to a few prominent vectors of social change. Yet, we will still be able to elucidate important patterns of evolution within the public spheres and the mass media's role within them.

I begin by briefly retracing the original arguments of Jürgen Habermas in regard to the public sphere to have as a sort of analytic yardstick to apply in the following discussion. From there I sketch some of the more significant features of transformation in the social landscape. Thereafter I turn to structural themes in the development of the media. The latter part of the presentation looks at the character of democratic politics in relation to the mediated public spheres of several countries, and I conclude with some reflections on the historical present. The chapters that follow pursue some of these themes in nationally more specific analyses: UK (John Corner), France, (Josiane Jouët), Poland (Wieslaw Godzic), and Turkey (Mina Gencel Bek).

Public spheres: the Habermasian floor plan

While general notions of the public sphere appear in a variety of ways in the writings of many authors in the twentieth century, such as Walter Lippman (1922), Hannah Arendt (1998) and John Dewey (1954), most people today associate the concept with Jürgen Habermas' particular version. What is all the more interesting for our purposes here is that his book appears almost at the very start of the period we have under scrutiny here, in 1962. Though the full text was not translated into English until 1989 (Habermas 1989), his concept had by the 1970s come to play an important role in the critical analysis of the media in the English-speaking world. Since the translation, use of the concept has grown considerably. Over the years there have been many critical interventions around the concept (see Calhoun 1992, for an excellent collection, including a reply by Habermas; Eriksen and Weigård 2003; Crossley and Roberts 2004; the processes of globalization have also entered into discussions of the public sphere, and some authors now underscore its transnational dimension, e.g. Drache 2008). While Habermas has not attempted a full-scale reformulation of the public sphere, it is clear that his view of the concept is evolving as his work in other areas develops (Habermas 1996, 2006); in brief, today he is more disposed to include many nontraditional and cultural manifestations in the media as legitimate expressions of the public sphere, signalling a more resilient frame of analysis.

In its original formulation, the public sphere is seen by Habermas to consist of two basic domains. The first is the political public sphere, which is our concern here. Yet we should not forget that Habermas also addresses the cultural public sphere, a domain constituted by the circulation of – and discussion of – literary and artistic works. Certainly in today's mediated world the cultural public sphere is of enormous import. All media output cannot be reduced to politics and, though Habermas did not develop the notion of the cultural public sphere as much as he did the political one, it still can be enormously fruitful to approach the mediation of culture from this conceptual angle. Not least, we should bear in mind that the boundary line between the political and the cultural is not something that we can take for granted, especially today when there are new forms of public engagement emerging (see below) that challenge traditional conceptions of what constitutes politics.

The political public sphere is comprised of the institutional space where political will-formation takes place, via the unfettered flow of relevant information and ideas. This space is constituted by both mediated communication and face-to-face interaction. That is, while in the modern world the institutions of the media are the structural core of the public sphere, it is the face-to-face interaction, the ongoing talk between citizens, where the public sphere comes alive, so to speak, and where we find the actual bedrock of democracy. In recent of years, of course, such civic interaction also takes place via the newer interactive digital media.

After an extensive historical overview, Habermas surmises that a public sphere began to emerge within the bourgeois classes of Western Europe in the late eighteenth and early nineteenth centuries. The institutional basis for this public sphere consisted of an array of milieu and media, such as clubs, salons, coffee houses, newspapers, books and pamphlets, all of which in various (though incomplete) ways manifested Enlightenment ideals of the human pursuit of knowledge and freedom. For Habermas, the key here was not only the institutional basis but also the manner in which communication took place in this burgeoning public sphere. However imperfect it may have been, he saw that interaction in this social space embodied the ideals of reason, i.e. the Enlightenment goals of rational thinking, argument and discussion. In this notion of the public as a rational, dialogic process, Habermas' account of communication and democracy bears similarities with that of John Dewey.

As he continues with his historical narrative, Habermas sees the public sphere growing and deepening in the first few decades of the nineteenth century with the spread of mass literacy and the press. Then gradually the decay sets in. Journalism increasingly loses its claim to reason; public discourse degenerates into public relations. As the logic of commercialism increasingly shapes the operations of the media, the domain of rationality diminishes. Moving into the twentieth century, Habermas observes with pessimism the trivialization of politics, not least in the electronic media, the industrialization of public opinion, the transformation of publics from discursive to consuming collectivities, and an array of other ills that many critics have often noted.

Observers have noted that this historical account bears many of the markings of the original Frankfurt School of Critical Theory. With Adorno as his supervisor, it is not surprising that Habermas in his analysis shares many of the attributes of the leftist high cultural critique of 'mass society', while at the same time anchoring himself in a neo-Marxian perspective of advanced capitalism and the cultural industries. There is also a decidedly nostalgic quality to the analysis, the sense that there once was an historical opening which then became closed off. Habermas certainly sees the limits of this bourgeois public sphere, not least in class terms – and feminists have been quick to point out the gender limitations – but there remains something powerfully compelling for him (and many of his readers) about this budding public sphere and its significance for Western democracy.

Here it is suitable to mention that there is some ambiguity with the concept: it is not fully clear whether what Habermas describes is an empirical reality of an historical situation, or whether he is fundamentally presenting the reader with a normative vision. Most readers conclude that it is both. He describes the structural mechanisms that erode the public sphere, yet at the same time he – and many of his readers – continue to be inspired by the vision of a robust public sphere serving a well-functioning democracy. Indeed, the idea of the public sphere has gravitated away from its neo-Marxian origins and joined mainstream discussions about media performance, journalistic quality, and the conditions of democracy. In practical terms, the normative horizons from the liberal or progressive traditions that promote 'good journalism' or 'information in the public interest' are not so different from ideals about the media inspired by the framework of the public sphere. Yet, Fraser (2007) reminds us of the importance of retaining the critical core of the public sphere concept: that its legitimacy and efficacy reside in its capacity to facilitate genuine, i.e. non-manipulated, public opinion. As has often been said in the past, the genuine realization of even liberal ideals would have truly radical implications for society.

In the present context, then, the notion of the public sphere invites us to look at the media empirically, but also with a normative eye on the character of democracy. Reality suggests that we should actually speak of public spheres, i.e. in the plural, not only because we are dealing with different European countries but also because within any one country we find an array of distinct, even if overlapping, social spaces that constitute different public spheres, for different publics. The major mass media of a society can be seen as creating the dominant public sphere, while smaller media outlets can generate clusters of smaller spheres defined by interests, gender, ethnicity, etc. This tendency is certainly growing with the Internet. Yet, because of both linguistic convenience and the fact that we are dealing here with precisely dominant mass media, we will continue to use the singular form. So as we, in the chapters ahead, compare the situation between 1960 and 2000, what do we find? Does Habermas' account of the structural changes in the media hold relevance for this period? Is his conceptual framework of use? What has changed during these four decades, and how shall we view these changes in the light of the normative visions of the public sphere? And not least, what relevance does the concept have in societies that have had a very different history from the Western European one on which Habermas' analysis builds? The chapters on Poland and Turkey take up this theme.

Power drifts, cultural shifts, and evolving democracies

In focusing attention on the fundamental power alignments of European society, we see in this four decade period a trajectory of change, accelerating with each decade. Capitalism has been a precondition for liberal democracy and yet remains perpetually problematic for it, in that it generates social power (economic-financial) that lies beyond democratic control. The post-war welfare state structures and the Keynesian policies associated with them were a successful strategy in their time for dealing with such tensions; the various shades of social democratic measures generally serving to extend democracy and citizenship in Western Europe. By the early 1970s this model was encountering serious difficulties. Since then, particularly during the 1980s, we have witnessed in Western democracies a political turn where market forces and private enterprise have been given much greater reign to define the social landscape, with a concomitant retreat of the state and a general decline in democratic accountability. This has led, in turn, to a shifting of the ideological climate to emphasize the congruence between democracy and capitalism while downplaying the dilemmas. While observers with a neo-Marxian background were quick to problematize these difficulties, the new neo-liberalism also became the concern of 'traditional' liberals (cf. Frank 2002; Hertz 2001; Self 2000).

In Central and Eastern Europe the major changes have been of course all the more dramatic, with the demise of the communist system and the reconstruction of the societies using the templates of liberal democracy and market forces. In several of these countries it may be still premature to write a history of the epoch; certainly we can observe differences in, say, the capacity to anchor a democratic culture or establish a minimal regulatory environment for private enterprise. The transition of power in some cases has been more complete, while in other cases remnants of the old guard, in new dress, are still present. The extension of rights and liberties has gone far in a formal sense, yet it is unrealistic to expect that between 1989 and 2000 all the mechanisms for social justice could be in place. Change, however, has been rapid and deep-rooted, and even if the introduction of market forces has not turned out to be the societal panacea some originally hoped for, it has served to trigger a societal development that has generated optimism on many fronts.

During these four decades, the formal political systems of Western Europe have become increasingly stagnant, reactive rather than proactive, eclipsed by developments in the realms of large-scale capitalism and technological innovations and outpaced by socio-cultural developments. The margins of governmental manoeuverability are narrowing. Institutions central to democratic life, in particular political parties, have become unresponsive in the face of the major changes of late modernity. The sovereignty of the nation-state itself is being downsized in the face of global circumstances; in particular the role of transnational corporations as well as – in the European context – the EU. In the case of the latter, this opens up the challenge of developing democracy at the regional level. In Central and Eastern Europe, there has been both wide-spread democratic engagement and political apathy among citizens as the new democratic institutions struggle to take root. In the late 1990s, many of these countries were knocking on the door of the EU (successfully, it proved), which takes a positive view of expansion. Also, in the present decade, Turkey is looking westward, albeit with ambivalence, as it is met with mixed responses in regard to EU membership. From within and from abroad comes movement to encourage enhanced democratization of Turkish society, though in some areas the power structure is slow to respond.

Among citizens, the arena of official politics similarly has witnessed a decline in support and participation. These trends became very apparent during the 1990s, when the 'crisis of democracy' discourses began to take hold. Voter turnouts are decreasing, even in countries such as Sweden, which has had considerable stability in its electoral patterns over the earlier post-war decades. Party loyalty is in decline, especially among the young. One sees signs of a growing contempt for the political class. A corrosive climate of cynicism is emerging in some places. The extensive disenchantment with formal politics and the crisis of citizenship and civic culture is a theme addressed by many (see Blumler & Gurevitch, 1995, for a summary statement from that decade). Economic insecurity, unemployment, low wages, declining social services, growing class cleavages, global financial crises, ecological dilemmas, and a sense of powerlessness among many citizens are all part of the picture.

At the same time, we have evidence of alternative developments, a more optimistic renewal of democracy largely outside the parliamentarian context that can be said to represent a form of 'new politics' (Giddens, 1991, speaks of 'life politics'). If we look beyond formal electoral politics, we can see various signs that suggest that many people have not abandoned engagement with the political but have rather refocused their political attention in new arenas, or they are in the process of redefining just what constitutes the political, often within the context of social movements. The boundaries between politics, cultural values, identity processes and local self-reliance measures become fluid (Beck 1997); civil and political society becomes less differentiated from each other. Politics becomes not only an instrumental activity for achieving concrete goals but also an expressive and performative activity.

This new politics is to a great extent a phenomenon that emerges at the end of this period. While such activity has long been a part of democratic societies, it is safe to say that they took a big step forward starting in the mid-1990s and are, not surprisingly, associated to some extent with the rise of the Internet (see Castells 1997; van de Donk et al. 2005;). These new, alternative politics are characterized by personalized rather than collective engagement, and by a stronger emphasis on single issues than on overarching platforms or ideologies, and often attract younger citizens (Bennett 2003a, 2003b; Dahlgren 2007; Loader 2007). Some claim that part of this development can be understood as a move away from politics based on production to one focused on consumption; political attention is geared more towards the needs of clients, customers and consumers than in the past (Gibbens and Reimer 1999). Further, political activity within the new politics is more ad hoc, less dependent on traditional organizations and on elites mobilizing their standing cadres of supporters. Whether or not these developments are genuinely fruitful for the enhancement of democracy is under debate, but they do open the door for new ways to think about the contemporary political landscape in Western Europe.

Finally, the people, the citizens of Europe, are becoming more heterogeneous and, seen sociologically, are to some extent fragmenting. Boggs (2000) in the US context speaks of a 'great retreat' from the arena of common concerns and politics; while less pronounced in Europe, we still observe here some patterns of withdrawal into 'enclave consciousness', away from larger collective identities and community sensibilities. These enclaves may have a political focus but more often do not. This fragmentation has several origins, but two are most significant. The first has to do with the pluralization of life-styles in late modernity. Generally, advanced consumer culture fosters increasing 'nichification', as the multiplicity of tastes, interests, and social orientations accelerate (Corrigan 1997; Desmondhalgh 2003; Miles 1998; Slater 1997). The second has to do with multiculturalism as the ethnic and religious pluralism of many Western European countries increase (*Journal of Ethnic and Migration Studies* 2005; Lavdas 2001; Petersson & Clarke 2003; Rex 1995). These centrifugal forces problematize a democracy predicated on a nation-state characterized by homogeneity, sharing a unified public culture. Both of these tendencies also serve to promote frames of reference and engagement beyond the borders of the nation-state (e.g. global youth culture, transnational social movements, diasporic communities).

In short, the societal and cultural landscape has become more differentiated; our social worlds that bit more pluralistic, and our identities – our sense of who we are and what we want – somewhat more heterogeneous. The cultural commonality of national populations – as manifested in everyday leisure activities and lifestyle identities – has declined, but by no means vanished. If we situate these developments in relation to media audiences, it suggests that, increasingly, audiences are expecting more choices in media consumption. It also means that media audiences themselves are becoming more fragmented. Indeed, the notion of a national audience is eroding to some extent as audiences split into smaller groups. This undercuts the vision of a shared public culture and common knowledge. Clearly there are exceptions and variations here, not least in regard to specific media, with terrestrial national television channels still representing the best approximation of national audiences.

Also, while citizens are becoming increasingly socially fragmented amongst themselves (i.e. seen horizontally) as specific market niches emerge, a hierarchical (i.e. vertical) differentiation is also becoming more pronounced. The distinction between 'informed elites' and 'entertained majorities' is on the increase in many countries, supported not least by media economics, as access to deeper information and knowledge beyond the popular mass media becomes more of a significant economic factor (James 2003). Overall, the strong concept of 'the public' as the voice of the inclusive citizenry moves more toward a weak version of media spectatorship, complemented by a plethora of smaller, more exclusive 'interpretative communities'. The citizen becomes increasingly marginalized by the consumer.

Media modulations

There are many factors shaping late modern society and democracy in Europe, and we would be foolish to lapse into media-centrism and reduce all these dynamics simply to the workings of the media: their impact is effected through their interplay with other forces. Moreover, the media do not function as a unified societal force, but comprise a set of institutions. They are shaped by internal organizational features as well as by external societal conditions. That said, I still underscore the media's key position in the transformation of democracy. I would also support the counter argument, that the media help maintain continuity for democracy, providing stability via their established ways of covering politics, the collective frames of reference they foster, and the rather ritualistic elements that characterize their modes of representation. The two positions are obviously not mutually exclusive: democracy and society manifest both stability and change in varying ways

Most fundamentally the media are social institutions, largely organized commercially for profit. As institutions, what they do is to provide the dominant symbolic environment of society, with patterns of communication criss-crossing the social terrain in complex fashion. Their activities are enabled and constrained by their political economy, as well as by the social and cultural environments in which they operate (such as the behaviour and views of their audiences). Also, their organizational structures and routines, and the occupational horizons and ambitions of the people who work within them are important elements. For example, the professional ideals of journalists at times come into conflict with those who make financial decisions. The legal parameters for their operations derive from regulatory policies, itself a key political terrain. Not least are the respective technologies of the media and technical developments that impact on how these institutions operate and develop (e.g. television can do different things from the press; both are being modified by digitalization).

Some of what is presented in the media derives from the media's own initiatives and professional mores (e.g. investigative journalism). Much arises from the symbiotic relationship the media have with external actors, notably the mutual dependence of journalists and political elites. Some of the media's output is a direct result of external initiatives (a politician calling a press conference, for example). Popular discourses tend to mythologize journalists as heroes (and sometimes villains). The answers to the classic questions of *why* the media's output looks the way it does generally, or why they covered a particular event in a given way, however, are to be found in a complex interplay of institutional circumstances. (See Schudson, 2005, for a classic overview of sociological perspectives on news production).

A key to understanding the media's role in the life of European society and democracy from 1960 to 2000 is to grasp how the structural conditions of the media are changing and what this means for the way they operate. We can specify six interrelated, and by now rather familiar, trends. The interplay between these six trends has been altering the media landscape of Europe in the past four decades: proliferation, commercialization, concentration, deregulation, globalization, and digitalization.

Proliferation: We have a whole lot more channels of communication today than we had forty and even twenty years ago. Cable and satellite television offers packages with dozens of channels; in some cities the number available is nearing 100. If the number of daily newspapers is contracting somewhat, the growth in magazines has been explosive over the past two decades. And the Internet offers not only a seemingly endless supply of information on its own but is also increasingly relaying the output of traditional media. The mediatization of society and culture is proceeding at a rapid pace, as the density of our symbolic environments, and the accessibility of information, mushrooms. While much of the media environment is geared to entertainment, leisure and consumption, it would be unfair to say that news and current affairs have been left in the dust; they too are proliferating, primarily on the Internet and on television.

Commercialization: All media have to arrange for their financing and with the exception of public service broadcasting, which has been strong in the Western European context and comparatively weak in the US, the media have been organized as commercial ventures from the start. They are institutions in the business of making money for their shareholders. In regard to the press, the profit incentive has traditionally been balanced – with varying degrees of success – by a sense of publicist purpose and responsibility. For private radio and television there had been a similar sense of social responsibility, though backed up by regulatory frameworks that, among other things, demanded a minimum of news and current affairs output.

For a variety of reasons, commercial imperatives have hardened over the past few decades and the balance between public responsibility and private profit has been steadily tipping in favour of the latter. Normative goals are increasingly giving way to economic calculation (Baker 2002; Croteau and Hoynes 2001). In the current commercial climate, many daily newspapers are having a hard time attracting readers, especially younger ones, as other media successfully compete for their attention. The elite press in most countries is in decline, and popular forms of journalism are on the increase.

Concentration: For the press and for private broadcasting, commercialization is inseparable from the concentration of ownership and the media's expanding character as big business; the media are following general patterns found in the economy. Massive media empires have emerged on a global scale, concentrating ownership in the hands of a decreasing number of corporations. Such giants as Time Warner, Disney, Rupert Murdoch's News Corporation, and Bertelsmann are among the dozen or so leading global media corporations, followed by another three or four dozen somewhat smaller corporate actors. Together they dominate the media landscape of the modern world. The holdings of these corporations encompass all phases of media activity, from production to distribution, hardware and software, across virtually all media forms and technologies.

Significantly, via mergers and co-operative ventures, the media industries are integrating with telecommunications (e.g. AT&T with DirecTV) and the computer industry (e.g. Microsoft and NBC, Time Warner and AOL). These trends and their implications for democracy are analysed in a growing literature (Artz and Kamalipour 2003; Demers 2002; Herman and McChesney 1997; McChesney 1999; Schiller 1999; Thussu 2006). Thus, in the context of an ever-hardening commercial climate within corporate conglomerates, the ideals of journalism as expressed in traditional news values increasingly give way to the economic logic of fast and high profits. The culture of journalism, with its critical watchdog functions and its protection of freedom of expression, is not the culture of these institutions.

Globalization: Michael Tracey (1998: 46) observes that among the top 500 corporations in the US, half proclaim that they belong to no single nation. Within the communication field we see also an increasingly global character of media ownership and activities. The major media corporations, as noted above, are global actors, operating transnationally. Media globalization can mean transnational ownership, which can raise such problems as responsiveness and accountability. However, globalization also can mean transnational media activities. For example, European countries had to relinquish claims to national sovereignty of their airwaves with the advent of satellite television, and the Internet certainly is indifferent to national boundaries. The implications of such developments are complex, yet we should not ignore the potential positive contribution of such developments for enhancing citizens' frames of reference and social engagement. For example, public engagement with many international events – political repression, environmental disasters, famine, etc. – has been made possible by globalized media coverage, especially on television. This remains true even while much criticism is justifiably aimed at the nature of the coverage (e.g. the Gulf War) and the vast black holes of non-coverage of much of the world. Globalization within Europe in the form of cooperative television ventures has, however, only been partly successful (see Weiten, Murdock and Dahlgren 2000).

Deregulation: If economic developments have given birth to intensified commercialism, concentration and globalization, deregulation has been the midwife. Deregulation is the policy process whereby the various laws, rules and codes that governments use to shape media ownership, financing and ongoing activities are withdrawn or weakened, a process which at bottom is a political one, reflecting the power and interests of various actors. Regulation and deregulation of the media are of course an area of intense concern in a period of profound restructuring of the media landscape.

Deregulation has been most strongly manifested in the area of broadcasting, with the transition in most Western European countries in recent decades from public service monopolies to mixed systems. Public service broadcasting itself was in need of institutional renewal. Virtually all such broadcasting organizations were facing financial difficulties by the 1980s, and charges of paternalism and stagnation, as well as in some countries a too-close relationship with the state, were not without validity. However, as many have argued (cf. Tracey 1998) the question is whether or not the politics of deregulation have contributed to the erosion of the public service mission, including enhancing democracy.

Public service broadcasting is predicated on the ideals of universalism – it is intended as a right for all citizens, and strives to serve society in its entirety via the diversity of its programming. Its premise is to address its audiences as publics, not markets. Clearly its degree of success in achieving these aspirations varied, but there remained, significantly, a normative consensus regarding its mission, and mechanisms of social accountability. The alterations in broadcasting's circumstances have significantly weakened this consensus and any possibility of accountability. While public service in most countries has restructured and streamlined itself, today it comprises a declining proportion of the overall broadcasting output, and its *raison d'être* is less self-evident. The new commercial broadcasters, for their part, had fewer restrictions placed on them in regard to programming, and enforcing the regulations that remained at times proved difficult.

Are these trends good for democracy? Herman and McChesney (1997: 1) describe the overall situation succinctly:

Since the early 1980s there has been a dramatic restructuring of national media industries, along with the emergence of a genuinely global commercial media market. The newly developing global media system is dominated by three or four dozen large transnational corporations (TNCs), with fewer than ten mostly US-based media conglomerates towering over the global market. In addition to the concentration of media power, the major feature of the global media order is its thoroughgoing commercialism, and an associated marked decline in the relative importance of public broadcasting and the applicability of public service standards. Such a concentration of media power in organizations dependent on advertising support and responsible primarily to shareholders is a clear and present danger to citizens' participation in public affairs, understanding of public issues, and thus to the effective working of democracy.

Digitalization: By the 1990's, digitalization had become the major technological media trend. This means that a common electronic language, based on the 'bits' of the computer, is emerging for all mediated communication. Thus, text, sound, voice, as well as still and moving images are increasingly being translated into a common digital form. The traditional media are all using digital technologies in various phases of their activities.

A major threshold that has been anticipated in recent years is the transition from analogue to digital television transmission, an at-present commercially uncertain development that is now just starting to take off. We see digitalization firmly entrenched in other media, for example in the CD-ROM formats of games and educational materials, DVD technology and, of course, on the Internet. Within the traditional media, the most developed manifestation of digitalization is the online versions of print newspapers which, by the end of the 1990s, was clearly a major factor in changing the way newspapers operated (e.g. enhanced interactivity with readers, altered periodicity of production, emergence of multimedia formats), even if many of the online versions were still not making much profit. We can anticipate continued digitalization and the convergence of media forms, not least that the mass media will increasingly be present on the Internet, as the Internet increasingly takes on the characteristics of mass media.

These structural changes in the media have arisen reciprocally with other societal trends, including the crisis of the welfare state, the dilemmas of the national project in a globalizing world, and the enhanced power of market forces. Together these challenge us to rethink the definitions and possibilities for democracy in the future. They also set the stage for a more focused discussion on the public sphere.

Public spheres and the space of politics

Against this background of change in society, culture, democracy, and the media, we can recuperate and integrate the various strands by turning to the notion of the public sphere. At this point in the discussion, it can be helpful to conceptualize the public sphere as consisting of three constitutive dimensions: structural, the representational, and the interactional. Evaluation of how well the public sphere of a particular society functions must take all three dimensions into account.

The structural dimension has to do with the formal institutional features of the public sphere. Most obviously this means media organizations and regulatory frameworks that include questions of ownership, financing, control, procedures for licensing, rules for access, etc. Also we have the legal frameworks defining the freedoms of and constraints on communication (e.g. libel and privacy issues). But beyond the media themselves, the structural dimension also analytically encompasses society's political institutions, which serve as a sort of 'political ecology' for the media and set boundaries for the nature of the information and forms of expression that may circulate. At this level, the public sphere's entwinement with society's overall political situation becomes paramount. A society where democratic tendencies are weak is not going to give rise to healthy institutional structures for the public sphere. Which, in turn, means that the representational dimension will be inadequate.

The representational dimension refers to the output of the media. In this dimension one can raise all the traditional questions and criteria about media output – e.g. fairness, completeness, accuracy, pluralism of opinion – as well as newer ones such as the diversity of cultural expression. There is a growing complexity about the representational dimension which has to do with the overall trend of mediatization, which I take up below. Here I just wish to note that while in modern societies the media constitute the core of the public sphere the media also generate a semiotic milieu which far exceeds traditional understandings of what constitutes a public sphere. Thus, consideration of the representational dimension must include not only that media output which we may selectively choose to treat as belonging to the public sphere but also the larger semiotic media culture which envelops it and intertextualizes it.

The dimension of interaction needs emphasis, since this element tends often to be neglected given the (understandable) mediacentrism which colours most discussions of the public sphere. Interaction consists of two aspects. Firstly, it has to do with the citizens' encounters with the media – the communicative processes of making sense, interpreting the output. The second aspect of interaction is that between citizens themselves. While this perspective was prominent in the older sociology of the media (I am thinking here especially of the 'two-step flow' tradition), it often gets ignored in discussions about the public sphere.

Here it is useful to recall Habermas as well as other writers, such as Dewey (1954), who argue that a 'public' should be conceptualized as something other than just a media audience. A public, according Habermas and Dewey, exists as discursive interactional processes; atomized individuals, consuming media in their homes, do not comprise a public. There are of course strong interests in society which have a stake in defining 'the public' in terms of aggregate statistics of individual behaviour and opinion and such approaches certainly do have their uses from the standpoint of marketing, the official political system, and not least from media institutions themselves. However, from the standpoint of democracy, it is imperative not to lose sight of the classic idea that democracy resides, ultimately, with citizens who engage in talk with each other, as the many proponents of deliberative democracy have argued (Dryzek 2000; Fishkin and Laslett 2003, Guttman and Thompson 2004).

I would underscore that in the period we are discussing, the public spheres of Europe became structurally and representationally more pluralistic and complex, and less bounded and ordered. Habermas' classic text on the subject appeared in 1962, in a period of dominant national media. He has revised his position (Habermas 1996), not only taking into account the more sprawling character of the public sphere – he now sees it virtually merging with civil society and all mediated culture – but also modifying somewhat his earlier more pessimistic tone. And certainly the socio-cultural changes noted above, with the rise of new politics and the easy access of the Internet, give new optimism to the viability of democratic life.

At the same time, if we keep our focus on the major mass media, their significance for the public sphere and political life more generally should not be underestimated. This does not per se give more weight to a pessimistic view; rather it simply seeks to keep a sharp sociological focus. Structurally, the major media still dominate the public sphere; it is these media that constitute much of the space of politics. As Castells (1997) and others forcefully argue, the media are transforming democracy because political life itself today has become so extensively situated within the domain of the media. This view does not mean that politics does not exist outside the media, or that politics has been reduced to a mere media spectacle. It does, however, posit that political actors who want to accomplish things requiring public visibility will always turn to the media. Political and economic elites make use of the media for the daily routines of governing, for opinion- and image-management, as well as for major initiatives or trouble-shooting in times of crises.

Moreover, it suggests that structures, organization and strategies of politics are increasingly adapting themselves to the media. This is manifested in everything from the strategic targeting of messages for specific audience niches to the rhetoric of press conferences and to the conscious adaptation of public discourse to sound-bites of suitable length and visuals with dramatic impact. Established elites as well as alternative or oppositional groups trying to shape public opinion (Greenpeace is a paradigmatic example) must all follow the same path. 'If it wasn't in the media, it didn't happen', as they say.

Further, this view emphasizes the emergence of an increasingly coherent media logic (Altheide and Snow 1991) that sets the conditions for participating in the media. These conditions comprise such features as timing and scheduling, forms of expression, tempo, informational density and modes of address. These factors have important consequences for how politics is organized and expressed. It is important to bear in mind that we are talking about the media as sites, i.e. in the plural form. While we can point to a rather coherent media logic, there are important distinctions to be made. Firstly, the various branches of the mass media – press, radio and television – have somewhat differing logics. Television as a medium, for instance, is visual and exists in time; the press is a textual medium that takes up space (though the processes of digitalization are pushing all media toward a technical convergence). The communicative logic and the processes of production are significantly different, and hence political actors using these media will have to use different approaches. Moreover, within any given medium there are important genre differences: a local radio talk show is not the same as a national news broadcast; a popular television magazine operates differently from a highbrow debate programme.

The concept of media logic contains an element of modest postmodern reasoning. It suggests that the traditional way of understanding the media's relationship to politics is being called into question, namely that the media simply represent, with varying degrees of accuracy, politics and, more generally, the real world 'out there'. What is asserted here is that politics no longer exists as a reality taking place outside the media, to then be 'covered' by journalists. Rather, politics is increasingly organized as a media phenomenon, planned and executed for and with the cooperation of the media. Note that I called this a 'modest' form of postmodern reasoning. It does challenge the traditional notion of media practices aiming to represent an external reality, but it does not claim that there is no real world outside the media, or that everything we see in the media is merely a form of simulation. The argument instead can be understood sociologically: in the modern world, many institutions, including religion and sports, but especially politics, have adapted their activities to the logic of the media, and in the process have transformed themselves.

We will have to continue to grapple with democracy, both conceptually and in our concrete life circumstances. Any and all such activity must have the media clearly in focus; indeed, we would do well to consider the media themselves as key focal points for struggles to enhance democracy. If the media have become the privileged sites of politics, then they must also become central objects of democratic engagement.

Power elites and the media

One port of entry into the analysis of the public sphere and democracy is to look at the relationship between the economic and political elites and the media. Each national case will have its own version here, and certainly the particular case of Turkey will be notably different from many of the patterns in Europe; Poland and other Central/Eastern European societies also vary. What follows is a brief schematic view from Western Europe.

The increasingly free reign given to market forces in society has had its corresponding impact on the media. It has also had a significant impact on the ideological climate in the media and in public culture more generally. In simplified terms, we can specify two major consequences here; these can feed off and reinforce each other, but it is useful to keep them analytically separate. On the one hand, there is the well-known trend towards popularization and tabloidization (cf. Sparks and Tulloch 2000). On the other hand, and perhaps at a more subtle level, there have been important ideological developments. The media, as sources of public knowledge and discussion, have increasingly come to give voice to views supporting market forces as the prime motor for more and more areas of social life. The realm of the political as defined in public culture has thus become diminished as issues and views relating to the democratic control and accountability of economic power increasingly faded from the political agenda. This is by no means a neat linear or uncontested development, but the pattern is clear. Certainly the role of economic elites in arranging sources for news and spin (see Cottle 2003) is important here. Their interventions have contributed to shaping popular perceptions and opinions have been instrumental in forming the current climate of public debate.

The power of the economic elites to shape information and debates in the media was facilitated by the general political direction of society, but also by circumstances in the media. With economics gaining as an area of journalistic coverage (and pressed for time and in need of material) journalists find it difficult to turn down ready-made informational 'packages' offered by the corporate world. Most journalists covering economics come from the business schools, not the journalism schools, and tend to have fairly homogenous views about economic matters. Further, we see not only a growth but also changes in economic journalism. The economy sections expand, but also economy as a dominant theme is spreading into news journalism and feature journalism. The economic experts used as sources and for interviews tend increasingly to come from the business world rather than from academia.

Coverage of the economy during the 1990s has strongly emphasized the crisis, but less often discussed its origins or where responsibility lies. Ideologically, market forces become abstract powers, less amenable to political intervention. Such a climate is favourable for business definitions and initiatives in the political realm. At the same time, expansion of coverage of economic matters cannot but help to bring with it a good deal of bad news for the general public; ideological climates are never air tight. In short, the power of the economic elite has steadily increased in relation to the media, though this does not prevent difficulties in the economy from becoming topics of public concern.

If the economic elite has witnessed a rise in its power relative to the media, the political elite's situation is more ambivalent in this regard. It is still the case of two sly foxes using the rules of the game to maximize their advantage; 'symbiosis' still prevails between journalism and the political class; there exists a mutual dependence. Political elites need easy access – and preferably favourable coverage – while journalists need good source contacts. However, the rules themselves have been evolving, and a different kind of journalism is emerging. It is this development that can have long-term impact on the power of the relative power of political elites.

Basically, what has been developing over the past decade or so is a gradual shift in the manner in which national politics is presented in the media. On the one hand, the imperatives of commercialization are serving to escalate the general level of drama associated with national politics, which in earlier decades had been characterized by more sedate forms of journalistic coverage as well as the overarching mentality of consensus. On the other hand, much of the drive-shaft of politics today comes at least indirectly from the corporate sphere. The flow of power from the formal political system to the upper echelons of the private sector has, as I suggested above, resulted in a relative decline in the power of the political elites. These developments have given rise to a new dramaturgical framework for journalistic practices, a framework that builds on traditional sensationalism in the context of contemporary media logic and power relations.

What has this to do with the relative power of political elite and the media? Under circumstances where the political elite is losing relative power to the economic elite, and where the economic elite is available to the media largely under circumstances that these elites themselves decide, the media dramatize and personalize current affairs most readily by pouncing on the political elites whenever possible. What emerges is a dramaturgical framework that becomes not only a game-plan for a lot of journalism, but also an ideological construction offered to (but obviously not always accepted by) the citizenry, namely that society basically consists of the political elite, the media and the citizenry. At its worst, this framework suggests the political elite is to be viewed with suspicion, as self-serving manipulators. The media present themselves as guardians of the public interest, while the economic elite basically gets edited out of discourses about power.

In recent years, there has been a good deal of complaint from the political elite that the media are fostering a popular contempt against them. While this view of political elites has not been totally undeserved, there is still some justification to the claim. The media have taken a more active watch-dog role, but they have been barking at too many shadows. The media have, in a sense, taken advantage of the political elites' relative decline in power but at the same time not focused their critical eyes on the economic elites. It can also be argued that the media have gained a notch in power over political elites in that contemporary media formats put so much emphasis on the forms, the modes, of representation. Television cameras, sound bites, etc., compel the political elites to some extent to dance to a tune composed by the media. Yet we should be careful in not exaggerating the shift in power balance here: the political establishment has also become more sophisticated in dealing with the media.

Realigning the triad

It should be clear that democracy in late modern society is at a turning point and even if we cannot predict exactly which directions it will take in the new century there is legitimate cause for concern. Moreover, the transformations we see in how democracy functions stand in complex relation to the dramatic changes in the structures of the media. Changes in both the traditional mass media and the Internet, as well as changes in the conditions and practices of journalism, and in the social trends of cultural differentiation and consumption, all come into play. These large social trends, in turn, connect with the increasing fragmentation and stratification of media audiences and the polity in general, and the altered dynamics between political and economic elites vis-à-vis the media. The stagnation of formal political systems, the emerging climate of 'anti-politics', the retreat to enclave consciousness, but also the growth of extra-parliamentary 'new politics', are not simply caused by the media but do articulate in a myriad of ways with media developments.

Cast in terms of Habermas' original view of the public sphere, it could be argued that, in the four decades of this period, the negative trends within the media's political economy, with the consequent patterns of deregulation, concentration and commercialization, have advanced. The critical trajectory of his earlier work has not lost relevance. At the same time, the proliferation of media, their globalization and not least their digitalization, have ushered in a new era in which the conditions for a viable public sphere have to some extent been positively altered. More people can get more information through the mass media, and more people can actively access more diverse information through the newer media. Politics is taking on new forms, the growing porousness of the nation state means that even new kinds of issues, mobilizing new kinds of publics, arise. Thus, we may wish to modify his rather strong pessimism – as he himself has done. At some point, optimism and pessimism become dispositions that exist beyond (or even in spite of analyses), and we would not wish to press too hard in either direction here.

If we highlight instead the triad of political elites, economic elites and citizens within Western Europe, we can see how the power constellations between them have evolved over the years. The power of economic elites has unquestionably expanded at the expense of the other two collective actors. Citizens are situated further from the centres of economic decision-making, not just because the economy has become increasingly globalized but also because the political elites, who ostensibly represent the citizenry, have lost power relative to the economic elites. Meanwhile, there is a declining confidence among the citizens in the formal political system's capacity to deal with contemporary problems. For their part, the citizenry's relative power has declined, as they have become increasingly fragmented by growing class divisions and cultural pluralization, including the relative non-integration of immigrant populations. On the margins, however, we find new forms of political engagement, especially making use the newer, interactive media.

Whether the democratic glass is half full or half empty we leave to the reader but we hope that the analytic overviews in this and the following chapters come to the service of a viable disposition for the reader. This narrative takes us up to the turn of the century/ millenium. Nothing is as precarious as the present and, certainly, in the coming interplay between society and the media, power elites and citizens, and media and developments and the evolution of the public sphere, the situation – including our hopes for a democratic future – remains open.

References

Altheide, David & Robert Snow (1991) *Media worlds in the post-journalism era*, New York: Aldine de Gruyter.

Arendt, Hannah (1998) *The human condition*, Chicago: University of Chicago Press.

Artz, Lee & Yahya R. Kamalipour (eds.) (2003) *The globalization of corporate media hegemony*, Albany: State University of New York Press.

Baker, C. Edwin (2002) *Media, markets and democracy,* New York: Cambridge University Press.

Beck, Ulrich (1997) *The reinvention of politics: Rethinking modernity in the global social order,* Cambridge: Polity Press.

Bennett, W. Lance (2003a) 'New media power: the internet and global activism', in N. Couldry & J. Currans (eds.) *Contesting media power*, Lanham, MD: Rowman & Littlefield, pp. 17–37.

Bennett, W. Lance (2003b) 'Lifestyle politics and citizen-consumers: identity, communication and political action in late modern society', in John Corner and Dick Pels (eds.) *Media and political style: Essays on representation and civic culture*, London: Sage, pp. 137–50.

Blumler, Jay & Michael Gurevitch (1995) *The crisis of public communication*, London: Routledge.

Boggs, Carl (2000) *The end of politics: Corporate power and the decline of the public sphere*, New York: Guilford Press.

Calhoun, Craig (ed.) (1992) *Habermas and the public sphere*, Cambridge, Mass: MIT Press.

Castells, Manuel (1997) *The power of identity*, Vol II of *The information age,* London: Blackwell.

Cottle, Simon (ed.) (2003) *News, public relations and power*, London: Sage.

Corrigan, Peter (1997) *The sociology of consumption*, London: Sage.

Crossley, Nick & John Michael Roberts (eds.) (2004) *After Habermas: New perspectives on the public sphere*, Oxford: Blackwell.

Croteau, David & William Hoynes (2001) *The business of media: Corporate media and the public interest*, Thousand Oaks, CA: Pine Forge Press.

Dahlgren, Peter (ed.) (2007) *Young citizens and new media: Learning for democratic participaion*, New York: Routledge.

Demers, David (2002) *Global media: menace or Messiah?* Cresskill, NJ: Hampton Press.

Desmondhalgh, David (2003) *The culture industries*, London: Sage.

Dewey, John ([1923]1954) *The public and its problems*, Chicago: Swallow Press.

Drache, Daniel (2008) *Defiant publics: The unprecedented reach of the global citizen*, Cambridge: Polity Press.

Dryzek, John S. (2000) *Deliberative democracy and beyond*, Oxford: Oxford University Press.

Eriksen, Erik O. & Weigård Jarle (2003) U*nderstanding Habermas: communicative action and deliberative democracy*, London/New York: Continuum.

Fishkin, James S. & Laslett, Peter (eds.) (2003) *Debating deliberative democracy*, London: Blackwell.

Frank, Thomas, (2002), *One market under god: Extreme capitalism, market populism and the end of economic democracy*, New York: Vintage.

Fraser, Nancy (2007) 'Transnationalizing the public sphere: on the legitimacy and efficacy of public opinion in a post-Westphalian world', in Seyla Benhabib, Ian Shapiro & Danilo Petranovic (eds.) *Identities, affiliations and allegiances*, New York: Cambridge University Press, pp. 45–66.

Giddens, A. (1991) *The consequences of modernity*, Cambridge: Polity Press.

Gibbens, John R. & Reimer, Bo (1999) *the politics of postmodernity*, London: Sage.

Guttman, Amy & Thompson, Dennis (2004) *Why deliberative democracy?* Princeton: Princeton University Press.

Habermas, Jürgen ([1984]1987) *The Theory of Communicative Action*, 2 vols. Cambridge: Polity Press.

Habermas, Jürgen (1989) *The structural transformation of the public sphere*, Cambridge: Polity Press.

Habermas, Jürgen (1996) *Between facts and norms*, Cambridge, MA: MIT Press.

Habermas, Jürgen (2006) 'Political communication in mediated society', *Communication Research* 16 (4) pp. 411–26.

Herman, Edward & McChesney, Robert (1997) *The global media*, London: Cassell.

Hertz, Noreena (2001) *The silent takeover: Global capitalism and the death of democracy,* New York: Arrow Books.

James, Jeffery (2003) *Bridging the global digital divide*, Cheltenham: Edward Elgar Publishing.

Journal of Ethnic and Migration Studies (2005) (Special issue) 'Media and Minorities in Multicultural Europe', Vol 31, no. 3.

Lavdas, Kostas A. (2001) 'Republican Europe and multicultural citizenship', *Politics* 21 (1), pp. 1–10.

Lippman, W. (1922) *Public opinion,* New York: Macmillan.

Loader, Brian (ed.) (2007) *Young citizens in the digital age: Political engagement, young people and new media,* London: Routledge.

McChesney, Robert (1999) *Rich media, poor democracy: Communication politics in dubious times,* Champaign: University of Illinois Press.

Miles, Steven (1998) *Consumerism as a way of life*, London: Sage.

Petersson, Bo & Clark Eric (2003) *Identity dynamics and the construction of boundaries*, Lund: Nordic Academic Press.

Rex, John (1995) *Ethnic minorities in the modern nation state*, London: Macmillan

Schiller, Dan (1999) *Digital capitalism: Networking the global marketing system,* Cambridge, MA: MIT Press.

Schudson, M. (2005) 'The sociology of news ', in J. Cuurran & M. Gurevitch (eds.) *Mass Media and Society,* 4th ed. London: Edward Arnold.

Self, Peter (2000) *Rolling back the market: Economic dogma and political choice*, New York: St. Martin's Press.

Slater, Don (1997) *Consumer culture and modernity*, Cambridge: Polity Press.

Sparks, Colin & Tulloch John (eds.) (2000) *Tabloid tales: Global Debates over media standards*, Oxford: Rowman & Littlefield.

Thussu, Daya Kishan (2006) *International communication: Continuity and change*, London: Hodder Arnold.

Tracey, Michael (1998) *The decline and fall of public service broadcasting*, Oxford: Oxford University Press.

Van de Donk, Wim, Loader, Brian D. Nixon, Paul & Rucht, Dieter (eds.) (2005) *Cyberprotest: New media, citizens and social movements*, London: Routledge.

Weiten, Jan, Murdock, Graham & Dahlgren, Peter (eds) (2000) *Television across Europe*, London: Sage.

Part II

Structures

Chapter 2

Four Decades of European Newspapers: Structure and Content

Lennart Weibull & Åsa Nilsson
University of Gothenburg

Introduction

The point of departure for this chapter on the developments of the European press over four decades is that newspapers are a means of understanding the changes of society, that newspapers, both as industry and as cultural product, reflect political, economic and social trends, thus reflecting the development of the social and the political sphere. The language of headlines, the character of pictures, and the layout of pages together reveal a perspective of the contemporary world. This chapter provides a brief description of changes of the newspaper industry in Europe, and presents an overview of trends in the development of form and contents of the main papers of twelve European countries.

The overview of newspaper structure is mainly based on available statistics, whereas the content analyses originate from a minor study carried out within the research project *Changing Media, Changing Europe*. In order to frame these analyses we will start with a brief introduction to the European newspaper tradition, mainly building on the important work by Daniel Hallin and Paolo Mancini (2004) and on the recent overview by Gustafsson and Weibull (2007).

The European press tradition

From early on the European press consisted of newspapers with roots in the economic as well as in the political world. In the small states of central Europe newspapers were mainly connected with trade, whereas in the nation-states the papers usually were part of the state propaganda. The public space created by the papers was an elitist one, as was the readership. In the eighteenth century new papers came to reflect the cultural sphere, but the readers were still the elites and the dissemination of newspapers grew only slowly. First in the nineteenth century the modern press emerged.

Rise of the modern press

The general press market profoundly changed as a consequence of industrialization. In the new urban areas the market expanded and new groups of readers found their way to the newspapers. As John B Thompson (1995) points out, newspaper expansion was part of the modern project. Just as industrialization took different directions in individual European countries, so did the press development. In the United Kingdom as well as in Germany and the Netherlands a strong newspaper press developed early in the nineteenth century, whereas in some Mediterranean countries, still dominated by agriculture, newspaper penetration was – and still is – considerably lower.

The expansion of the newspaper market not only reflected socio-economic changes, but the democratization of political life, and opened up for a real public sphere providing space for new voices. Often newspaper publishers themselves took part in the struggle for political change. Liberal newspapers, established in the middle of the nineteenth century, were normally closely involved in the modernization process. The cause, however, could differ between countries. In Italy, the early liberal press fought for the political unification of the country; in Sweden, liberal papers were strongly involved in the movement for universal suffrage. The expansion of the labour movement gave rise to a socialist, later also a communist, press, normally owned by party organizations.

In the early twentieth century the European press market was to a large extent characterized by a political pluralism, even though the structure differed between countries as a consequence of the political situation. The leading political newspapers were generally published in a metropolis such as Berlin, London, Milan or Paris, and spread nationally. However, in northern Europe, political pluralism also characterized the local and regional press markets.

Another important change was the expansion of a popular press reaching new segments of readers. Whereas the traditional political newspapers in most European countries were elitist in their journalistic style, focusing on the political and economic institutions, the popular press widened the scope of journalism. The *Petit Parisien*, the *Daily Mail* and the so called *Boulevardblätter* in Berlin and Vienna – all established in the late nineteenth or early twentieth century – represented a new type of low-cost newspaper, aiming at readers within the expanding working class (see Gustafsson 1996). Both in journalistic style and in language they tried to approach a social segment that was later to be called the downmarket.

The rise of the modern press was to a large extent determined by the increasing role of advertising, which itself was a consequence of the urban market economy. However, in contrast to the elite press, the popular papers were less dependent on advertisements. They were sold as a single copy, building their economy on high circulation and an efficient distribution system. To attract large readership they offered a personalized journalism, devoting much space to human-interest stories, including populist campaign journalism. Their political profile was sometimes less evident but in most countries the popular press consisted of both leftist and conservative, often populist, papers.

Newspaper systems in Europe

From the brief overview of the rise of the European press we can identify at least three main dimensions structuring the newspaper systems of the individual countries: the party political, the geographical and the journalistic dimension (Färdigh 2008; Gustafsson and Weibull 2007; Terzis 2008).

The *political dimension* traditionally has been an important structuring factor. In some countries the party political factor maintained its strength into the second half of the twentieth century, but in most countries it gradually lost importance in parallel with the weakening of the traditional political parties. Party loyalty was no longer an advantage, and in countries with a dictatorship in the 1930s and 1940s a partisan press was regarded with suspicion. Also market concentration in the 1950s meant that leading newspapers loosened their party political ties and opened their pages to broad news coverage, even if they did not leave their traditional political loyalty on the editorial page (Weibull 1993).

A second dimension concerns market ambition and the actual spread of a newspaper – what can be called the *market dimension*. There have often been distinguished between three or four levels in order to describe the newspaper market: the national, the regional, the local and the sub-local (Høst 1991). The meaning of each level may shift between countries, but normally there is a strong demarcation line between the national press on one hand and regional/local press on the other. However, so-called national newspapers normally have a strong local penetration in their publishing area, where they are more or less local, whereas their national penetration is restricted to certain social groups.

The *journalistic dimension* is here used to distinguish between 'quality' and 'popular' press. The latter term has traditionally been used in order to classify the national tabloids in the UK, but this type of differentiation is also obvious in most European countries. The meaning of quality and popular may vary between countries, but it is essentially based on a distinction between a broad-issue approach, covering most parts of society, and a personalized journalism focusing on a few spectacular news stories or on a certain topic, like sports. In most countries the dimension coincides with upmarket versus downmarket newspapers, i.e. papers read mainly by the upper classes and by the working class respectively.

The three dimensions of the newspaper system encompass the main traditions of European press. Thus, it is a sort of framework suitable for understanding development trends and differences between the countries. Here it will be used as a frame for the analysis of European press development in the last four decades.

Changes in European newspaper structure 1960–2000

In 1960 newspapers still represented the dominating mass medium in most European countries. It is true that broadcasting had been introduced in the 1920s, but in Europe it had normally been organized as public service companies and its news coverage could not compete with that of the written press and normally it contained no advertising. Also, television in its first decades functioned mainly as a complement to newspapers, even though there were considerable differences within Europe in the interest in television (Scannell & Cardiff 1991; Smith 1998).

In the 1970s and 1980s radio and television came to represent a tough challenge to newspapers in news reporting. The increasing number of private TV channels also meant increased competition in the advertising market. Even if the newspaper market has turned out be relatively stable, changes have taken place and the press has lost shares in both readership and advertising. However, as we shall see, this relative decline does not so much seem to be a direct response to the introduction of new media but rather as a consequence of a changing European society in a wider sense, including social segregation and new lifestyles.

The focus for our overview is the period 1960–2000, where we have studied the content development of the news press. However, the trends of market development presented in the next sections build on structural data up to 2006.

Measuring the European press market

Undertaking comparative analyses is always difficult, and the study of newspaper structure is no exception. The field is characterized by strong national traditions in defining a newspaper. The most internationally-accepted newspaper definition goes back to the UNESCO definition: 'a general paper published at least four days a week'. By tradition it includes only paid-for newspapers. Most comparative overviews, like most of the international statistics, are based on such a definition. It is also the definition used here.

However, we have to consider that the use of the UNESCO definition might mean that we exclude some important characteristics of national newspaper systems. Especially, it has to be pointed out that papers published two or three times a week represent a strong segment of the press, e.g. in Finland. From the definition it also follows that free sheets are excluded, even though the new type of free metropolitan papers like *Metro* or *20 Minutes* might play the same role as a traditional paper. In many countries, like Denmark, France and Spain, free papers play a vital role on both the national and the local media scene (cf. World Press Trends 2007). However, they are left out because of lack of comparative statistics over time.

There are traditionally two measurements of newspaper penetration. One is paid circulation, in comparative statistics normally the number of newspaper copies per 1,000 inhabitants. This measurement is in principle based on sold copies[1] (even though the definition of 'sold' might vary between countries) and, as such, offers only a rough measure since it does not take into account the fact that a paper might be shared amongst readers. However, the measurement is reasonably reliable in analyses of individual countries over time and it is also a convenient tool in comparative analyses of similar countries of Western Europe.

The second measurement is based on readership surveys. Most surveys have been designed according to the needs of advertisers. Thus, they mainly try to estimate the probability of exposure of a certain issue of a newspaper, or a certain type of newspaper, not analysing the reading habits. Since the 1990s there are at least fairly comparative readership surveys available in most European countries. For most years, however, we are obliged to resort to official circulation figures, although the level of paid circulation may vary a lot according to national definitions.

A final observation concerns the problem of national comparisons, where the national state is the unit of analysis. With regard to data on paid circulation as well as readership surveys, we have to rely on national statistics. This means that regional variations are mainly excluded from the analyses. For some countries, e.g. Italy and Spain, differences in regional cultures might be even bigger than differences in relation to other countries. In other cases, e.g. Belgium and Switzerland, language variations within the country might mean that national figures are not representative for the whole country.

European press structure

In the year 2000, about 1,500 newspapers were published regularly in Europe, meaning a regularity of at least 4 issues a week. The country with clearly the highest number of papers is Germany. In relation to the national population, however, the figures for Norway, Switzerland, Sweden, Estonia, Iceland, and Finland are significantly higher, with more than ten newspapers per one million inhabitants (Table 1). In this comparison, Germany's newspaper penetration is weaker with fewer than five papers per one million inhabitants, though the penetration is even weaker in countries like Italy or the UK (about one newspaper per one million inhabitants). It is, however, important to keep in mind that the definition of newspapers might vary between countries according to national traditions, e.g. concerning general and specialized papers.

The total circulation of European newspapers in 2000 was about 95 million copies per publication day. In this case as well Germany is found at the top: with about 24 million copies it is responsible for a little over a quarter of the total European newspaper circulation. Europe's biggest newspaper, the *Bild-Zeitung*, is published in Germany, but the biggest paper in relation to country size is the Austrian *Kronen-Zeitung*, which, including its local editions, represents more than half of the newspaper market in Austria. The highest average circulation is found in the UK, Austria and the Netherlands, and the smallest in Estonia, Greece and Portugal.

As has been mentioned above, the most widely-used measurements in comparative newspaper studies are the number of paid copies ('sales') per 1,000 inhabitants or the reading measure ('reach') based on surveys. With regard to newspaper sales, Norway is found at the top with about 600 copies, followed by Finland, Sweden and Switzerland; at the bottom we find Italy, Portugal and Greece, all three with 100 copies or less per 1,000 inhabitants. Newspaper reading generally follows the same pattern. In the Nordic countries and Switzerland about four fifths of the population are regular readers, whereas in the south less than half of the population reads a newspaper on a regular basis.

Table 1: Number of newspapers, circulation, newspaper reach, in 24 European countries 1994–2006.

Country	Number of papers						Circulation (1,000)				
	1994	1998	2000	2002	2006	Papers per million inhabit.	Total	Average	Biggest	Copies per 1,000 inhabit.	Daily Reach (Per Cent)
Austria	16	17	16	17	22	2.7	3,014	156	1,052	341	73
Belgium	32	29	28	29	29	2.8	1,650	56	286	163	52
Croatia	9	10	12	12	16	3.6	747	54	252	152	86
Czech Rep.	26	18	18**	n.a.	n.a.	1.7**	1,704	95	338	196	50
Denmark	39	37	31	33	42	8.2	3,381	47	180	287	83
Estonia	15	16	13	12	13	9.7	334	20	66	242	67
Finland	56	55	55	56	55	10.5	2,424	42	447	515	82
France	87	85***	84**	88	93	1.9	9,302	97	785	156	44
Germany	411	398	382	374	374	4.5	21,254	63	4,390	298	74
Greece	23	28	32	39	42	6.6	1,491	21	86	282	3
Hungary	45	40	40	30	31	2.7	1,775	41	212	145	50
Iceland	5	3	3	3	3	9.7	250	30	55	198	96
Ireland	8	6	6	6	12	2.9	965	96	168	245	54
Italy	91	92	88	96	101	2.0	10,319	68	718	156	42
Netherlands	39	35	35	38	32	2.0	4,769	126	808	287	73
Norway	83	83	82	81	77	16.4	2,270	31	391	601	83
Poland	84	56	59	47	47	1.2	5,743	20	457	139	66
Portugal	27****	29	28**	14	18	2.2	947	25	103	75	82
Slovenia	6	5	6*	6	8	4.0	350	68**	93	204	52
Spain	125	130	136	136	178	4.1	9,072	32	435	110	42
Sweden	102	100	93	93	91	10.0	4,721	40	387	466	84
Switzerland	105	97	104	102	98	13.1	3,510	26	314	371	78
Turkey	n.a.	47	45	55	81	2.6	5,143	90	685	167	33
UK	99	99	104	107	116	2.4	18,444	183	3,461	335	33

Comment: ****) Figure refers to 1995. ***) Figure refers to 1997. **) Figures refer to 1999. *)Figure refers to 2001. Source: World Press Trends, 1999 and 2001 editions., including own calculations.

Three European newspaper regions

Even if measures of sales and reach show about the same tendency, there is an obvious difference between the levels of the two. The gap in sales between the highest and the lowest figure is much higher than that of readership. In Norway more than five times as many newspapers per 1,000 inhabitants are sold than in Italy, but the reach is less than the double. If we look more carefully at the figures, it seems that a single newspaper copy is shared among a lot more readers in the south of Europe than in the north, but also that a northern newspaper reader more often reads more than one paper regularly. Thus, the circulation and exposure statistics demonstrate much of a North-South line. To make it comprehensible we can divide Western Europe in the early twenty-first century into three newspaper regions:

1. Norway, Finland, Sweden, and Switzerland
2. Austria, United Kingdom, Germany, Denmark, the Netherlands and Luxembourg
3. Belgium, Ireland, France, Spain, Italy, Portugal and Greece

The grouping of the countries differs somewhat from that made by Hallin and Mancini (2004), especially the second one – the countries of which they place in the first group. The reason for the discrepancy is that their analysis focuses on the interplay between media and politics, and in that perspective most of the countries of the second group are similar to the first group, with the UK as the notable exception. Here, however, only the total penetration is the basis for the categorization in the three groups. In 2000 the Eastern European countries are, in terms of penetration, close to the third group but later, mainly because of their common post-war history, they have gradually formed a group of its own, although there are big differences (Gustafsson and Weibull 2007; c.f. Färdigh 2008).

Some of the differences in newspaper reading habits between the three groups can be explained by differences in general development patterns: cultural traditions, political development, social welfare, communication structure, household character and employment rate. Differences, however, can also be found within individual countries, e.g. between metropolitan and rural areas. In the long perspective, background factors like educational level and religion, and even climate, might influence newspaper development (Gustafsson and Weibull 2007).

Relating to the structuring factors used in the dimensions of national newspaper systems discussed earlier, we can use both the market (*local-regional-national*) and the journalistic (*quality-popular*) dimensions to understand country differences. The dimensions sometimes go together, meaning for instance that the most prestigious paper (e.g. an elitist business paper) and the most sensational paper (e.g. a popular tabloid) both tend to be national. Regional or local papers often have a less-pronounced profile in this respect, aiming at informative coverage of prestigious issues as well as at entertaining coverage of more popular topics. In other words, the countries at the top of newspaper circulation have a strong local press *as well as* strong national papers. They have, so to speak, two distinct layers in the newspaper market – Norway having almost three because of its many very small papers. The countries at the bottom have a press of mainly national character, which is not very strong. The group in between seems to be characterized by either a strong national or a strong local press.

European newspaper trends

The European newspaper market has, since the 1990s, been declining. Although the press is generally strong it has been weakened with regard to both sales and readership. However, the pattern differs for individual countries. If we use the relatively most reliable measurement over time – the sales measure with copies sold per 1,000 inhabitants – it is possible to present a comparable overview. Figure 1 shows the development trends from 1965 to 2006 based on this measure.

As was already observed, the expansion of new types of media has not basically changed the European newspapers landscape, even though trends may vary for individual countries. Where the printed press has a relatively low penetration the situation is extremely stable whereas, in most countries at the top, the 1990s represent a small decline. Detailed surveys on the developments in the Nordic countries points mainly at socio-economic factors, most importantly at the general economic decline in combination with a price increase on newspaper copies (Gustafsson and Weibull 2007). The price increase, reinforced by a weak advertising market, has further opened the door to other media, in the big cities especially with reference to free papers.

However, the late 1990s with a booming economy in most of the countries included in the analysis meant an increase in newspaper penetration, especially in the Nordic countries at the top, but also in the UK and the Netherlands. Thereafter all countries, with the exception of those at the bottom, show a significant decline. The explanation is probably not only economic factors, but the expansion of new digital media, not least the Internet-based ones, as well as free papers. Analyses based on time series survey data from Sweden also shows that the decline in reading habits is especially pronounced among generations born in the 1970s and 1980s, where regularity in reading is dropping faster than in older generations (Nilsson 2005).

In spite of the gradual changes concerning long-term trends the European newspaper market has been remarkably stable. An indication, at least so far, is that no country has totally changed its position in relation to the others. Sweden holds a top position most years, whereas Italy and Portugal are found at the bottom. At the same time there are certain long-term changes in range order to be observed. The UK in the 1950s and 1960s was one of the strongest, if not *the* strongest, newspaper nations in the world, and its news press structure with the quality and popular papers was a model for others, but in the 1990s it is down to about the European average. A country moving in the opposite direction is Norway: in 1965 Norway was slightly above the average in Europe but after the mid 1990s the nation is clearly at the top.

If we look into the parallel but opposite developments in the UK and Norway we find a common factor in local newspapers. For the development of the Norwegian press, the increasing strength of the local newspaper market has been the backbone of its expansion, whereas the British newspaper decline in newspaper penetration is closely related to circulation problems of the local press. In Norway there is a strong newspaper penetration at all geographical levels (national, regional and local), but in the UK the originally strong

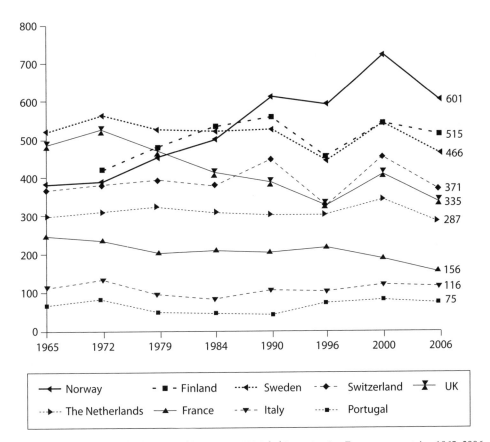

Figure 1: Paid circulation for the printed press per 1,000 inhabitants in nine European countries, 1965–2006.

Note: Data for Finland in 1965 n.a.
Source: For 1965–1996 UNESCO, for 2000 and 2006 World Press Trends (cf. Sommar, 1981). The basis for the calculation differs somewhat, since World Press Trends include only the adult population and this present a slightly higher figure. Also note that the time scale is not totally equidistant.

non-national papers have gradually declined, partly because of a concentration process, where the main conglomerates have protected their national-profile papers.

Finally, it can be observed that the three regions have been the same for at least three decades. One important reason for this stability was the slow movement of the advertising market. Where newspapers had high readership they also had a strong advertising share making it possible to develop its content; with low readership they had problems entering the advertising market and, thus, a problem in developing their profile. In the latter case television or magazines are the dominating advertising medium (Gustafsson and Weibull 2007). After 2000, however, there was an increasing volume in

Internet advertising, which gradually influenced the development of the newspaper market. Although most of that money stays within newspaper companies it is reasonable to believe that it is going to affect newspaper strategies. According to recent statistics from the industry, published in *Newsweek* magazine in March 2009, almost half of the newspaper advertising in France goes to the online editions. It is true that the French press traditionally has attracted little advertising so the total amount is fairly small, but also in a relatively strong newspaper country like the UK online advertising attracts more than 35 per cent of the total newspaper advertising.

Content changes of European newspapers 1960–2000

The conclusion on stability of the newspaper structure refers to newspapers as organizations. It obviously omits the continuous changes characterizing newspaper content. In terms of journalist products, newspapers are different from day to day, but we all know from personal experiences that the content character also changes over the years. We may not see those alterations as day-by-day readers, but when we compare today's paper with a paper from about a decade ago they are quite obvious. Actually, it is reasonable to believe that content adaptation to societal changes and to the contents of other media is one important factor behind the relative stability of the press structure.

The following section deals with the question of what changes have taken place when it comes to the form and content of newspapers, with a basic overview of content changes in the European press. The results cover not all of Europe, but twelve countries: Belgium, Czech Republic, Denmark, Finland, France, Germany, Norway, Italy, Poland, Sweden, Turkey and the UK. The analyses aim at a very general overview of main tendencies and are restricted to the leading quality and the leading popular newspapers for one single autumn week in 1960, 1980 and 2000 (see Appendix 1).

Measuring newspaper contents

To make content analyses over time is difficult; to do them across countries is even worse. The undertaking, from which some main tendencies are presented here, is a rudimentary one: there has been no ambition to go in-depth, but only to scan the main characteristics and changes over time. Only one week has been selected from each year – the first week of October (Monday–Sunday) – and only three years selected as points of references: 1960, 1980, and 2000. As already mentioned, twelve countries have participated in the project, covering the three years in focus; with five of them – Belgium, Czech Republic, Finland, Norway and Sweden – newspapers from the years 1970 and 1990 have also been included in the analysis. The same is true for the UK popular press.[2]

Within the week covered by the analysis, the main study of the content character is further restricted to two days within each week: Tuesday and Thursday. However, all issues during the week were considered when it comes to supplements; and also notes were made of the kinds of section themes occurring in other than the Tuesday and Thursday issues.

The selection of newspapers has not been based on individual newspaper titles but of the leading newspapers in each country, each year of study, where *leading* has been defined in terms of circulation. However, leading papers might be very different in different countries. To make comparisons plausible, two papers were chosen: one representing the quality press and one representing the popular press. As has been pointed out, the distinction between quality and popular press stems from a British tradition, which is typical for many other European countries, but not for all countries in our study. Further, the fact that the papers with the largest circulation have been selected implies that the papers are not necessarily the same over the years, even though this often is the case.

The analysis of the newspaper contents is divided into four parts: (1) volume, including the volume of specific sections as well as of supplements; (2) listing of thematic sections other than those covered in the measure of volume; (3) story contents on the front page and in various sections,[3] and in the biggest adverts; and (4) visualization in the newspaper, including a counting of all editorial illustrations in the main issue.[4] The main purpose of the content analysis has been to briefly characterize the newspapers' content profile by their volume priority of editorial sections and by their front-page coverage. Questions asked when analysing the material have been for instance: What volume of the papers is reserved for traditional news sections like home news, foreign news and local news over the years? To what degree do the papers contain general news pages without headings informative as to their thematic focus? What priority is given to sections specifically treating issues such as economy/business, culture, entertainment/popular culture and sports? How much space is devoted to leisure material, family pages and TV/radio material? More details of the procedure of analysis are given in Appendix 1.

Given this design, the obvious question is what really can be concluded on the basis of a few days' newspaper contents? Of course, one must be very careful when interpreting the data. However, we have chosen to focus on volume and content changes that are not too dependent on weekly or seasonal changes but reflect potential long-term alterations. The way in which a newspaper gathers and presents its contents under various headlines as well as the share of advertising is more stable than the contents of single articles published, for instance, on the front-page. Hence, the analysis that is presented first of all deals with newspaper content *profiles* over time. Contents in front-page stories and in home- and foreign-news material can only be interpreted in terms of indications. Generally, all results have, whenever possible, been validated by experiences within a wider scope of knowledge, e.g. by comparisons with available, more detailed studies within individual countries (cf. Nilsson and Severinsson 2001).

A second problem is related to reliability of measurement. It is almost unavoidable that a comparative undertaking of this kind, based on measurements carried out in individual countries, can easily lead to coding misunderstandings. Thus, it has been attempted to follow up the material thoroughly and to integrate only material that has been analysed in the same way.[5] This is the reason why not all countries are included concerning all variables. More details are given in Appendix 1.

A third and more general problem has to do with the selection of newspapers. As has been pointed out, our interest has been to include the largest 'quality' and the largest 'popular' paper in each country. However, as has been concluded from the overview of structural newspaper developments, quality and popular are not mutually-exclusive press categories in all European countries. In some countries the distinction does not fit very well for all or for some years, e.g. France, Italy and Turkey. In these cases, the participating countries have been asked to select the relatively most quality and the relatively most popular paper.[6] The newspaper titles included for each year/group are presented in Appendix 1.

Finally, it has to be pointed out that our focus on two weekday issues means that the tendencies reported first of all reflect a weekday newspaper, the product of 'weekday journalism' aimed at a weekday reading audience. In order to widen the analysis somewhat we refer also to other occurring themes in sections from the other days of the week, themes that might be included in the newspaper precisely on a weekly basis. The classification of supplements is part of this extension of the analysis in order to be able to say more of one week's newspaper contents from a reader's perspective.

Changes in newspaper formats

Newspapers of the beginning of the twenty-first century are not the news products they once were. The small leaflets which saw light in central Europe in the seventeenth century, offering a limited selection of news, have been replaced by voluminous newspapers filled with a broad variety of news topics, feature material, service information, and advertisements. Changes in communication systems, production technology, economic market, politics, welfare systems, education, people's everyday life conditions, and changes within the notion of journalism itself, have in various ways contributed to these changes. Of course, big shifts took place and great changes evolved a lot earlier than 1960, the starting point for our empirical analysis of the flagships of the European press. However, the form and content in the leading European newspapers at the turn of the century compared with forty years earlier still speak of quite big changes in the way the newspaper product has developed during this period of time.

Towards a smaller page format
The change to a smaller page format has been a trend over some decades. The origin was the boulevard papers and later what was to be called 'tabloids' because of their size and – later – their content. They were modern, single-copy sale papers with a focus on sensation and human interest ('tabloid journalism'), but also papers for people on the move, where they had to be easy to handle. When looking at the situation in most European countries up until the 1980s, it

seems clear that the tabloid size of the paper was linked to expectations for low-quality content, compared with broadsheet format that was normally associated with quality, though with national exceptions.[7] The association between newspaper size and journalistic quality restrained quality papers from adapting the smaller format – even if it could be argued to be both handy and cost efficient. Also demands from advertisers – more important to quality than to popular press – wishing to expose the readers to big adverts has been an obstacle to change.

It was the small local papers in the Nordic countries which were the first to change their format, aiming at cost reducing measures (Høst and Severinsson 1997). The tabloid size very soon became popular among the readers and also forced bigger paper to rethink their format.[8] As a consequence, size became less associated with journalistic quality. Further, in Sweden and Norway the free-sheet *Metro*, offering non-sensational news in the tabloid format, has most likely contributed to wiping out the sensationalism associated with tabloid sized newspapers (Sternvik 2007). Also, in our sample of leading European newspapers, we find a trend towards the smaller-page format. In 1960, 18 of the selected 24 titles were broadsheet papers; in 2000 the number is down to 13, the other 5 having changed into tabloid format. Amongst the quality papers, the bigger format, however, was still, in 2000, the most common (9 out of 12 titles). However, when it comes to the popular papers, only 4 out of 12 are broadsheet format: *Bild-Zeitung*, *Het Laatste Nieuws*, *Il Messaggero* and *Milliyet*. The German and Belgian sensational papers have kept to the old British format model which the British sensational press itself has abandoned. But it has to be kept in mind that Italy's *Il Messaggero* and Turkey's *Milliyet* represent newspapers with a less sensational profile than its European counterparts.

Among quality papers of broadsheet size there are also cases of tabloidization of a more cautious and hidden kind. Keeping the main part of the paper in full format, many newspapers offer other parts in tabloid, e.g. the lifestyle section or the television magazine. This is true for the quality papers in, among other countries, Denmark, Norway, Sweden, and the UK. In the UK, *The Independent*, soon followed by *The Times*, in 2003 both began to publish every daily issue in two format versions: the old broadsheet and the new tabloid format – for each reader to choose.

An increased volume

The observed trend with newspapers changing into smaller-page format should not be interpreted in terms of a dwindling newspaper press. During the studied time period – especially between 1980 and 2000 – the number of pages in the leading European newspapers grew significantly, in both quality and popular papers (Figure 2). The expansion trend is also valid when taking into consideration the changes in page format, something which is far from evident how to interpret in terms of volume.

There is one main exception to the general expansion between 1980 and 2000, namely the Swedish quality paper *Dagens Nyheter*, which, between 1990 and 2000, almost halved its number of pages, which meant fewer pages in the main issue in 2000 than in 1980. A similar pattern, however not as strong, is observed for *Helsingin Sanomat*. In both cases, the main

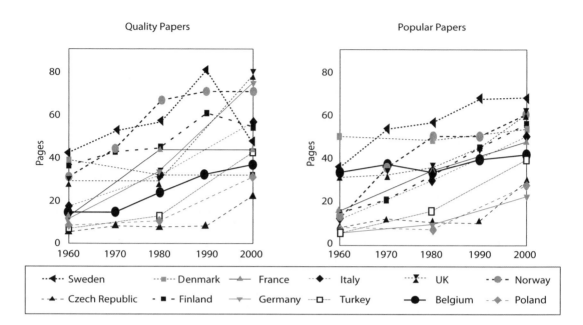

Figure 2: Average number of pages, Tuesday/Thursday issue, 1960–2000 (pages).

Quality papers	1960	1970	1980	1990	2000
Belgium	16	16	21	28	32
Czech Republic	5	8	8	8	22
Denmark	39		27		27
Finland	36	41	42	60	52
France	16		40		40
Germany	15		30		70
Italy	17		32		56
Norway	27	42	64	66	66
Poland	7		9		32
Sweden	42	52	56	80	46
Turkey	6		13		40
UK	26		25		78

Popular papers	1960	1970	1980	1990	2000
Belgium	27	32	27	36	38
Czech Republic	6	8	8	8	26
Denmark	48		42		48
Finland	16	20	31	42	50
France	18		30		42
Germany	5		9		20
Italy	12		27		46
Norway	16	32	44	44	54
Poland	6		8		24
Sweden	36	50	52	62	62
Turkey	6		14		32
UK	32	28	32	39	56

Note: All countries were not included in the coding of the 1970 and 1990 papers (empty cells). The increases in the number of pages in the Czech and Polish quality papers are affected by changes into smaller format; the same goes for the Czech, Norwegian and Polish popular papers (see Appendix 1).

explanation is a decline in advertising volume, leading also to some decrease in editorial volume. The observation illustrates the quality press' dependency upon a constant supply of advertisers, which in it its turn is dependent of the national economy. It is reasonable to believe that this factor is especially crucial to the Nordic quality press with its fairly broad readership. *Le Monde* also represents an exception from the general expansion trend, the number of pages being the same in 2000 as in 1980 – in spite of the fact that the paper during this period changed from broadsheet to so-called Berlin page format. In this case it seems to be a matter of reduction of costs.

So far we have concentrated on the volume of the main paper. However, the expansion trend is strongly manifested in the growing number and the growing volume of supplements (Table 2). It is even reasonable to say that one of the most important features of the news press at the end of the twentieth century is 'supplementation'. Newspaper supplements have widened the concept of a newspaper into something that offers the reader not only *more* to read but also a wider selection of themes and subjects. The most remarkable growth of supplement volume we find in the UK and its prestigious *Times*; in this case we note in 1980 a four-page economy supplement and, two decades later, a little less than 400 supplement

Table 2: Total number of supplement pages and number of supplements, all week, 1960–2000 (pages).

Quality papers						Popular papers					
Number of pages	*1960*	*1970*	*1980*	*1990*	*2000*	*Number of pages*	*1960*	*1970*	*1980*	*1990*	*2000*
Belgium	0	0	32	0	158	Belgium	0	0	0	0	104
Czech Republic	0	0	0	0	0	Czech Republic	0	0	0	0	0
Denmark	0		96		104	Denmark	0		0		124
Finland	0	0	0	0	56	Finland	0	0	0	n.a.	66
France	0		0		170	France	0		0		0
Germany	10		171		176	Germany	0		0		0
Norway	0	0	24	0	n.a.	Norway	0	0	0	0	0
Poland	0		0		193	Poland	0		0		79
Sweden	0	20	60	64	206	Sweden	0	48	60	116	324
UK	0		0		386	UK	2	0	2	9	12
Number of supplements	*1960*	*1970*	*1980*	*1990*	*2000*	*Number of supplements*	*1960*	*1970*	*1980*	*1990*	*2000*
Belgium	0	0	2	0	9	Belgium	0	0	0	0	7
Czech Republic	0	0	0	0	0	Czech Republic	0	0	0	0	0
Denmark	0		5		7	Denmark	0		0		7
Finland	0	0	0	0	1	Finland	0	0	0	5	3
France	0		0		6	France	0		0		0
Germany	2		5		7	Germany	0		0		0
Norway	0	0	2	0	n.a.	Norway	0	0	0	0	0
Poland	0		0		12	Poland	0		0		4
Sweden	0	1	3	2	7	Sweden	0	2	3	6	5
UK	0		0		12	UK	1	0	1	1	1

Note: All countries were not included in the coding of the 1970 and 1990 papers (empty cells).

pages. Still, the main issue grew from about 25 pages in 1980 to almost 80 pages in 2000 (the main issue in 2000 comprises a separate part named *Times 2*, including feature material, culture, TV, and other more theme specific topics). The volume of advertising was almost doubled in the main issue of the paper during these years. Also, those newspapers that declined in editorial volume, like *Dagens Nyheter* and *Le Monde*, increased the number of pages in weekly supplements

Supplements seem mostly to be a feature of the quality press, but the popular newspapers have also in recent years come to publish supplements. However, here we find no common European trend and the number of supplements per week is not as many for the papers that do use this way of presenting their more voluminous and varying contents. Sweden might represents a notable exception in this regard, since its leading popular paper in 2000, *Aftonbladet*, offered 324 supplement pages (mainly containing TV material, entertainment and leisure reading) spread over five separate supplements the week included in the analysis. It is a quite remarkable change compared to the situation in 1980, when the main popular paper at that time, *Expressen*, included 60 supplement pages in the analysed week.

The role of advertising

We have already mentioned the dependency upon advertisers among the quality papers, which – with a few exceptions – are mainly subscribed to and have an upmarket readership. In our selection of leading European quality papers, the average share of advertising volume between the years in focus varies between no advertising at all and almost three quarters of the volume. In the popular press the share is generally smaller; no paper average reaches above 43 per cent any of the analysed years. Most papers have a larger share of advertisement content in 2000 than in 1960 but, especially among the quality papers, there are the already-mentioned exceptions in the Nordic countries.

The generally growing share of advertisement volume has led to newspapers with a more similar balance between the volume of editorial contents and that of advertising. Amongst the quality papers the share of advertising in 2000 varies between 22 and 61 per cent between the papers (in 1960: between 0 and 65 per cent); the popular papers, between 8 and 36 per cent (1960: 0 and 41 per cent). The change from state control to free market in Eastern Europe is especially evident in advertising. The newspapers representing the Czech Republic and Poland have increased their commercial profile most dramatically. Back in 1960 the share of advertising in the Polish quality paper *Trybuna Ludu* was no more than 2 per cent; in 2000 *Gazeta Wyborcza* consists of 30 per cent of advertising material. In the Czech papers, the increase was already partly visible in 1980. The Turkish paper *Hürriyet* has also increased its share of advertising to quite some extent.

The development of the volume of advertising reflects mainly economic trends of the individual countries but also to some extent the character of the paper. However, in a competitive newspaper market advertising is an important condition for editorial coverage, both in terms of resources and volume. Thus, an interesting observation is that there has been an expansion of advertising in the quality press over the period of years, meaning that the papers have a strong position in their societies. But a general observation is that quality papers with a socially broader readership seem to be more exposed to economic changes than the real upmarket papers.

Editorial approach: Sorting the new world?

The increase in the number of supplements can be regarded from various perspectives. One is that a weekly supplement might be a neat solution when wanting to expand the coverage of material of a less time-bound character, such as leisure reading, culture and topics of more specific interest such as housing, auto, travelling and ICT. Such material is often cheaper since it is preproduced and often bought from freelancers. Secondly, and no less important, a supplement is an efficient way of selling readers to advertisers looking for a special segment of interests. Thirdly, for more specific topics, a supplement is an effective way of presenting the contents exactly as 'optional reading', often making it easier for a household, etc. to share the newspaper according to individual reading preferences.

The factors behind 'supplementation' of newspapers are also crucial in structuring the main issue of the paper. Both editorial organization and the reading of a newspaper can be made easier by sorting and dividing all content under section headlines, informative about their theme or geographic focus – a newspaper strategy sometimes called departmentalization. In the newspapers from 1980, and especially 2000, we generally find more of such effort than in 1960. In 1960 several quality papers consisted of roughly one third of unsorted material without any headline about its thematic or geographic focus, the extreme example being the Norwegian *Aftenposten* with more than 60 per cent of its content without page headlines. In 2000 no paper consisted of more than one fifth of unsorted material.[9] A detailed study of Swedish newspapers confirms the observation as valid for the Swedish press in general (Nilsson and Severinsson 2001).

It could be argued that the growing departmentalization of the contents reflects a new bureaucratic organization of the editorial work, which in the last decades has become much more structured, based on a new organizational rationality. From a reader's point of view it means an increasing 'fragmentation'. But the fragmentation is, in all likelihood, also motivated by a journalistic ambition to present the reader with a newspaper easy to read and scan through, also when its volume increases. Another probable factor of importance is the widened scope of newspaper journalism, with the introduction of new, more theme-specific, content genres. Examples of topics which have been emphasized in the modern newspaper – in separate sections in the main issue as well as in supplements – are economy, travel, computer/ICT and food/cooking – adapting the paper to fundamental changes in interests and lifestyles among readers. Another way of seeing it is that the newspapers of the early twenty-first century are more explicitly target-oriented than they were in 1960. Other examples are the frequent feature sections specifically addressing a certain audience, such as women and young people.

What has been said about both supplementation and departmentalization is true for the quality press, but less so for the popular papers. It seems that this is one of the most profound differences of the two newspaper types. The big quality papers depend increasingly on bureaucratic structures whereas the popular press is more flexible in its organization. The observation implies that popular papers in themselves are less organized, but that the central news desk is very strong in handling the news material. An illustrative example is the change of the Norwegian *Dagbladet* from a traditional broadsheet morning paper to a popular single-copy sale paper. A classical study, based on participant observation, clearly showed the increased power of the central desk to meet the daily needs of the news market (Klausen 1986).

Even though there is a clear difference between quality and popular papers in terms of content structure, there is also a tendency among the latter to organize its content in a stricter form. Such changes are most clear for some of the Nordic popular papers, but also for the Turkish *Milliyet*.

Content profile

If there is a general trend towards a more clearly-defined editorial profile of the contemporary European newspaper, especially the quality paper, the diversity is bigger when it comes to the actual profile: which sections to be included and, not least, to what extent – in relation to other sections. Even for a voluminous newspaper there are, of course, priorities to be made between subjects and what themes to cover.

Less general news
First looking at the quality press, it is evident how the leading newspapers generally have come to reduce their news profile between 1960 and 2000. Pages filled with home news, foreign news or unsorted general news have not expanded in the same way as other content, especially when it comes to the economy and TV/radio material. Taking into consideration the supplements as well, the trend is even clearer. With the supplements, the news profile of the contemporary newspaper has been further toned down in favour of a paper offering more leisure-reading, popular culture and entertainment.

In the 1960s, Poland, France, Norway, Italy and the Czech Republic were the countries with the most pronounced news profile in the leading quality papers; in 2000, Italy, France and the Czech Republic still hold the top position in this respect (Table 3). At the other end, Germany, Sweden and the UK are the countries in which we find the weakest news profile – countries which (alongside Denmark) are also found at the bottom in 1960, with already a varied range of topics offered in specific sections.

Of course, we have to bear in mind that our sample week does not allow too many conclusions on the level of individual papers or countries. For instance, in Poland in 1980, the sample week coincides with the week of the Communist party plenary assembly – a political event that wiped out a lot of the content genres generally covered in the paper. Still, such a situation says something about the relation between the Polish mass media and the Polish government at that time.

From a general point of view, the foreign focus in the news reporting has been somewhat strengthened since 1960, at least when it comes to foreign news gathered together and presented under a specific foreign news heading, thus high-lighting the foreign news profile of the newspaper. The average share of foreign news of the total news volume has varied from 21, 35 and 31 per cent over the investigated years. The strengthened foreign news profile is especially marked in Italy, Turkey, Norway, Sweden, Czech Republic and Poland; in 1960 the newspapers in the Scandinavian countries as well as those in Turkey had no

Table 3: The editorial profile in the quality papers, 1960 and 2000 (per cent, Tuesday/Thursday average).

1960	News	Economy	Sports	Culture	TV/radio	Opinion	Other	Sum
Poland	80	0	14	4	0	2	0	100
France	64	12	2	11	1	5	5	100
Norway	62	8	11	10	2	7	0	100
Czech Rep.	57	11	13	7	0	4	8	100
Belgium	49	7	7	5	4	6	22	100
Finland	48	0	13	13	1	5	20	100
Turkey	39	0	33	0	6	14	8	100
Germany	36	26	5	10	0	10	13	100
UK	35	15	11	8	2	9	20	100
Sweden	34	5	12	11	3	6	29	100
Denmark	33	17	11	7	6	7	19	100

2000	News	Economy	Sports	Culture	TV/radio	Opinion	Other	Sum
Poland	34	27	12	9	0	1	17	100
France	47	19	3	11	4	7	9	100
Norway	26	16	16	11	4	8	19	100
Czech Rep.	38	14	21	4	2	6	15	100
Belgium	24	36	6	11	7	4	12	100
Finland	33	13	10	8	8	7	21	100
Turkey	34	19	29	3	1	13	1	100
Germany	12	45	6	14	4	3	16	100
UK	21	10	7	13	9	7	33	100
Sweden	20	22	11	15	6	7	19	100
Denmark	38	25	5	12	8	5	7	100

distinct foreign section. It is also notable that the local news profile in 2000 is generally more pronounced than before. On average, the share of sectionalized local news of the total news volume in the quality papers has grown from 4 to 15 per cent since 1960. The newspapers of the Nordic countries, together with *Právo* in the Czech Republic, answer for the lion's share of the change: it is almost exclusively these papers that make up the trend. Once again, it seems reasonable to conclude that middle-market quality papers, like the Nordic ones, have a somewhat different profile, probably as a consequence of their more local anchorage.

The reinforced local and foreign news profile in the quality press might in part reflect the increased organization of the contents discussed above. The average volume-share of general news pages of the total news volume in 1960 is halved in 2000 – in effect already in 1980. Local and foreign news coverage that formerly has been offered on general news pages today is more often placed in specific sections of the newspaper. Looking at changes at the level of individual papers, it becomes clear, however, that it is mainly the foreign news profile that seems to have been enhanced by the stricter organization of the newspaper contents. The growth of local pages to a larger extent seems to lead beyond the mere mode of presentation.

High and low in quality papers

The leading quality papers in Europe have, to quite some extent, reinforced their economy profile during the four decades of study. In two countries, Poland and Turkey, the leading quality paper of 1960 did not contain any economy section at all, and in other countries the section was marginal. The most pronounced economy profile is found in the German *Frankfurter Allgemeine Zeitung*, in which the share of the economic section rose from about one quarter of the editorial contents to almost half between 1960 and 2000. Furthermore, it covers economy in weekly supplements. On the other hand, the paper has the least-pronounced basic news profile, with only a little more than 10 per cent news volume of the editorial contents in the main issue. The tendency is the same in almost all quality papers in our study and, in the year 2000, the economic material constitutes between 10 and 36 per cent of editorial contents of the leading paper's main issue.

But there is one important exception to the general rule. In the UK, the coverage of economy and market issues in *The Times* has not expanded between 1960 and 2000, relatively speaking. The average page volume has in fact doubled between the years but with the great general expansion of the newspaper between 1980 and 2000 – including the launch of *Times 2* – the economy section has not kept its former position. Looking more closely into the development, it becomes obvious that *The Times* has chosen a different way from other quality papers, namely broadened its contents and changed from a harder to a softer editorial profile. Actually, in 1960, the *Times* offered about as much economic material (2 to 3 pages) as *Frankfurter Allgemeine Zeitung* (2.5 pages) but has since then increased its coverage on culture more than on economy, not only in the main paper, but also in supplements.

The volume of sports coverage in the quality papers has generally grown since 1960, but its share in relation to other editorial sections has been about stable. However, in some papers there is a relative growth, e.g. in the Czech *Právo* and the Norwegian *Aftenposten*. Also *Le Monde* in France has increased its sports contents but its share is still on a very marginal level. By comparing the quality newspapers across Europe, it becomes obvious that Turkey's *Hürriyet* has a remarkably larger sports share compared to the other European quality papers in 1960 as well as in 2000, keeping one third of the editorial volume for sports material. This exceptional pattern puts forward the question of whether, in the end, *Hürriyet* should be defined as a quality paper (see above discussion).

The share of culture and entertainment content has not changed that much as long as our focus is restricted to the main issue of the papers. In Turkey and the Czech Republic, the culture/entertainment profile of the quality papers was weak in 1960 as well as in 2000, whereas in Sweden, Germany, and the UK the quality papers show a most marked culture/entertainment profile in 2000, but were already strong in this respect in 1960. For TV/radio material, however, there is a general trend of increase, especially in 2000 compared to four decades before. In all countries, except Poland and Turkey, the volume has grown, not the least in relation to other types of editorial content categories. Together with the growth of supplements in 2000 covering TV/entertainment/leisure, it is reasonable to conclude that the quality press has a generally-growing entertainment profile.

The opinion profile of the quality newspapers has generally been quite stable between 1960 and 2000. However, with the general volume expansion, there is a tendency *within* the opinion material that debate material and letters to the editor have gained more room in relation to editorials and columns. The latter kind of material does not possess the same potential for expansion as does the former – or indeed other types of newspaper content. In this sense, the newspaper's role as a public forum has become more pronounced during the last four decades; this is especially noticeable in the UK, Finland, Denmark, and France, in which the leading quality paper in 2000 devoted one-and-a-half pages or more to debate material and letters to the editor. Finlands' *Helsingin Sanomat* and Italy's *Il Corriere della Sera* both display the most popular democratic touch in publishing a full page of letters to the editor. In the leading papers of the Czech Republic, Poland and Turkey respectively we find the very opposite: very little of debate and few letters in relation to editorials, columns etc.

Increasingly popular: the popular papers

The popular press have, by definition, a somewhat different content profile from the quality press, even though the weakened news profile is a common denominator between the two groups. In 2000, most of the popular papers included in the study contained on their editorial pages about 25 to 40 per cent general news (Table 4). There is one main exception: *Il Messaggero*, which, like its quality counterpart in Italy, *Il Corriere della Sera*, devotes approximately 70 per cent of its editorial contents to general news. Back in 1960, the corresponding news share in the popular papers ranged between 26 per cent (Turkey) and 88 per cent (Norway).

The economy profile in the popular papers is generally weak – with two exceptions: the papers in Turkey and the Czech Republic. Instead, the sports profile is relatively strong, especially in Sweden's *Aftonbladet* and Germany's *Bild-Zeitung*, where this material constitutes about one third of the contents – in *Aftonbladet* almost 40 per cent. In Denmark and Finland the papers, with comparatively little sports coverage in their Tuesday/Thursday issues, publish sports supplements on Mondays.

The culture/entertainment coverage gets most room in the popular papers of the UK and the Nordic countries – between 13 and 19 per cent of the editorial contents in 2000. Another Swedish study has shown that culture/entertainment is the most expansive editorial content in Sweden since the 1980s (Domellöf 1999). Less interest in culture is shown in the papers of Turkey and of the Czech Republic, which, as we have seen above, is true for the popular and

Table 4: The editorial profile in the popular papers, 1960 and 2000 (per cent, Tuesday/Thursday average).

1960	News	Economy	Sports	Culture	TV/radio	Opinion	Other	Sum
Norway	88	0	1	0	0	9	2	100
Poland	57	5	15	5	3	3	12	100
Italy	53	12	12	23	0	0	0	100
Belgium	52	4	18	7	3	2	14	100
Denmark	51	1	19	3	2	3	21	100
France	50	4	15	10	3	0	18	100
Finland	49	0	13	0	2	8	28	100
UK	48	4	20	14	4	7	3	100
Czech Rep.	47	0	25	5	0	3	20	100
Germany	43	0	14	0	0	8	35	100
Sweden	41	0	20	13	2	6	18	100
Turkey	26	2	31	0	4	9	28	100

2000	News	Economy	Sports	Culture	TV/radio	Opinion	Other	Sum
Norway	32	0	16	16	10	7	19	100
Poland	23	0	19	11	8	4	35	100
Italy	72	8	10	8	2	0	0	100
Belgium	42	8	22	8	8	2	10	100
Denmark	39	0	11	19	5	11	15	100
France	30	9	25	7	11	1	17	100
Finland	34	5	15	16	7	8	15	100
UK	26	3	24	19	6	7	15	100
Czech Rep.	36	18	18	7	3	15	3	100
Germany	42	0	28	0	7	3	20	100
Sweden	27	0	37	13	6	5	12	100
Turkey	31	26	24	1	1	12	5	100

the quality papers alike. However, the problems with the distinction between quality and popular papers in these countries, especially in Turkey, should be kept in mind.

As is the case with the quality press, the TV/radio material has grown during the last decades in the popular papers. In 2000 it constituted in between 1 per cent (Turkey) and 11 per cent (France) of the editorial pages – not counting the frequent supplements.

The Visualized newspaper

With the growing number of pages in the newspaper, the number of visual elements accompanying editorial material has expanded alongside the number of articles. At the same time visuals often connote a more popular paper, whereas text is associated with quality. Thus, it is expected that there are fewer pictures in quality papers than in popular papers. Concluding from the earlier observations of more popular contents, the hypothesis would be an increase in visuals per editorial volume over the years. To test this we have simply counted the number of visuals in the Tuesday and Thursday issues. Finland, Italy, Norway, Sweden, and the UK are included in this part of the analysis.

Concerning visualization in the quality press, there is no simple tendency, at least not regarding the mere *number* of visuals on the average page. The number of illustrations per one broadsheet page of editorial contents varies between 1.6 (*The Times*, of which, in 2000, approximately one half consists of tabloid pages: *Times 2*), and 4.8 (*Aftenposten*). In Finland's *Helsingin Sanomat* and Sweden's *Dagens Nyheter*, the average number per page unit has even decreased in 2000 compared with the 1960s and 1970s. Turning to the popular press, the picture is partly different. In the leading popular paper in Italy, *Il Messaggero*, the average number has doubled from 1.2 visuals per one tabloid page of editorial contents in 1960 to 2.3 in 2000. In the other countries/papers,[10] the average number has increased as well.[11]

Looking specifically at the front pages, there are differences to the degree in which the top stories are illustrated. In our quality-paper sample, roughly every other front-page story of the top five is illustrated, in 2000 as well as in 1980 – and in 1960. There are however big national variations: in 2000, the average ranges between 31 per cent (*Il Corriere della Sera*) and 77 per cent (*Hürriyet*). In the sample of popular papers, the total average is about the same; in this case, however, the material indicates a trend of enhanced visualization during the studied period, with an increasing share of illustrated stories – from 44 per cent in 1960 to 67 per cent in 2000. The results suggest that in 2000, the popular paper has a more visualized news profile compared with the quality paper.

Conclusion: Stability and change

In the four decades from 1960 to 2000 the European newspaper system from one perspective has been remarkably stable – yet, from another it has been characterized by important changes. To put it simply, the stability refers to the newspaper structure, the changes to the newspaper contents. The content changes, however, have also been related to the structural development of the European press.

Structural patterns

The most general observation is that the newspaper structure of Europe in many ways reflects the economic, political and socio-cultural traditions of individual countries. In this respect it is not meaningful to speak about *the* European press. The strength of the daily press of an individual country is explained by economic conditions, urbanization, educational level, political development and employment rates. Since these differences encompass a north-south dimension, the press structure also differs between a region of northern and small European countries with a strong press, a Mediterranean belt with a weak press, and in-between countries with a press with a European average readership (cf. Hallin and Mancini, 2004).

From such a structural point of view, little has changed since the beginning of the 1960s. The observed tendency is a decline of the British press from the top level to the middle, and a rise for the Finnish and Norwegian press from the middle to the top level. Further, the 1990s mean a decline of the press in countries at the top level, whereas the situation is very stable, or even somewhat increasing, in the low-level countries.

At least on the surface, most individual newspapers in the countries included in our analysis seem to have kept their position. It is mainly the same leading quality and popular papers in 2000 as it was in 1960. Even in Eastern Europe, in spite of the political changes of the 1980s and 1990s, the main papers have normally succeeded in changing their profiles to keep up with the changed political, economic and social conditions. However, our focus on the biggest papers as well as our choices of countries might be somewhat misleading. New papers have emerged and contested the dominating ones, both on the quality and the popular market. In Italy, *La Repubblica* has challenged *Il Corriere della Sera*; *The Independent* is a newcomer on the British quality market and in Poland, *Gazeta Wyborcza* developed from an opposition leaflet to the country's leading quality paper –to name only some examples. Also specialized business papers have sprung up, like *Dagens Industri* in Sweden and *Dagens Næringsliv* in Norway. In the former Eastern Europe, the expansion of new sensational tabloids is a striking feature, e.g. *Blikk* in Hungary and *Dnes* in the Czech Republic, both owned by the Swiss newspaper company *Ringier*. A common denominator of the new papers established since the 1960s is a more popular profile compared to that of their competitors, or they are very specialized in news focus.

Content changes: Volume and profile

A general tendency for almost all newspapers covered by this study is a strong increase in volume. The expansion can be observed both in the main paper, especially in the establishment of new sections but also in the increasing number of supplements. We have pointed out two important aspects of this development: the *fragmentation* of news contents, meaning more distinct content sections than before, and the *supplementation*, meaning a paper in several parts, some of which has an editorial profile of their own, often like weekly magazines.

In this development at least three important observations can be made. The first is that the news profile of both quality and popular papers has become gradually less accentuated. Of all contents the reader is offered, less is devoted to the very daily news and more to background material, in-depth analyses and leisure reading. The second observation is that an increasing share of non-news content is devoted to entertainment and popular culture. There are some differences between individual countries – in Germany there have been almost no changes, in Britain the newspapers have changed a great deal since the 1980s – but for the average European paper, the tendency is quite clear. The third observation is that the volume increase, especially with regard to the supplements, is mainly a matter of weekend reading. For example, many quality papers increasingly bring out a Saturday or Sunday magazine. In Germany, *Frankfurter Allgemeine Zeitung*, the most traditional quality paper in our sample, has launched a Sunday paper with a somewhat more popular profile. The British press differs somewhat in this respect because of its long tradition of popular Sunday papers, a market more or less of its own.

A fourth, more general, observation can be added: the development of the European press has – with few exceptions – increasingly resulted in a more popular editorial profile than before. For the quality press it presupposes fewer political items (however more economic) and more leisure material. Thus, the quality press in parts imitates the journalistic style of the popular papers, whereas the popular press has gone further in content areas like entertainment, television and gossip. The tendency is true for all countries, though the level and the pace might differ.

It seems reasonable to interpret the developments of the editorial profiles as adaptations to economic, social and cultural changes in Europe. Changing social structure, new lifestyles and more leisure time have created other demands among European citizens. Moreover, newspaper companies, since at least the 1980s, are more market-oriented than before, not least because of the increasing competition with other media. They want to present a wide selection of topics relevant to the readers, when the readers have time to read it, but they also want to position themselves on the advertising market and offer the advertiser interested target groups. Thus, a stricter structure of the expanding contents, delivered in separate sections or supplements, and more leisure material at the end of the week, all seem to be ways of adapting to changes in people's everyday life as well as to the individual interests of the readers. Furthermore, the popular papers seem to adapt themselves to issues put on the agenda by television. They have increasingly come to focus on people inhabiting the world of television.

A changing newspaper market?

When the ideas behind this study were laid out, it was a non-debated point of departure that it was easy to distinguish between quality and popular papers. As has been mentioned in the section on methodology, it soon turned out that the distinction was not relevant in some countries, e.g. in Turkey, and also less so in France and Italy where the specialized sports papers take the place of the popular daily press. Furthermore, our empirical observations have clearly demonstrated that the traditional distinction between quality and popular is not as clear at the turn of the century as it has been, at least not if we interpret the dimension in terms of editorial form. It is especially interesting to note the British press here, once a sort of ideal model of this distinction, where so-called quality papers have undergone the most evident changes. One could even be tempted to talk about a tendency towards content convergence.

Our observations make it important to focus on the relation between popular form and popular content. With popular form we mean a paper with a format that is easy to handle and that is more flexible towards individual tastes (the tabloid-size; separate sections; supplements) as well as pages with a clear structure and a layout attractive to the eye. With popular content, on the other hand, we refer to 'soft' content like entertainment, television, celebrities and personalities as well as sensational news and to some extent sports. Until the 1980s, popular form and popular content coincided in the so-called popular press. Later, the popular forms have been taken over by the quality press, including big headlines, colour photographs and, in some cases, smaller format. This is not the same as to say that

Figure 3: Prestigious or popular: A question of both content and form.

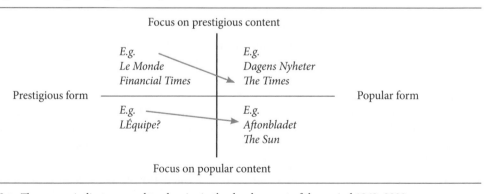

Note: The arrows indicate general tendencies in the development of the period 1960–2000.

the content per se has become more popular, even if this is true for some areas, like the specialized material and the supplements.

However, the traditional distinction between popular and quality in itself contains a hidden normative statement that it is better to stand for quality than to be popular. Such a distinction is not very useful, we argue, when looking at today's so-called quality papers which offer their audience a product of an increasingly popular format. We find 'prestigious' a word more apt than 'quality' when wanting to describe the dimensions in press types that fit the news press market of the twentieth as well as the twenty-first century.

By using a four-field table to demonstrate the market changes, it is thus possible to distinguish between, on the one hand, 'prestigious' papers and, on the other hand, 'popular' papers – with regard to both form and content (Figure 3). The classical prestigious papers are found in the upper left; but at the turn of the century, many of these have moved to the upper right. In the upper left we suggest that we still find a paper like the French *Le Monde* together with the main business papers, like the *Financial Times* or the German *Handelsblatt*. The popular press of today is found in the lower right, but was probably placed somewhat to the left of this position in the 1960s, if not exactly in the lower left. The latter box might perhaps be the home of specialized sports paper, like the French *L'Equipe*.

The figure also illustrates the observed tendencies of the leading European newspapers over the four decades. The general impression is that the leading papers are drifting in a popular direction in form as well as in content. It seems reasonable to conclude that a newspaper in today's media world has to be more popular than before to attract large segments of the general public. The reason behind this can be found in the societal changes in all European countries as well as in the increasing competition in the media market. As has already been pointed out, the expansion of television, especially since the early 1980s, is probably one very important factor, affecting especially the profile of the popular papers. However, it is reasonable to say that the gradual change of the quality press has been influenced by television, albeit indirectly. Another driving force might have been the expansion of the business press, which compelled traditional quality papers to broaden their contents, e.g. in economic as well as cultural material.

The observed changes show the strength of the European press in adapting to a changing environment. It is probably true that it will be difficult for the press to keep its strength with the expanding availability of old and new media, not least so-called free media. But most predictions of the future of newspapers so far seem to have failed as a result of having underestimated the capability of newspapers to adapt to new situations.

Finally, we have to ask what the changing newspaper market means for the European public sphere. A first observation is that it is difficult to regard the combined newspaper structure of individual European countries as one European newspaper sphere. Even if some newspapers are similar in profile there are too many differences between the countries to speak of one European newspaper system. Secondly, the fragmentation and segmentation of newspapers challenges the idea of the newspaper as one comprehensive platform for information and ideas. The papers are split into sections targeted at different readers that might never meet. Thirdly, actual changes of the European newspapers probably have consequences for their role as a national public sphere. The observed tendencies clearly indicate that economic considerations are important for the content in the early twenty-first century, probably much more so than was the case in 1960. Thus, the Habermasian criticism of the commercialized media sphere of the 1960s (Habermas 1962) might be even more true four decades later.

Notes

1. The measurement standard used by UNESCO.
2. The weeks cover the following dates: 1960: 3–9 October; 1970: 5–11 October; 1980: 6–12 October; 1990: 1–7 October; 2000: 2–8 October.
3. The biggest or otherwise first appearing home and foreign news stories, 20 and 10 stories respectively, are selected, disregarding whether or not they are found under a headline informative as to their geographic orientation. As to other sections, the Nth biggest stories (2, 3 or 5) are selected from occurring sections treating: Economy/Business (3 stories); Culture (5); Entertainment/Popular culture (3); Sports (3); Editorial/Opinion/Commentary (2); Debate (2); Letters to the Editor (2). Regarding the coding of home and foreign news stories some countries were left out of the analysis after a preliminary and limited coding (see appendix).
4. A reduced national basis for analysis: Finland, Italy, Norway, Sweden, and the UK (the latter only regarding the quality paper).
5. The coordination has been handled at the Department of Journalism and Mass Communication, University of Gothenburg.
6. Further, in the UK, *The Times* has been chosen throughout the period of analysis, despite the fact that it had not the biggest circulation in 1980; *The Guardian* had by then a bigger circulation than *The Times*, but the difference was small (*The Times*: 316'; *The Guardian*: 379') (Seymour-Ure 1996).
7. For example, the biggest sensational newspaper in Germany, the *Bild-Zeitung*, is a broadsheet.
8. In 2002, the percentage of tabloid-sized newspapers in Sweden had increased to about 60 per cent, in 2007 to almost 100 per cent (Sternvik 2007).
9. In 1960 the news coverage in *Aftenposten* was above all local (Oslo), which reasonably reduces the need of presenting the news under specific section headlines, informative as to the geographic orientation of the news. In 2000 the newspaper, after a period of heightened national news ambitions, changes its focus back to mainly local reporting; by then, however, the more structured paper had come to stay.
10. UK is not included in the analysis of popular papers.
11. In Norway, the average number is in fact bigger in 1960 than in 2000; however in 1960 the leading popular paper (*Dagbladet*) is of broadsheet format. Since 1970, when the leading paper (*Verdens Gang*) became printed in tabloid format, there has been an increase in the average number of illustrations per page.

References

Domellöf, Maria (1999) *Mycket nöje! Nöjesjournalistik i förändring*, Report no. 94, Dept. of journalism and mass communication, University of Gothenburg.

Färdigh, Mattias (2008) *Mediesystem i Europa (Media systems in Europé)*, Research report. Department of Journalism and Mass Communication, University of Gothenburg.

Gustafsson, Karl Erik (1996) *Origins and development of the Swedish tabloid. Expressen 1944–1994*, Report 38. Mass Media Research Unit, School of Economics at Göteborg University (Sweden).

Gustafsson, Karl Erik & Weibull, Lennart (1997) European newspaper readership. Structure and development, *Communications*, Vol 22: 3.

Gustafsson, Karl Erik & Weibull, Lennart (2007) An overview and detailed description of European newspaper readership, in Valtteri Niiranen (ed.) *Europeans read newspapers*, Brussels: European Newspaper Association.

Habermas Jürgen (1962) *Strukturwandel der Öffentlichkeit*, Neuwied: Politica.

Hallin, Dan & Mancini, Paolo (2004) *Comparing media systems: Three models of media and politics*, Cambridge: Cambridge University Press.

Høst, Sigurd (1991) The Norwegian newspaper system, in H. Rønning & K. Lundby, (eds.) *Media and Communi-cation: Readings in methodology, history and culture*, Gjøvik, Norwegian University Press, pp. 281–301.

Høst, Sigurd & Severinsson, Ronny (1997) *Avisstrukturen i Norge og Sverige – 1960 til 1995. Arbetsrapport nr 1 fra projektet Norsk-svensk dagspresseutveckling*, Report no. 77. Dept. of Journalism and Mass Communication, University of Gothenburg.

Klausen, Arne Martin (1986) *Med Dabladet til tabloid*, Oslo: Universitetsforlaget.

Nilsson, Åsa (2005) 'Tidningsläsandets åldrar och generationer', in Annika Bergström, Ingela Wadbring & Lennart Weibull (eds.) *Nypressat – Ett kvartsekel med svenska dagstidningsläsare*, Dept. of Journalism and Mass Communication, University of Gothenburg.

Nilsson, Åsa; Severinsson, Ronny; Wadbring, Ingela & Weibull, Lennart (2001) *Trender och traditioner i svensk morgonpress 1987–1999*, Dept. of Journalism and Mass Communication, University of Gothenburg.

Scannell, Paddy & Cardiff, David (1991) *A social history of British broadcasting, Volume 1922–1939*, Oxford: Blackwell.

Smith, Anthony (1979) *The Newspaper: An international history*, London: Thames & Hudson.

Smith, Anthony (ed.) (1998) *Television: An international history*, Oxford: Oxford University Press.

Sommar, Carl-Olov (1981) Dagspressens spridning i ett internationellt perspektiv, *Dagens Nyheter verksamhetsbrättelse för 1980*, Stockholm, Dagens Nyheter.

Sternvik, Josefine (2007) *I krympt kostym. Morgontidningars formatförändring och dess konsekvenser*, Dept. of Journalism and Mass Communication, University of Gothenburg.

Terzis, Giorgios (ed.) (2008) *European media governance: National and regional dimensions*, Chicago: Intellect Books.

Thompson, John B (1995) *The media and modernity. A social theory of the media*, Cambridge: Polity Press.

Unesco (1992) *Unesco statistical yearbook 1992*, Paris: Unesco.

Seymour-Ure, Colin (1996) *The British press and broadcasting since 1945*, Oxford: Blackwell.

Weibull, Lennart (1993) The status of the daily newspaper: what readership research tells us about the role of newspapers in the mass media system, *Poetics* 21, pp. 259–282.

World Association of Newspapers (2007) *World Press Trends 2001–2007*, Paris: World Association of Newspapers & Zenithmedia.

Chapter 3

50 Years of European Television: An Essay

Jostein Gripsrud
University of Bergen

Introduction

L ooking back on the history of television in Europe over the last five decades, one is struck by the extent to which its institutional and textual history reflects the economic, social, political and cultural history of the continent. This is partly due to the centralized structure of the medium, resulting from the limited nature of the radio spectrum and relatively high cost of production and distribution, which has meant that only governments or companies with vast financial resources can establish and run television services. Consequently, television was, in Europe, at first distributed on only one or two national channels. Thus it also had to be a major topic of public debate and an issue of considerable political and economic importance.

Television's close dialogical and reflective relations with the rest of society are manifested in its contents, day by day following historical developments of all kinds, on all levels and planes. The archives of European broadcasters hold audiovisual historical source material of immense scope and multifariousness. It may well be a more-or-less-skewed or even broken mirror of general social and cultural history, but a mirror it was and still is – even if also an actor, a force in its own right, in social, political and cultural developments.

Television has had a leading position in the public sphere in more ways than one. It is not only located institutionally and geographically close to the centres of economic and political power. It not only draws the largest simultaneous audiences of all media. It also, to a considerable extent, sets the agenda for public discourse. It supplies resources for political participation and also supplies material for, and shapes, the cultural identity of viewers. Television has thus been essential to the experience and practices of citizenship for five decades or more. And it will be argued in this essay that it will continue in this role, albeit somewhat differently positioned, in the age of the Internet.

All of this is more or less the same for all countries. But there have also always been big differences. The specific arrangements of television provision were not only marked by national peculiarities. In line with Dan Hallin and Paolo Mancini's observation (2004: xiii) that there are 'clusters of media system characteristics' that tend to 'co-occur in distinct patterns', one can also point to differences between groups of countries related to certain historical, social, economic, cultural and political circumstances they share.

Since the European continent from the second half of the 1940s until 1989 was divided by the so-called iron curtain into two parts with radically different social systems, this of course also marked the organization, contents and overall development of television. In addition to the east-west division, there was also one between the southern and the northern/central parts of Western Europe. Hallin and Mancini (ibid.) have conceptualized this difference as one between the 'democratic corporatist model' of north/central Europe on the one hand and the 'polarized pluralist model' of southern Europe on the other. With special reference to television, other terms might be more adequate, but the dividing line is quite similar.

This chapter is called an essay since it is indeed an attempt at something very difficult: to chart the overall developments of European television over roughly half a century. It will provide a simple chronological overview by suggesting four distinct phases. Some of the differences between different parts of Europe and individual countries, whether bygone or still in existence, will be pointed out. It should be stated right away, however, that the main focus and the main basis for the chronology is the development in Western Europe and in particular the north western part. This reflects, firstly, the fact that this corner of the continent has been leading developments in important ways. Secondly, it reflects the fact that television research is older and stronger in this same area than elsewhere. Thirdly, and this is most regrettable, it reflects the present author's limitations. Comparisons will be made not only internally, among different European states, but also externally with the television system in the US, a politically crucial 'other' in the politics of European TV.

The article argues that the television systems in Europe may now have become more similar to that of the US in important ways – commercialism and a multitude of competing channels were introduced from around 1980 on – but also that very important differences remain. These are primarily due to the strong position, historically and contemporarily, of public service television, including the pan-European cooperation between public broadcasters through Eurovision. Finally, the question is raised what the role of television might be in the formation of a truly pan-European public sphere.

The pioneering phase: Television in Europe before 1960

Regular European broadcast television started in the mid-1930s after years of various experiments. The overall simultaneity of these developments is striking, even if technical and other details vary. Regular television services were first launched in Germany, where programmes were transmitted three days a week from March 1935, using a 180-line mechanical scanning system much superior to, for instance, the 30-line system employed by the British pioneer John Logie Baird in his (and as of 1932, the BBC's) experiments. France's first official television broadcast took place in April 1935 on a 60-line system, which in December of that year was replaced by a 180-line system. Regular, nightly, broadcasts started in January 1937. The world's first regular 'high definition' television broadcasts – 405 lines – were started by the BBC in November 1936, while Germany started using a 441 line system in February of 1937 and France declared a 455 line standard as of July 1938.[1]

In all three countries, television was, to begin with, largely a medium experienced in a public setting. In Britain, a television set would cost about the same as a small car, or a year's wages for an industrial worker, and so the number of sets in use before the Second World War was low: estimates vary from 12,000 to 20,000 for 1939, all located within a twenty-mile radius of the transmitter in London. The best chance ordinary people had of experiencing television was therefore to watch the sets located, for instance, in Waterloo Station and in restaurants. (Corrigan 1990) In France the numbers of sets in use as late as 1939 has been estimated at only two to three hundred and many of these were also located in public places, including rooms specifically assigned to this purpose.

Strikingly contrasting developments in the US, where a commercial and more decentralized television system emerged, the new medium was launched by public-sector agencies in all of these three leading European countries – the BBC in Britain, the Reichspost in Germany and the Ministère des Postes, Télégraphes et Téléphones (PTT) in France. The same was the case in almost all other countries on the continent. This is an indication of significant differences in the ideological and actual roles of the government and the public sector in Europe and the US. These differences would mark also developments after the Second World War.

Systems of public broadcasting monopoly re-emerged or were developed from scratch practically all over the European continent from 1945 on. But they took radically different forms.

In the half that belonged to the Soviet bloc, governments took total control of all broadcasting activities and exercised detailed political censorship right up until the collapse in 1989. This has also marked later developments. Karol Jakubowicz has argued that 'elements of social consciousness and culture' have played 'a crucial role' in attempts to change the media systems in line with the systemic change in general since 1989 (Jakubowicz 2004: 54). Authoritarian ideology remains in many countries so that authorities stress the need for journalistic media to be 'cooperative' and 'loyal' to the processes of change led by the government. Jakubowitz sees a broader cultural change as a necessary prerequisite for the establishment of a media system functioning in line with the principles of the public sphere of developed democracies. (ibid: 59)

The Western part of Europe largely continued or re-established a public service broadcasting monopoly financed wholly or partially by a licence fee. But this formulation covers up the fact that there were fundamental differences between the broadcasting systems of the north and south.

In Portugal and Spain, fascist regimes that had been sympathetic towards and outright supportive of Nazi Germany and Fascist Italy were still in place – and would remain so until the mid-1970s. Their broadcasting systems also remained tightly controlled by political authorities. In Spain, for instance, private enterprises were allowed to operate radio networks from 1952 on, but only on conditions such as 'having owners linked to the regime, maintaining a stringent political control through government intervention in the selection of their directors; prohibition of news and current affairs programmes; strict self censorship, etc.' (Bustamante 1989: 67ff). Since the mid-70s, however, these two countries have developed a system of combined public service broadcasting and commercial channels largely similar to that of north-western Europe.

The two losers in the World War re-designed their broadcasting systems, but to different extents and in different ways. In 1944 Italy re-named its privately-owned but state-controlled broadcasting company, which had been called Ente Italiano Audizioni Radiofoniche (EIAR) since 1927, Radioaudizioni Italia (RAI). But there was little immediate organizational change and the company kept its nationwide monopoly. [2] In 1954 RAI became Radiotelevisione Italiana, the Italian state became the company's only shareholder and regular television broadcasts began. RAI's channels were always tied to the party-political system to a quite unique degree. As put by Cinzia Padovani, the history of Italian public service television

runs from the time when the Christian Democratic Party had almost full power within the RAI (1954–1975), to the time when influence was distributed among parties (1975–1992) [the *lottizzazione* system, JG] to the post-*lottizzazione* phase (1993–) when commercial imperatives became predominant concerns for the broadcaster. (Padovani 2005: 2)

Regulatory reform in the mid-1970s allowed for private local television, and Silvio Berlusconi took advantage of this and a vast untapped demand for television advertising in a booming economy when building his media empire. As prime minister, Berlusconi thus has had unparalleled media power as de facto leader of both RAI and Mediaset, his privately controlled set of television channels.

Germany, on the other hand, completely reorganized its broadcasting services. In the West, the US, the UK and France established the Arbeitsgemeinschaft der öffentlich-rechtlichen Rundfunkanstalten Deutschlands, the ARD, a cooperative organization of regional public service broadcasting networks controlled by the Länder of the Federal Republic. Television was first started in the British zone in 1948, while a 'general test phase' opened in September of 1950 with programmes transmitted for two hours every night. In the East, the Soviet Union set up a separate system of radio and TV stations, what was to become the Deutscher Fernsehfunk (DFF) of the German Democratic Republic (GDR). A television service based on the Soviet model begun its test phase in June 1952, while regular programming officially started in March of 1956.

The BBC resumed its television services in 1946, and towards the very end of the decade the new medium started to spread outside of the London area. Having gathered experience with live outside television on previous occasions (e.g. King George VI's funeral in 1952), BBC television had a breakthrough with its coverage of the coronation of Queen Elizabeth II:

That day the TV audience, for the first time, was almost double the sound radio audience. Of the adult population of Britain, numbering about 36,500,000, fifty-six per cent watched the Coronation on TV – 20,400,000 viewers. Sound radio had 11,700,000 listeners. In the longest-established TV areas the TV audience exceeded the listening one to an even greater extent; in London and the Midlands there were three times as many viewers as listeners. More than half the viewers all over the country watched in the homes of friends. About a million and a half watched big-screen relays in cinemas and other public places.[3]

The coverage was also watched live by at least one million people in France, Belgium, the Netherlands and West Germany. This enormous achievement had required solutions to technical problems associated with the fact that the standards were very different: Britain had its 405-line system, France its 819-line system, while Germany and the Netherlands had a 625-line system. Film from the ceremony was furthermore transported by military aircraft to North America, where over 85 million watched it, and film material was broadcast also in other European countries, such as Denmark.[4]

This success resulted in a tremendous growth in the sales of TV sets: for television as a medium, this had been a highly convincing tour de force. It actually provided the viewers with tele-vision, i.e. the ability to see what simultaneously is going on far away. At the same time, it demonstrated, equally convincingly, that broadcast television could take the identity-producing capability of broadcast radio, which had once radically improved the identity-producing function of newspapers (cf. Anderson [1983]1991), to quite another level. Television's visual, aural – and oral – rendition of a central event in the country's history became a ritual encompassing and integrating the entire population. Later events, such as the 1954 football world cup finals from Bern in Switzerland and the 1956 wedding between Grace Kelly and Prince Rainier of Monaco, also boosted sales of sets and helped install television centrally in the daily lives of most, and eventually practically all, Europeans.

A very important event in the history of European television was the establishment of the European Broadcasting Union in 1950. It was, early on, involved in organizing multinational, live television transmissions – the first was the coronation of Queen Elizabeth II. A Eurovision programme exchange coordination centre was established in 1956, and the EBU organized the first Eurovision Song Contest in Lugano, Switzerland in that same year. Since then this has been a yearly phenomenon which always draws considerable attention for a few weeks. In 1958, experiments with the exchange of news items were started, resulting in daily news exchanges as of 1961. The EBU and Eurovision, thus, without much attention from the general public, already contributed significantly to coordination of television output in Europe before 1960. Thereby they also contributed to a reality-base for the notion of a form or style which can be called 'European television' and imagined as different from that of other continents, in spite of myriads of differences between the televisions of European countries.

The second phase: The heyday of classical television

In Raymond Williams' television theory classic, *Television: Technology and Cultural Form* (1975), television is described as a medium with social functions and textual features that are still in existence. According to Williams, broadcasting as a cultural form reflected a pronounced centralization of resources and power on the one hand and the 'mobile privatisation' of people's lives on the other – that is to say, social and geographical mobility of individuals and nuclear families that in a sense are isolated, cut off from stable, traditional social communities.

Broadcasting's two main functions in this situation were, according to Williams, first, efficient distribution of essential information to all citizens and, second, the production of a shared, primarily national, but also regional, identity.

This perspective thus emphasizes how broadcast television is adequate to the needs of Government in nation states. But as a central institution within the public sphere it can also make essential information, knowledge and cultural experiences available at the same time to all members of society. This is evidently of great importance to a functioning modern democracy, and it means that broadcasting may serve the interests of the governed as much as those of the government and other centres of power.

But the validity of these functions as catch-all defining features of the medium is considerably less clear today than it was, when Williams did his research and writing, in the UK and the US in the early 1970s. The centralized, top-down structure was recognizable even in the US with its commercially dominated and quite decentralized system. But it was especially clear in Europe, where public service monopoly or duopoly systems were totally dominant until the early 1980s. Around 1960, the last few countries without regular television services had them introduced, and the medium caught on among people faster than anticipated: it was as if television had been sorely missed for quite some time. In France, for instance, 6 percent of households had a television set in 1958, 62 percent in 1962 (Le Champion & Danard 2000: 32).

The heyday of the classical form of broadcast television was, in other words, roughly between 1960 and 1980. Key textual features of the medium such as *liveness* and *flow* were very much in existence, but characteristic of programming to quite different degrees: while 'liveness' primarily for technical reasons was considerably much more prominent than today, 'flow' was, especially in Europe, considerably less developed than it would become in the multichannel competitive system brought on by satellite and cable technologies from about 1980 on.

'Liveness' is still central to televisual aesthetics – all programme formats, pre-taped or not, strive to achieve the sort of immediacy and presence associated with the true, direct 'seeing-at-a-distance' experience. But in the 1950s and into the 1960s it was also a necessary feature, resulting from the lack of video machinery. Liveness was thus characteristic of much television drama, a variety of entertainment genres and 'events'. Flow, on the other hand, was much more unevenly present, since the impression of broadcast television as 'a single irresponsible flow of images and feelings' (Williams 1975: 92) depends, as Williams noted already back in the early 70s, on there being a situation of more or less intense competition between television channels, all eager to get a grip on viewers and keep them throughout 'an evening's viewing' (ibid: 93).

While this competitive mechanism was known already from the struggles over viewers in the British duopoly situation, and was repeated again, for instance, when the Swedish public broadcaster introduced its second channel in 1969 (Dahlgren 1995: 30), it became all the more important when the number of channels on offer exploded around 1980 with the introduction of cable and satellite technologies of distribution and the simultaneous liberalization of broadcasting regulation. It was not only that each channel tended to intensify its character of flow by, for instance, increased cutting speed and other forms of variety-suggesting elements in programmes but also by much more effectively utilizing the space between programmes. In the 60s and 70s public broadcasters tended to use space between programmes for nothing much at all: the Norwegian public service broadcaster for instance, the NRK, used to show an aquarium in longer breaks between programmes and a clock in somewhat shorter breaks.

So the heyday of classical television was an epoch where television was characterized by much liveness, little flow and only a small (or *very* small) number of channels. Especially in Europe it was largely organized in national, pyramidal structures, broadcasting from a centre to a periphery of mobile and privatized citizens and consumers. Wherever and whenever it was introduced with regular services it very quickly established itself as the leading medium; the medium other media referred to in any number of ways. This meant that television to a great extent decided the agenda of the public sphere in the broad sense of 'whatever goes on more and less prominently in public'. And it meant that the mass media production of national identity, once begun by the press and made a lot more efficient by broadcast radio, was significantly further strengthened. If the world did not become a village, the nation certainly did. Television's programming became an organizing force in people's everyday lives, setting the rhythms of the days, weeks and years more efficiently than the religious calendar had managed. TV provoked and staged debates, it produced celebrities of a new sort, it revealed scandals and was itself scandalized, spread top-class dramatic art and low-brow shows, world events as well as national ones – thus building a national public more inclusive and less divided than probably ever before.

In this sort of system, even imported programmes could contribute significantly to the (re)production and strengthening of national identity. The immense popularity of the British crime/detective series *The Saint* may have been particular to my native Norway, as was probably the enormous popularity of the US classic western series *Gunsmoke* and the German crime/police series *Derrick*. These shows may have been well-liked elsewhere but in Norway they were central ingredients in the cultural environment in the 1960s and 70s, cornerstones of the Friday and Saturday night schedules of the only television channel for years. Drama series were few and far between in the TV menu back then, and so the ones that appeared could reach heights of popularity in large parts of the population in ways that are hard to imagine nowadays.

But the 1960s were also a decade where signs of later radical changes in broadcasting systems first occurred. The first active communications satellite, Telstar, was launched in 1962, and on 27 July of that year President Kennedy addressed European viewers in a first live transmission of television sound and images across the Atlantic Ocean. The technology that enabled television from space improved quickly and had another grand victory when viewers around the world on 20 July 1969 could follow Apollo 11's moon landing. This was a 'live broadcasting of history' (Dayan & Katz 1992) which was a first manifestation of a practically global television audience – potentially a global public – foretelling not only of many similar occasions to come but also the emergence of a new, much more far-reaching stage of globalization.

At the same time, the immigration from Africa and Asia that had barely started in the 1950s caught speed and started to change the ethnic makeup of major West European countries, especially from about 1970 on. The audience became more diverse – while television still, for over a decade, remained neatly centralized in one or at most a handful of channels.

Phase number three: Two decades of commercialism – and diversification

From around 1980, television in Western Europe went through rapid and profound changes that were brought on by two forces: the successful, rapid introduction and spread of satellite and cable technologies and the success of neo-liberalist deregulation media policies in most countries. There was no direct link between these two phenomena, but the technological capacity for multichannel TV meant that especially capital but also many consumers would sooner or later press for a realization of these possibilities. It is probably correct to say that the changes in the organization and content of television that took place were generally very positively received by a majority of audiences. It was as if a strong demand for a different sort of broadcast television had been built over many years in the era of 'classical television' described above.

This demand could, in principle, have been met and satisfied in different ways. For instance, the monopoly or duopoly public service television channels could have introduced more channels, changed the way they addressed viewers in the direction of the popular or colloquial, introduced more popular drama and entertainment formats that could differ from the most common commercial ones in various ways, made sure some of the new channels catered to special interests of different sorts, etc.

But only an opening of broadcasting markets, regarded as markets much like any other, introducing commercialism and competition, seemed politically possible at the time. The result was a development where cable and direct broadcasting satellites were added to the traditional terrestrial, analogue broadcasting distribution system, so that the number of available channels grew extremely rapidly, while contents were not diversified in a corresponding manner. Competition led to a strong drift towards a programming menu that would please as many as possible. This development would not surprise those familiar with 'Hotelling's law' from the 1920s. Very simply put, it goes like this: vendors will tend to do their business in the middle, not over to one side or in a corner, in order to be as close as possible to as many as possible (Hotelling 1929).

Various attempts were made to counter this very strong tendency toward mainstreaming or uniformity of programming offers. One of them was the establishment of the British Channel 4, which opened in November 1982. It was to be a commercially-funded public service channel explicitly devoted to experimental and minority-oriented programming. Its first chief executive (1981–87), Jeremy Isaacs, also took the channel's remit very seriously and set a style for the channel which was truly distinctive. After 1993, however, when there were changes in the regulation of commercial broadcasting, it seems as if programming moved toward the entertainment-dominated mainstream, addressing younger viewers especially. Sports and 'reality' formats such as *Big Brother* became central elements. This development should be understood in light of the concurrent changes in the British television landscape.

The UK had only 3 channels (BBC 1&2 and ITV) until Channel 4 was launched. But that same year, 1982, the first commercial television channel also started operating via satellite. The company behind it, Satellite Television Ltd, was set up by a former CEO of the commercial London channel Thames Television. In 1984 Rupert Murdoch bought the channel and (re)named it Sky Channel. It was distributed in a number of Western European countries with well-developed cable systems, such as the Netherlands and in Scandinavia, introducing blatantly commercial fare such as a music video programme called *Sky Trax* and children's programmes like *Fun Factory* and *The DJ Kat Show*. Due to the sparseness of cable systems in the UK, this early phase of 'Sky TV' did not have much impact there. A change came after Murdoch stopped the broadcasts to European cable operators in 1989 and created the Sky Television Network, which he then, in 1990, merged with British Satellite Broadcasting, eventually forming BSkyB, soon the leading Pay-TV supplier in the UK and Ireland. Throughout the 1990s, the satellite-based competition became stronger, and much more difficult to ignore for the BBC, ITV and Channel 4 when deciding about their programming and strategies more generally. But as late as 1997, when cable alone reached 96 percent of households in the Netherlands and cable and satellite combined covered 63 percent of Norwegian and 62 percent of Swedish households, only 10 percent of households were cabled and 18 percent had satellite TV in the UK (NORDICOM 1999). A fifth terrestrial channel, Channel 5, which opened in March 1997, was also supposed to be a commercially-funded public service channel. But unlike its predecessor, it was very clearly commercially oriented in all of its output from the start, thus illustrating the general trend of the times, i.e. that unabashedly commercial television was on the offensive and conquered large parts of the viewing audiences.

But there were also other important trends. A number of channels devoted to themes such as history and wildlife were launched and, even if seemingly more immediately commercial themes such as fashion, food, and tourism may have dominated among these newcomers, a considerable variety of thematic channels were launched, survived and continued to develop. Television was beginning to look a bit more like the highly-differentiated, yet thoroughly-commercial magazine market. France and Germany together established the cultural channel Arte in 1992, in television context clearly a high-brow enterprise and not aiming for the mass market. But its existence through 17 years (so far), regularly drawing about a 5 per cent share of the French audience and 1per cent of the German,[5] has enriched television's offering as a whole, and leaving many viewers outside France and Germany with a wish that they had either mastered German or French better or that there was an English language version as well.

A feature of particular interest and social significance is the globalization of European television by way of satellite and cable. This unfolded in two major ways: the introduction of pan-European channels with global reach of Western origins, such as CNN, Disney Channel, Discovery, and BBC World, and the availability across the continent of Turkish, North African, Middle Eastern, Chinese etc. channels serving the various non-European ethnic minorities that have grown immensely since the early 1960s. The significance of this latter phenomenon is difficult to overrate. Arjun Appadurai also brings in other media and refers to the US in the following passage, but the point is clearly relevant also for Europe and its television audiences:

The story of mass migrations (voluntary and forced) is hardly a new feature of human history. But when it is juxtaposed with the rapid flow of mass-mediated images, scripts, and sensations, we have a new order of instability in the production of subjectivities. As Turkish guest workers in Germany watch Turkish films in their German flats, as Koreans in Philadelphia watch the 1988 Olympics in Seoul through satellite feeds from Korea, and as Pakistani cab drivers in Chicago listen to cassettes of sermons recorded in mosques in Pakistan or Iran, we see moving images meet deterritorialized viewers. These create diasporic public spheres, phenomena that confound theories that depend on the continued salience of the nation-state as the key arbiter of important social changes. (Appadurai 1996: 4)

The public broadcasters in Western Europe, early on, started special magazine programmes that were addressing the new ethnic minorities. First among them was the German ZDF, which already in 1963 launched *Nachbarn, unsere Nachbarn* ('Neighbours, our neighbours'), followed by *Ihre Heimat, unsere Heimat* ('Your homeland, our homeland') on WDR. 'The titles speak for themselves: the aim was to combat homesickness with features often produced by Greek, Italian, Polish or Yugoslav television. Each community had its own slot, in its own language, with German subtitles.' (Frachon & Vargaftig 1995: 4) BBC followed in 1965 with a programme intended for Indian and Pakistani immigrants. An important goal for the programme was to teach immigrants English and show them ways to cope with British culture and solve everyday problems. The same year, the French public service TV in Belgium, RTBF, launched its first programme for immigrants and over the next few years practically all the major immigrant communities had their own programmes – Italian, Spanish, Portuguese, and North African. France, however, was different, according to Claire Frachon and Marion Vargaftig (1995: 5): the first French magazine for immigrants, *Mosaïques*, did not appear until 1976, on FR3, and was from the outset 'patronising' in its tone, aiming for the assimilation of its viewers rather than their integration. But what really made it special, was the fact that its production was not paid for by the public broadcaster, but by the Fonds d'Action Sociale (Social Action Fund), a public body answerable to the Ministry of Social Affairs. The same was the case for the programme's follow-ups, called

Rencontres and, from 1993–94, *Premier Service*. And after 1994, no such specific magazine seems to have been on air in France (Frachon & Vargaftig 1995).

The major reason for that is most probably that such magazine programmes lost much of their point when satellite television could address these minorities more specifically and also with a quite different, positive attitude. A study of these magazine programmes, roughly between 1960 and 2000, would on the other hand probably be quite telling as to the question of how the new immigrants, directly and indirectly invited by the global economic inequalities, were understood and treated in their new home countries. Television history and national history – as well as European history – are not only intimately related, they are thoroughly intertwined.

The satellite channels addressing ethnic minorities are of two different kinds. On the one hand there are the satellite-transmitted channels from non-European countries in, say, North Africa. On the other, there are a number of channels broadcasting from Europe itself, especially the UK,[6] addressing Indian, Pakistani, Chinese, Persian, etc. minorities. They are all, however, only one corner in a very rapidly growing system of transnational television services in Europe.[7]

The number of cable and satellite channels available in Europe grew from 145 in 1991 to 1013 in 2000: 165 and the number has grown considerably since then. The kinds of channels that flourish in particular are (as of March 2001) children's channels (57), documentaries and movies (122) and sport (63) (Chalaby 2005). The numbers of households across the continent that can receive them 'broke through the 100 million barrier' in 2000, according to Chalaby (ibid: 165). The number grows so fast it has now most probably passed 200 million. 17 transnational channels stand out (stood out) from the rest in that they are 'pan-European in scope', 'have a strong distribution in at least five European countries' and have 'a commitment to international expansion': Arte, BBC Prime, BBC World, Bloomberg, Cartoon Network, CNBC, CNN International, Discovery, EuroNews, Eurosport, Fox Kids, MTV, National Geographic, Sky News, TV5, Universal Studios Networks and VH1. 'On average', Chalaby says (ibid: 186) 'these channels broadcast to 24 European territories and are received in nearly 40 million European households.' Many of them have subtitles, dubbing or even special versions for particular areas or countries, since European audiences are so diverse in terms of tastes and culture more generally.

When we add to this the enormous growth in local and regional television services all over the continent, usually commercially financed and distributed via cable and/or satellite, we end up with a situation for the medium of television which is radically different from that of the 1960s and 1970s. There are still vital national television channels, and public service channels are central among them, which continue to function as central national arenas and providers of national identity. There is still a vital European Broadcasting Union, still organizing a daily exchange of audiovisual clips between its members and also still organizing, among other things, the yearly mega-event the European Song Contest. But an intricately patterned, multi-layer system of television services, most of them commercially funded, many of them transnational, pan-European or even global, generalist or thematically limited, ethnically specific or not, indicates and contributes to a very different social and cultural diversity than was the case around 1960.

What lies behind this change toward decentralization and diversity, on the other hand, is a radical strengthening of the power of private, corporate interests in European television. Public service television remains strong in many countries, especially in North-Western Europe, but there are also many countries and whole areas, particularly Eastern Europe, where public service broadcasting is now in a weak position, attracting only a small share of audiences. Television services on the whole now tend to be distributed much more like any other media in accordance with social borderlines such as gender, age, income and education. The resulting confirmation and reproduction of social cleavages is one major cause for critical reflection on the pros and cons of developments over the last 20 years.

General trends and infinite variety

So far the focus has mostly been on the general trends in developments. While such trends no doubt exist, it is also common knowledge that Europe is a very complex continent in any number of ways, so that variations and deviations from the overall picture may well be innumerable. In order to determine the relations between overall pattern and underlying variations, empirical studies are necessary.

In the project *Changing Media, Changing Europe,* which ran from 1999 to 2004, the research team that worked on the theme *Citizenship and consumerism: Media, the public sphere and the market* decided to do a simple comparative study of media developments between 1960 and 2000 in the European countries represented in the team. One would study each country's leading (in terms of circulation) 'quality' newspaper and also each country's leading 'popular' newspaper for the first week of October in 1960, 1980 and 2000 (in some countries, other years were added). One would thus also study television in two ways – its newspaper coverage and, not least, simply the programme listings in the papers. Concentrating on developments in public service television, the latter sources indicated certain main trends very clearly.[8]

Firstly, the number of broadcasting hours rose sharply from about 1980. Though variations were great from country to country, it seems clear that public service television in what I have here called its classic years (1960–80) broadcast roughly between 30 and 50 percent of what was to become its output in the year 2000. Once commercial television really gains ground in Europe and a new era of competition sets in, broadcasting hours are radically extended and round-the-clock or near-round-the-clock television become normal.

If we then have a look at how these developments affected programming, we get the following picture for a key genre – the news: The time given to news programmes is increasing everywhere in the classic era, while developments appear somewhat less unidirectional between 1980 and 2000. While the increase continues in most countries, and Turkey escalates to 96 minutes or 30 percent of the evening hours, the time awarded to news

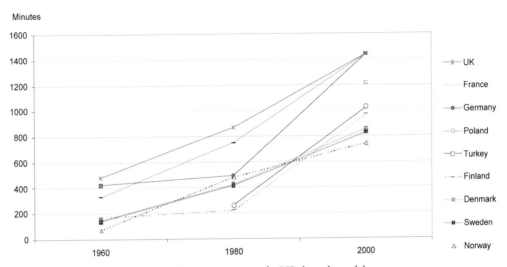

Total broadcasting time, average for PSB channels, weekdays.

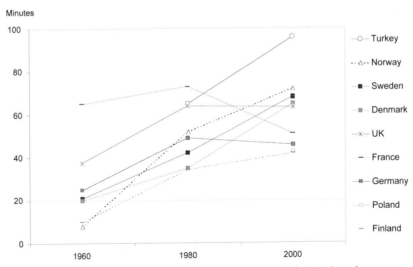

Daily news programmes on weekdays, in minutes, average for PSB channels.

programmes remains roughly the same in the UK and it seems to drop in Germany and, in particular, France.

On closer inspection, however, developments are somewhat less differentiated. In 1980, France was where the public broadcaster devoted the most time to newscasts, with the UK following closely. This means France and the UK were already ahead of the rest. It would be difficult to increase the time spent on newscasts any further without cutting down on other important and popular genres. So even if news, for various reasons, is a genre that is of considerable weight in competition among channels, it cannot grow beyond certain limits in a general programming channel. The UK basically remained at the same level. If we have a closer look at Germany, we find the downward turn there is not very pronounced at all. The 2000 situation there is not very far removed from the British one. The reduction in France is real, though, and the explanation is complex.[9] One would first of all have to point to radical changes in the broadcasting system in the 1980s. The main public service channel was privatised in 1987 (TF1) and the new regime of channel competition contributed to a shortening of news programmes (which used to include several longer reportages and last some 45 to 50 minutes) to a standard half-hour format. The establishment of specialized cable/satellite news channels such as LCI and 1 Télé may also have contributed to this development. Furthermore, one channel's (F2) late night newscast was moved to after midnight.

If the news genre developed differently in different countries from 1980 to 2000, this was not generally the case for drama series. With the exception of Turkey, where there was a marked drop in the number of minutes devoted to drama series, and Sweden, where the

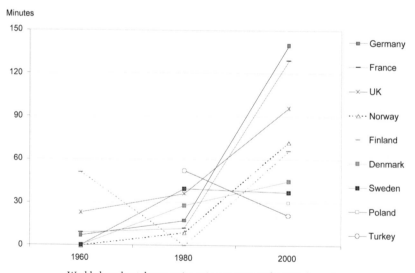

Weekly broadcast drama series, minutes, average for PSB channels.

situation was more or less unchanged, the number of minutes devoted to drama series on workdays increased dramatically. When competition over audiences got tough, an important part of the answer of public broadcasters was quite clearly to offer more drama – not least drama imported from the US.

These very coarse indications of general tendencies are based on the public service channels in the countries listed. There is no reason to imagine the commercial channels deviate from the overall trend here. As the new millennium started, then, there were more hours of television than ever on offer, and in the programme menu there were more news and more drama series than before. As a medium, television was now more than ever 'an entertainment machine with news'.[10]

This is the situation as the Internet has become a household fixture in Europe and the US.

Into the fourth phase: Television and the Internet

As proposed above, the television history of Europe can (roughly) be divided into three chapters up until the new millennium: The pioneering phase (mid-30s until about 1960), the classic decades (1960–1980), and the phase of commercialization and diversification (1980–2000). As the new century started, so did a new chapter in television history: that of interplay and symbiosis between television and the internet.

Certain prophets of the digital era (e.g. Rose & Brown 1996) long claimed that television would soon be a thing of the past. The box in the living room would be replaced by personal computers connected to the Internet. These prophets did not foresee the last few years' explosive sales of large, flat-screen TV sets. These sets are mostly used for broadcast TV, and also for digital games and watching DVDs. They are *not*, however, used for banking, the ordering of airline tickets, or e-mail correspondence. In other words, the TV set has become a multi-purpose screen but it is extremely rare to use it as a screen for services specifically associated with the Internet. People maintain a division between labour and leisure in the uses of TV and the PC so that TV is associated with leisure while the PC is associated with work or work-like personal activities. This is why several studies, at least in Europe, show that the rapidly increasing use of computers and the Internet has not led to a reduction in the total time used on television.

In fact, the tendency is rather the opposite, at least in some countries: Norwegians have never watched more television per day than now, even if Norway also is near the world top in terms of the distribution of broadband connections, home computers, Internet activity and, say, Facebook membership. The average Norwegian's viewing of television on an average day was up roughly a half hour from the mid 90s to the middle of the present decade, and the average viewing time on an average day among those who actually were watching TV went up almost 40 minutes and hit 3 hours for the first time in 2006.[11] The same year, people in Japan and the US were averaging 4.5 hours, while the figure was 3.5 hours a day for the

UK, and only 2.5 hrs in Sweden.[12] At the same time, from 2000 to 2006, the average use of the Internet in Norway on an average day rose from 18 minutes to almost an hour and from almost an hour to one-and-a-half among those who actually used the Internet. This is in a country where 79 percent of the population had internet access from their homes in 2006, a year when 63 percent had broadband connection at home, compared to just over 50 percent with broadband at the end of 2006 in the UK and 50.8 percent in the US in October 2007 – the latter estimate apparently being based in poor methodology.[13] It seems evident, then, that increased use of the Internet, and a growing number of households getting broadband connection, does not necessarily lead to a reduction in the viewing of broadcast TV.

Broadcast television will thus most likely continue to exist for as long as we can now reasonably claim to see into the future. The fundamental social conditions that, according to Raymond Williams, made broadcasting so socially relevant and valuable generally remain: we still have centralized political and economic power on the one hand and seemingly ever-more mobile, privatized people on the other. We still live in nation states that are not at all dead, even if in some respects quite different and perhaps weaker than before, and so broadcasting will continue to deliver national identity composed of shared cultural references across social, geographical, generational and other divisions.

But television does not remain the same. Traditional broadcast media now must relate to and rely on not only print media and the music and motion picture industries; they also have to take into account in a more fundamental way the existence and possibilities of the Internet, a very special addition to the media ecosystem. We now see the emergence of a symbiotic relationship between TV and the Internet. The Internet is not only an increasingly important channel or platform for the (re)distribution of radio and television programmes, it is also, to a considerable extent, a broadcaster in its own right through its distribution of sound, moving images and text from countless websites – some much more prominent than others. Television channels have long since discovered that their websites are very useful in tying viewers to them, in forming virtual communities tied to certain programmes, in communicating additional material and further information tied to particular news or documentary programmes and much, much more. Many public service broadcasters have realized this and now see online activities as an important part of their mission (see Moe 2009). The sort of symbiosis developing between television and the Internet is evidenced also in the fact that some of the most intense person-to-person, egalitarian communicative activities once seen as a hallmark of the Internet as such are actually public conversations about TV shows (see, for instance, Jenkins 2006, chapters 1 and 2, about *Survivor* and *American Idol* respectively).

The most important question concerning television and the internet is what the outcome of the new, digitized, situation will be for the structure of the public sphere and the very existence of a public in the sense Habermas used the term in his classic book. Since broadcast television will remain, chances are that a central arena also remains where informed citizens discuss the norms that should regulate the exercise of power and where the critical confrontation between the government and the public can take place. What one might still ask, however, is how small – or big – this arena and this public will be, or, rather, to what extent it is going to represent the entire population. Television is not a medium addressing the whole population of a nation state simultaneously anymore. Viewers will at any given time be distributed across a large number of channels – plus the Internet and all other media. But while this may be a major problem for, say, advertisers (see, for example, Bianco 2004), it may be less problematic with a view to the functioning of a general public sphere. Overestimating the importance of the mere existence of a number of channels would be simplistic technological determinism. In reality, viewers still flock to a few channels while showing up only sparingly for the many dozens of others. The current situation in the US, which has had a much-segmented television situation for three decades, is indicative: a traditional US free-to-air network can still, with a good show, draw 30 million viewers at once. No other medium can do that. In the course of a week practically all Americans will have watched one or more network channels. A handful of cable channels are extremely much more watched than others. In other words, the times when broadcast television can constitute a central stage in a country's public sphere are not quite over yet. The danger of *cyberbalkanization* (Sunstein 2001 & 2007) should not be overestimated.

So what about 'europeanness'?

What will, in the situation just described, happen to a certain 'europeanness' which many would have it characterizes European television, in spite of all its internal differences, and marks it as different from the television of, say, the US, South America, or South-East Asia?

The idea of such a 'unity in difference' was, it seems, first put forward by the German television critic Gerhard Eckert. He argued that

> a certain European style of television developed in the 1950s, despite the different institutional settings and political contexts. This European television style was shaped by the idea of a nationalised, largely independent media entity and persisted – despite the introduction of commercial television – as a dominant characteristic. Following Eckert, public service ideology with its strong educational and pedagogical emphasis is perhaps the strongest common denominator of the diverse and colourful European television landscape. (Eckert 1965, according to Bignell & Fickers 2008: 76)

One can hardly speak of a 'strong educational and pedagogic emphasis' as the hallmark of current public service television in Europe, neither in theory nor in practice, not in the north, not in the south, and not in the east. What is perhaps more of a common trait all over the continent is the considerable volume of US drama, particularly serial drama but also movies (see Bondebjerg et al. 2008). This is, however, not a fact that in itself contradicts the idea that there is a specifically European profile to television in Europe. In many or most countries, one might say the presence of the American material only serves to highlight the difference between US commercial television and European television whether commercial or not.

Firstly, there is the simple fact that European television programme schedules outside of their US fiction constantly refer to Europe, mostly of course to the country where the channel in question operates, but also to other European countries and to Europe as such. There is hardly anything about anything European on US television. On any European channel worth mentioning there is extensive coverage of, say, European soccer and/or European royalty, European high culture artists and events, EU processes and politicians, European pop music, European history, fashion, nature, etc. This is the 'content element'.

Secondly, there is the continued presence of public service television and the influence it has also on commercial competitors in the countries where it has long and strong traditions and also as model in countries where it is much less developed due to the continent's political history. The public service ethos is not best described as 'pedagogical', 'paternalistic' or other euphemisms for 'authoritarian'. It is about addressing audiences as citizens in significant parts of the programme output. The classical years established this ethos so firmly in many countries that it has not been simple to do away with completely: the public is used to being addressed this way and may reject those who deny them this degree of dignity. In addition, regulatory regimes have in many countries tied commercial operators to public service obligations or otherwise limited their following a purely commercial logic. This means US fiction, at least in several central channels, appears in a context that is marked by such citizenship-oriented programming. While this may also be found outside Europe, it does at least contribute to make Europe different from the US. This is the 'public service ethos element', which is both about programme content and scheduling.

Thirdly, there are Eurovision and pan-European channels such as Eurosport and Euronews. The almost invisible exchange of programme bits and the extremely visible organizing of pan-European mega-events such as the Eurovision Song Contest are both significant contributions to the establishment and continuation of a situation where Europeans, across the continent, actually see, experience and talk about the same thing more or less simultaneously, in line with broadcasting's classic identity-producing functions. This is the 'Eurovision element'.

What has constituted 'europeanness' in European television for the last few decades, then, is the combination of these three elements with a significant presence of US drama series and movies. Even if the Internet might increase globalization in general, and US influence in particular, this is no reason to believe that European television will cease to appear European along these lines. The opposite might just as well prove to be the case, i.e. that the European features of television channels get strengthened as part of a defensive response to globalization and a strong US influence.

Notes

1. Most of the figures in this and the following paragraph are drawn from the article 'History of television' on Wikipedia (http: //en.wikipedia.org/wiki/History_of_television. Accessed 27 January, 2009), but have been checked against various other websites, such as www.british-tv-history.co.uk, http: //www.scheida.at/scheida/televisionen.htm, http: //www.televisionheaven.co.uk/history.htm
2. http: //www.cisi.unito.it/marconi/raieng.html. Accessed 29 January 2009.
3. http: //www.apts.org.uk/coronation.htm . Accessed 29 January 2009.
4. Ibid.
5. Wikipedia definition,, http: //en.wikipedia.org/wiki/Arte. Accessed 8 March 2009.
6. In the early 2000s, about 80 out of the over 100 transnational channels operating in Europe were registered in and broadcast from the UK. One important reason for this is that a licence from the then regulatory agency for commercial television, the Independent Television Commission, would be fairly easy to get and also quite inexpensive (£250). Plus the programme code and the rules for advertising have been quite lax compared to those of other European countries. (Chalaby 2002: 185).
7. The following two paragraphs are almost identical to two paragraphs in my article 'Television, Culture and the European Public Sphere', in the *European Journal of Communication,* 2007, 22: 479–492.
8. The tables underlying the diagrams in this section are the following, where the number of minutes for each country is either an average for the two leading public service broadcasters, however funded, or refers to a single public service broadcaster. In addition, included below are the shares of 'an evening's viewing' occupied by news and drama series respectively.

News in the leading public service channels, 18–24 hrs: Weekday average in minutes

Country	1960	1980	2000
France	65	73	51
Denmark	20	35	65
Finland	10	35	42
Germany	25	49	46
Norway	8	52	72
Poland			42
Sweden	21	42	68
Turkey		65	96
UK	37	64	63

News in the leading public service channels, 18–24 hrs: Weekday average share (percent)

Country	1960	1980	2000
France	25	22	14
Denmark	19	11	18
Finland	6	17	12
Germany	7	14	13
Norway	11	18	20
Poland			12
Sweden	18	14	19
Turkey		23	30
UK	12	18	18

Drama series in the leading public service channels, 18–24 hrs: Weekday average in minutes:

Country	1960	1980	2000
France	9	12	129
Denmark	0	28	45
Finland	51	0	66
Germany	7	17	140
Norway	0	9	72
Poland			30
Sweden	0	40	37
Turkey		52	21
UK	23	36	96

Drama series in the leading public service channels, 18–24 hrs: Weekday average as share (percent)

Country	1960	1980	2000
France	4	4	36
Denmark	0	9	12
Finland	33	0	18
Germany	2	5	3
Norway	0	3	20
Poland			9
Sweden	0	14	10
Turkey		18	7
UK	7	10	27

9. I thank Tristan Mattelart and Guy Lochard for their suggestions on this point.
10. A characterization used by the actor Rolv Wesenlund in the Norwegian debate over the US prime-time soap opera *Dynasty* in 1984.
11. Source: Norsk mediebarometer/Statistisk Sentralbyrås medieundersøkelser.
12. Source: http://www.ofcom.org.uk/media/news/2007/12/nr_20071213, accessed 4 March 2008.
13. Source: http://www.consumeraffairs.com/news04/2008/01/ntia_broadband.html, accessed 4 March 2008.

References

Anderson, B. (1983]1991) *Imagined communities: Reflections on the origin and spread of nationalism*, London and New York: Verso.

Appadurai, A (1996) *Modernity at large: Cultural dimensions of globalization*, Minneapolis and London: Minnesota University Press.

Bianco, A. (2004) 'The vanishing mass market', in: *Business Week*, July 12, pp. 61–8.

Bignell, J. & Fickers, A. (eds.) (2008) 'Introduction', pp. 1–4, and 'Conclusion: Reflections on doing European television history', in their *A European Television History*, Malden MA, Oxford, Victoria: Wiley-Blackwell, pp. 229–57.

Bondebjerg, I. et al. (2008) 'American television: Point of reference or European nightmare?' in J. Bignell & A. Fickers (eds.) *A European television history*, Malden MA, Oxford, Victoria: Wiley-Blackwell, pp. 154–83.

Bustamante, E. (1989) 'TV and public service in Spain: A difficult encounter', in *Media, Culture and Society*, vol. 11, no. 1, pp. 67–87.

Chalaby, J.K (2002) 'Transnational Television in Europe. The Role of Pan-European Channels', *European Journal of Communication*, vol. 17, no. 2, pp. 183–203.

Chalaby, J.K. (2005) 'Deconstructing the transnational: a typology of cross-border television channels in Europe', *New Media & Society*, vol. 7, no.2, pp. 155–75.

Corrigan, P. (1990) 'On the difficulty of being sociological (historical materialist) in the study of television: The 'moment' of English television, 1936–1939', in T. Syvertsen (ed.) *1992 and after: Nordic television in transition*, Report no. 10, Dept of Media Studies, University of Bergen, pp. 130–60.

Dahlgren, P. (1995) *Television and the public sphere: Citizenship, democracy and the media*, London, Thousand Oaks, New Delhi: Sage Publications.

Dayan, D. & Katz, E. (1992) *Media Events: The Live Broadcasting of History*, Cambridge, Mass. & London: Harvard University Press.

Eckert, G. (1965) *Das Fernsehen in den Ländern Westeuropas: Entwicklung und gegenwärtiger Stand*, Gütersloh: Bertelsmann.

Frachon, C. & Vargaftig, M. (eds.) *European television: Immigrants and ethnic minorities*, London, Paris, Rome: John Libbey.

Gripsrud, J. (2007) 'Television, culture and the European public sphere', *European Journal of Communication*, 2007. 22, pp. 479–92.

Hallin, D. and Mancini, P. (2004) *Comparing media systems: Three models of media and politics*, Cambridge, New York: Cambridge University Press.

Hotelling, H. (1929) 'Stability in Competition', *Economic Journal*, vol. 39. 153, pp. 41–57.

Jakubowicz, K., 2004 'Ideas in our heads. Introduction of PSB as part of media system change in Central and Eastern Europe', *European Journal of Communication*, vol. 19. 1, pp. 53–74.

Jenkins, H. (2006) *Convergence culture: Where old and new media collide*, New York and London: New York University Press.

Le Champion, R. & Danard, B. (2000) *Télévision de pénurie, télévision d'abondance: Des origines à Internet*, Paris: La documentation Française

Moe, H. (2009) *Public Broadcasters, the Internet, and democracy: Comparing policy and exploring public service media online*, PhD dissertation, University of Bergen.

NORDICOM (1999) 'TV i Norden, Europa och Världen', *MedieNotiser*, 2, University of Gothenburg: Nordicom.

Padovani, C. (2005) *A fatal attraction: Public television and politics in Italy*, Boulder, CO: Rowman & Littlefield.

Rose, F & Brown, E. (1996) 'The end of TV as we know it. Forget HDTV. Forget interactive television. Forget the 500-Channel universe. Instead start thinking PCTV', in *Fortune* December 23, 1996, http: // money.cnn.com/magazines/fortune/fortune_archive/1996/12/23/219864/index.htm. Accessed 3 March 2008.

Sunstein, C. (2001) *Republic.com*, Princeton: Princeton University Press.

Sunstein, C. (2007) *Republic.com 2.0*, Princeton and Oxford: Princeton University Press.

Williams, R. (1975) *Television: Technology and cultural form*, New York: Schocken Books.

Part III

Intermedia

Chapter 4

The Public Reception of Early Television: When Television was New in the Nordic Countries

Taisto Hujanen
University of Tampere

Lennart Weibull
University of Gothenburg

Introduction

The history of art shows that each new means of expression is misunderstood at the beginning. This conclusion of a music critique published in the cultural section of the main Finnish newspaper Helsingin Sanomat (9 October 1960) serves as a useful point of reference for the description and analysis of newspapers' reception of early television. The author, reviewing a concert in electronic music in Finnish television, was critical of 'musical' composers who made electronic music sound like instrumental music and did not understand the 'authentic' potentials of the new music form.

The notion of broadcast television implies that television as a new medium of communication was institutionalized in the form of broadcasting. In other words, following the above example of electronic music, broadcasting, and more particularly radio broadcasting, was the old media form closest to television and, in this way, dominated its early understanding. Not only technically but also socially and culturally, radio broadcasting was, as we shall formulate later, a meta-concept for television. Respectively, with reference to the public reception of television, one could say that broadcasting and the history of sound radio were the most immediate contexts of reception that framed not only public debate on television but also its adoption as technology. A concrete example is that many popular radio shows were soon adapted to the new television medium (Brooks & Marsh 1988; Mintz 1985).

Although radio broadcasting was certainly the dominant intermedial field in the construction of early television, several other connections should be noticed. In later theory about television, such interplay between television and cinema as means of expression and as social and cultural institutions has been a major theme (see Ellis 1992). A mere glance at early television schedules reveals a number of other relevant interconnections which include theatre, concerts, variety shows, circus, etc. (on research concerning early television schedules, see Barnouw 1977; Sterling and Kitross 1990; Tiedge and Ksobiech 1987). So, from the beginning, television was interpreted from different angles, which in part complemented but also contested each other. Similar to the above example of electronic music, the conflicting views created the basis for social and cultural hierarchies, which contested over the 'true nature' of television.

In the Nordic countries newspapers played an important role in the social construction of television. Although television had been demonstrated in shop windows of the big cities, mainly as a means of promotion for the new medium (see Hadenius 1998; Jensen 1997), for people in general, reports in newspapers were the main source of information. Moreover, the written press in the Nordic countries was strong in international comparison and reached most groups of the population. Thus, it is reasonable to conclude that the press was the most important context in the public reception of early television. In the introductory phase of television in the 1950s, and for a long time thereafter, the Nordic newspaper industry generally regarded television as a potential threat to its position in society, as it had earlier seen radio (Djerf-Pierre and Weibull 2001; Salokangas 1997). Gradually, however, television was regarded as a very important subject of newspaper journalism.

From our perspective, newspaper journalism by definition reports of, and gives a voice to, other social agents, but nevertheless has its own voice and an independent role to play. Accordingly, as for the newspaper press, its reception of a new medium can here be understood in two ways. On one hand, it concerns newspapers as actors in the media field, having their views on the new medium. On the other hand, newspapers in their coverage also reflect a general social attitude to television and, at the same, offer a forum for other social actors to formulate and express opinions about television. Of course, it is very difficult to distinguish between the two, not least because newspapers might filter public opinion and other actors according to their views.

Approach and data

The introduction of television in the Nordic countries has been treated in many studies (see Dahl and Bastiansen 1999; Endén 1996; Hadenius 1998; Jensen et al. 1997). These studies focus mainly on the institutional history of broadcasting, including description and analysis of organization and programming, whereas the interplay between television and society has been paid less attention (cf. Djerf-Pierre & Weibull 2001; Edin 2000; Ruoho 2001). This chapter will complement the institutional history with an approach that could be characterized as a history of reception.

With reception we mean a process by which individual people and their communities, social organizations and institutions make sense of their individual or collective experiences about the world in which they live. As with reception studies in general, the history of reception deals with construction of meanings and, in this case more particularly, with meanings of television (see Jensen, 1993). Our primary interest is to describe and analyse dimensions of meaning, which could be characterized as *intermedial* contextualizations of early television, and, secondly, to pay attention to a few broader social and cultural perspectives of the introduction of television (on intermediality and multimodality see Kress 2001; Lehtonen 2001). Our main data, in the form of a newspaper sample, means that we focus on *public* reception of early television; in other words, to constructions of meanings as they appeared in the newspapers under study. Newspapers are the most readily available sources for any analysis of reception history, although the relatively short history of television still allows the use of methods like interviewing or construction of individual media biographies (on the former, see Boddy 1994; Salmi 1992; Spigel 1992; on the latter, Graf 1997; Kytömäki et al. 2003; van Zoonen & Wieten 1994).

The description and analysis below is based on a newspaper sample from the first week of October in the years 1960 and 1970. The newspapers under study include both quality and popular papers from three countries, Denmark, Finland and Sweden, with the main focus on Finland and Sweden. The time span of the data from 1960 to 1970 covers a process of development that could be characterized as the emergence and establishment of modern television (see Kortti, 2003, on television advertising). Within this period, television grew from an emergent new medium to what Umberto Eco (1984) calls *paleo television*, a national institution which formed the centre of the national public life (for other periodizations of television, see Ellis 2000; Djerf-Pierre & Weibull 2001; Hujanen 2005). The aspect of modern in our reference to television can be understood as the social and cultural context of our analysis, meaning the constitution of the so-called modern society.

Early television in the Nordic countries

Whereas most European countries introduced television in the early 1950s, regular transmissions in the Nordic countries started in mid 1950s or later: 1954 in Denmark, 1956 in Finland and Sweden, and 1960 in Norway. At first the programming consisted of only a couple of hours at night, but the new medium was met with great interest by Nordic citizens and the number of TV sets sold soon exceeded all predictions. Finland's national broadcaster was first with two TV channels, the second one established in 1965; Sweden introduced TV2 in 1969, whereas the second channels in Denmark and Norway started first in the 1980s. In Denmark, Norway and Sweden television was broadcast by public service organizations and did not carry advertising, whereas Finnish television included both public service and commercial broadcasts.

During the first years, programming was restricted to less than two hours at night, and some weekdays were what was then called 'TV free'. In the late 1950s there was an increase in broadcasting time and in 1960 Danish, Finnish and Swedish television all broadcast almost three hours on weekdays, mainly from 8 through to 10 p.m., and a little more on Saturdays and Sundays. The typical 1960 programme schedule started with news and often included some film or documentary. A short children's programme was broadcast in the early evening around 5 p.m. The programming was dominated by national productions, including sports and theatre, but also US-produced shows, like Perry Como, were offered, but American TV series in general did not have a strong position in Nordic television until the late 1960s.

In 1970 the situation had changed. The volume had increased, particularly in Finland and Sweden. The Finnish public broadcaster had bought the independent commercial broadcaster and made it its second channel. The Swedish Channel 1 in 1970 normally broadcast from 6 through to 11 p.m., with educational TV in the mornings. The new second channel transmitted at first only for a couple of hours, but within less than a year it had an evening programme, almost on the level of Channel 1. Danish television in 1970 broadcast normally from 7 through to 11 p.m., but included school television in the mornings and a block of old programmes in the late afternoon.

Newspaper coverage on early television: general features

Although the quantity of television coverage in 1960 was small in comparison to the present situation, television was already an everyday phenomenon in all newspapers from the sample. In addition to programme listings, and a few previews of individual programmes, the new TV technology was presented both in news and features, and the political aspects of the organization were reviewed in editorials and commentaries. Longitudinal data from Sweden clearly shows that the expansion of newspaper coverage on TV, not surprisingly, coincides with the start of the programming in 1956. During the first TV years the newspapers seem to have a certain balance between coverage of television as a social phenomenon and the promotion or reviews of the actual programmes. Soon, however, the programmes take over and start dominating in reports and comments (Johansson and Törnqvist 2002; cf. Andersson 2003).

It is reasonable to believe, in the light of the Swedish data above, that the expansion of television coverage in newspapers was a consequence of the start of TV, although individual papers, for policy reason, could act differently (cf. Bastiansen 2003). The total number of articles during the weeks under study in 1960 and 1970 (see Table 1) is somewhat higher in Denmark than the respective figures in Finland and Sweden. One should notice that the launch of television clearly took place earlier in Denmark than in the other two countries. The average amount of coverage is around four articles per day, not including the programme listings.

Table 1: Average number of articles per issue on TV in six Nordic Newspapers the first full week in October 1960 and 1970.

	Denmark		Finland		Sweden	
Year	QP	PP	QP	PP	QP	PP
1960						
Number of articles	2.9	6.5	2.3	1.8	1.9	1.3
Front page articles	–	0.2	–	–	0.1	–
Editorials	–	0.2	–	–	–	–
Articles on individual programmes	1.6	3.3	1.6	1.5	1.1	0.4
1970						
Number of articles	5.1	3.3	6.4	3.8	3.7	2.7
Front page articles	–	0.2	–	0.3	–	0.1
Ediorials	–	0.2	0.1	0.2	–	–
Articles on individual programmes	3.4	2.2	4.1	2.0	2.7	1.9

Comments: Denmark: Quality press (QP) 1960 and 1970 *Berlingske Tidende* (7 days a week), Popular press (PP) 1960 *BT* (6), 1970 *Ekstrabladet* (6); Finland: QP 1960 and 1970 *Helsingin Sanomat* (7), PP 1960 and 1970 *Ilta-Sanomat* (6); Sweden: QP 1960 and 1970 *Dagens Nyheter* (7), PP 1960 and 1970 *Expressen* (7).

Except for programme listings, the standard newspaper coverage on television in 1960 consisted of a short review of yesterday's TV programme and an often even smaller preview, presenting two or three programmes with a few lines each. The headlines were normally very simple: just 'TV' or 'Television'. The review material and previews did not appear in one special section, as in 1970, but could be found on different pages depending on the topic. In the Finnish sample, however, culture was clearly the dominant context for reviews and previews. The latter material appeared rather in the form of small news than direct promotion of programmes in style of puffs, typical of the 1970 newspapers.

The variety and fluctuation of how newspapers presented television shows that the conventions of coverage were still, in 1960, in their developmental phase. Reviews adopted the conventions of radio critique or applied more generally to the tradition of cultural critique. Previews and programme promotion more generally already existed in the time of radio broadcasting. But the question of how television coverage was related to radio, whether its context was culture or leisure time or television as such, was all open in 1960. On the whole, the space devoted to TV was still somewhat less than that given to radio. Also the general news pages included some material on TV, mainly reports on the national TV organization or development of television in other countries. The news reports on TV were generally descriptive in their approach and presented television in a fairly neutral way. The few commentaries on television, mainly on its political role, were focused on understanding, not criticizing, the new medium.

The increased attention to individual programmes was the main difference between the newspaper samples of 1960 and 1970. In 1960 roughly half of the articles – programme listings excluded – of both Danish papers dealt with individual programmes; in 1970 the share was about 80 percent. For Sweden the corresponding figures were about 30 and about 60 percent. The Finnish popular paper of the sample was an exception to the general trend; in 1960 almost all its articles concerned individual programmes, whereas the respective share went down to a half in 1970. The Finnish quality paper similarly concentrated, in 1960, on individual programmes, but their share remained on the same high level in 1970 (two thirds of the articles). The overall conclusion is that, in relative terms, the coverage goes from a broader spectrum of television issues to a more focused treatment of programme content.

Along with increased attention to content, television also became, in 1970, to a greater extent a controversial issue in general news and commentaries, including editorials. Documentaries as well as TV debates were followed up by articles which treated both political controversies and human-interest issues. The readers' television-viewing as such was not an issue any more, but was taken for granted by newspaper editors. Even in relation to individual programmes, or programme categories (like TV theatre in Finland), more criticism was evident in 1970. The more critical tune of reporting and commentary was probably a consequence of the growing volume of TV programming, but also of the increasing importance of television in society. In reviews and promotion television started matching, and even exceeding, the respective space for radio. This kind of observation from only one week must of course be treated carefully, but the results are clearly in line with Swedish longitudinal data based on a broader material.

The 1960 newspaper sample contained a lot of advertising on television. Both the quality and the popular paper in Denmark included one or two TV advertisements on an average weekday. The same applied to the Swedish quality paper, whereas there were fewer ads in the popular one. The Finnish quality paper *Helsingin Sanomat* represented, however, an extreme case among the papers with 76 advertisements in the sample week of October 1960 (making in average about 11 ads per day). That is essentially more than the respective volume of the quality papers in Denmark and Sweden. Furthermore, the Finnish quality paper had a lot more advertising on TV than editorial content on the medium. The Finnish popular paper was, however, marginal as an advertising forum and included only a few ads on television.

The national differences in TV advertising in 1960 may be debated because of the small sample and the character of the selected papers. However, there are a couple of reasons which may explain why advertising was so central in the public reception of television in Finland. One factor was certainly the later expansion of television in Finland, but one should not forget the commercial influence in the introduction of Finnish television. Sponsored programming together with advertising funded early private television, and that created a form of programme promotion that was unique in the Nordic context. The interesting aspect of these ads was that they clearly represented the dominant form of programme promotion and preceded the later convention of puffing.

On the basis of the newspaper sample it seems quite clear that the volume of TV ads declined between 1960 and 1970. But even ten years later *Helsingin Sanomat* had a lot more TV ads than the other papers, although its number of ads was one-third less than 1960. The decrease is not surprising if one thinks that the volume of advertising is related to expansion of television technology. In 1960 television was a new medium in rapid expansion, especially in Finland. Ten years later the market was close to saturation and the new boom of colour TV was just beginning.

Programme listings

As a newspaper convention, the programme listings of television are based on a long tradition of radio listings, and that is why they remained rather consistent through 1960 to 1970. In 1960 most papers of the sample presented the daily TV programme as a minor part of the radio listings; even, in the Danish quality paper, under the headline 'The Programmes for the Radio Listener' and in both Finnish papers simply under 'Radio Programmes'. Listings in all three countries included foreign television: in Denmark, Swedish as well as German TV from both east and west; in Finland, Swedish and Estonian TV; and in Sweden, normally Danish and Norwegian.

Ten years later, in 1970, the TV listings had expanded and normally had their own column, even if this was still connected to the radio listings at the end of the paper. Especially in the popular press, TV now differed from the radio listings by small previews and promos of individual programmes, often including photos or other illustrations. In the 1970 sample, the Finnish quality paper was an exception since it still offered radio and television programmes under a joint heading: 'radio and television'. As to contexts of television, the interesting aspect of both Finnish papers was that the programme listings were located side by side with comics, which in Denmark and Sweden was true only for the popular papers.

The emerging television society was demonstrated by the specialization of TV coverage in the popular press in the style of 'TV This Week'. This convention was used in 1970 by Danish and Swedish popular papers, which offered a four-page section on Thursday presenting next week's TV, including extensive programme previews. The Finnish popular paper applied to a similar convention in relation to weekend programmes under the heading 'Weekend's TV and Radio'. So again, different from other countries, the Finnish case covered both radio and television, but as in the title of the section, television was now the first priority.

Reception of television as technology

The identification of early television as 'visual radio' expresses the technical and institutional continuation between television and radio broadcasting. In programme listings, the newspapers in 1960 took this kind of continuity for granted and connected television listings with radio. In Finland as well as in Sweden, television as visual radio was often used both in public policy and in the professional language of broadcasting in the early 1950s. However, with the actual introduction of the new medium, the language changed and the English-language word 'television' was rapidly domesticated. The change of language implied a growing awareness that functions and practices of television were different from traditional radio. But despite efforts for distinction, radio remained a 'meta-concept' for television a long way into the 1960s. In Finland this first phase of television is called by Silvo (1988: 157) the era of visual radio, which was characterized by comparison of television with radio and, secondarily, with theatre.

In the Nordic countries, the dominant role of the old national broadcasting institutions as such symbolized the continuity of television as visual radio. In all three countries under study the names of the national broadcasters made a direct reference to 'radio' – Danmarks Radio (Denmark's Radio) in Denmark, Yleisradio (General Radio) in Finland, and Sveriges Radio (Sweden's Radio) in Sweden – and did not change the name with the introduction of television. In Denmark and Sweden the existing national broadcasters took over television from the very beginning. In Finland, a new, private television company was founded and, in addition to that, public service television operated in a duopoly with a commercial programming company (on the Finnish TV duopoly, see Hellman 1999: 94–104 and Hujanen 2002: 14–18). The Finnish exception demonstrates that technological changes in media had the potential to affect institutional and organizational features of media, as well as division of power in the field.

Television as visual radio is a typical example of what could be called an intermedial construction. In addition to the taken-for-granted connection between radio and television, film appeared several times as a point of reference to television in our newspaper sample. Not least was film a standard element of television's programme supply but already, in the 1960 sample, the impact of television on film appeared as a social and political issue. A news story in *Helsingin Sanomat* (6 October 1960) reported that film and television competed over viewers in Western Germany. The story pointed out that such a competition was nothing new in the US. A few reviews in the 1960 sample also referred to aesthetic differences between film and television, and made the point that good film was not necessarily good television.

The importance of advertising in the early reception of television, particularly in Finland, is a good reminder that television from the beginning was closely connected with meanings and pleasures of the new consumer society (Spigel, 1990, emphasizes this point). One should notice that the introduction and spread of consumer goods like refrigerators, vacuum cleaners and, among them, television, was parallel to a political project which became known as the Nordic Welfare Society. Before establishment of programme promotion conventions like puffing, advertising of television receivers played an important role in communicating television content. In that sense, it is particularly interesting to look at the graphic and visual design of adverts about television receivers.

In the sample from 1960, most adverts depicted the actual receiver and also often gave a hint on the screen about the content of television. In Finland, these ads represented television typically as pleasure equipment and secondarily as a source of information. Tensions between consumer pleasures and the rational construction of welfare society were apparent in advertising about television. Thus, in terms of preferred reading, advertising often had a double message: it addressed those readers who were tempted by the popular pleasures of television and those who were interested in television as a reliable window on the world.

The latter type of advertising was more often found in newspapers from Denmark and Sweden, with their less-commercial television culture: 'Your living room is the centre of the world' said an ad from the brand S.P. in the quality paper Berlingske Tidende (BT 3 October 1960). And in the same paper, a few days later, Philips television boasted that it is 'far reaching' – showing TV sets with inscribed pictures from Stockholm, Cologne and Berlin, countries whose television channels could be watched in Denmark (BT 11 October 1960). In the Swedish quality paper Dagens Nyheter Philips presented an ad under the headline 'The most bought TV in Sweden' (DN 6 October 1960). The set was called 'Reportage' and, in the design of the ad, it was placed on top of a globe. Aspects of pleasure were not, however, totally absent in Danish and Swedish ads, but it seems that comfort and reliability were the most widely used arguments in relation to TV sets.

In the Finnish sample, one of the ads was playing with the reality effect of television. The ad for the Philips receiver depicted on the screen a fish in a bowl that was chased by a cat from outside the receiver (*HS* 3 October 1960). The text of the ad played with the double meaning of the phrase 'it is clear' in the Finnish language – Philips is clear in terms of a choice of receiver but also in terms of the picture quality. It seems that, still, in 1960 the nature and quality of television picture was a major obstacle when trying to build credibility for this new technology. That is why the most typical narrative convention of the ads tried to convince the reader of the technical qualities of receivers as 'top class' or 'world class'. Expert and science discourse was typically used in the legitimation of quality, including photos of scientists who had tested the equipment, or of merchants who sold it – all of them male.

Editorial construction of early television: Television in society

The role of television in society, of course, is not only a matter of watching, although it connotes the importance of TV in the daily life for pleasure or information. When considering the editorial construction of television in the newspapers, one should not forget that television is a social and cultural institution that affects, but is also affected by, other societal factors like politics, economy and culture. In terms of social construction, one could say that television contributes to politics, economy and culture but is mutually constructed by them.

Promises of television...

When looking through the sample week of October 1960, it is clear that the editorial construction of television by the newspapers is generally positive. The predominant perspective is the potential of TV as a productive socio-political factor. In two big articles, the Swedish quality paper *Dagens Nyheter* described school-television. The first one was focused on organization and production. In the second one, which started on the front page and was given almost a full page inside, the advantages of school-television were treated from a school perspective, where 'one expects that the new medium will function as a stimulus for both teachers and pupils and it will be a valuable complement to other forms of education'. (*DN* 4 October 1960) On the inside page, both teachers and school administrators commented on the potential of television and proposed ideas for school-TV programming. A representative of the parents said that 'with good TV education – no long documentaries – the time spent with homework could be reduced'. The reporter supported the conclusion in the final paragraph, and concluded by stressing what a gold mine school programmes could be for adults.

The Swedish discussion on the potential importance of school-television had obviously also been noticed in Denmark. In the same week, the Danish popular paper *BT* (4 October 1960) devoted almost a page to TV in schools, mainly presenting the Swedish model. The article was critical of the delay of school-TV in Denmark and the low interest shown by Danish television in the Nordic cooperation in the field.

The almost idyllic picture of the promises of television can be seen also in other articles from the newspapers. The Swedish *Dagens Nyheter* informed its readers in a headline that 'TV strengthens the family bonds' (*DN* 3 October 1960). The article, originating from the paper's London correspondent, presented results from a study conducted by BBC audience research, showing that a consequence of television is that families, to a greater extent, stay at home together at night. But it added that in big families, however, television means less cohesion. In the end the correspondent addressed directly the readers and said:

> Another fact that the Swedish TV-owners probably already know too well has been confirmed by the study: ownership of a TV set automatically brings more guests to your home. (DN 3 October 1960.)

It seems clear that in 1960 television was regarded as an important medium, associated with prestige and power. When the Swedish Prime Minister was supposed to be interviewed on US television (by Walther Cronkite of CBS), it was a news item in the Swedish popular paper *Expressen* (3 October 1960). And, of course, it was regarded as politically important news in all papers that the Soviet leader Nikita Khrushchev, that week visiting the United Nations in New York, had been allowed to speak on television in the US (e.g. the Danish popular paper *BT* 7 October 1960). The Finnish popular paper *Ilta-Sanomat* noted in particular that Khrushchev participated in an open-end transmission and pointed out that the Soviet leader's participation was not pre-censored in any way (*IS* 6 October 1960).

...and possible threats

The political importance of television also caused some critical concern in the 1960 newspapers. In the sample week, the Nordic newspaper readers were offered an illustrative example of the political role of television: the famous TV debates between the US presidential candidates, John Kennedy and Richard Nixon. The first debate, in late September, had resulted in a discussion of how television as a medium affected Nixon's poor appearance – looking sick and tired. Before the second debate, on 7 October, this was mentioned in almost all newspapers of the sample. The Danish quality paper *Berlingske Tidende* already paid attention to the forthcoming TV debate on Monday (3 October 1960) with the headline 'Nixon's TV Make up'. The article quoted Nixon's press secretary who stated that the poor appearance was a mistake by the Nixon staff when arranging the cameras, and 'will not happen again'. Later in the week the story was in the Swedish popular paper *Expressen* with the headline 'Make-up Experts Help Nixon' (7 October 1960).

The Nixon-Kennedy debate focused on the role of television in politics. The Finnish quality paper *Helsingin Sanomat* contained a column by Walter Lippman – copyright by New York Herald Tribune (*HS* 3 October 1960) – where he claimed that in political debates like this the cameras should 'behave neutrally', and that is why he considered it necessary to clarify what the technical reasons were which made Nixon look older and more tired than he was. As the Danish popular paper *BT* formulated it in an editorial, illustrated with a big portrait of a tired Nixon, the question was why the cameras were 'angry' with Nixon (*BT* 5 October 1960). It concluded that the example shows the danger of television – television reveals and has effects. Lippman's perspective was more positive, and he regarded television as 'a truth machine' that does not immediately affect opinions but which influences how people subconciously relate themselves to politicians.

In addition to the Lippman article, *Helsingin Sanomat* published later in the week a story about the second Kennedy-Nixon debate, which concluded that television made the election 'a nightmare' for public opinion researchers because of its impact on public opinion (*HS* 7 October 1960). It seems reasonable that the particular attention in Danish and Finnish newspapers on television's role in politics was influenced by current or forthcoming elections in these countries: Finland had local elections on Sunday, 2 October, just prior to the sample week; Denmark was preparing for national elections to be held in November; Sweden had had an election in September.

Danish coverage of television and politics clearly linked the campaign plans of the Danish political parties to the US experience. For example, the popular *BT* published a news article on the social democratic campaign film to be broadcast on TV, and especially noted that the party has hired a professional director for the film (*BT* 4 October 1960). *Berlingske Tidende*, the Danish quality paper, offered a feature article some days later (*Berl Tid* 9 October 1960) which focused on 'Television – the revealing medium' with sub-headlines like 'The new dangerous weapon of the election campaign' and 'What television requires from the politician'. *BT* argued that the election campaign on TV must not be theatre, since the issues of the elections are too important for that (*BT* 5 October 1960).

In contrast, the Swedish press seemed to play down the role of TV in the elections two weeks earlier, often called 'Sweden's first TV election'. The quality paper *Dagens Nyheter* commented on a TV programme which reported a study arguing that television meant relatively little: 'So one could go to bed with the knowledge that television was a relatively harmless medium and the Swedes a congregation of very resisting viewers' (*DN* 8 October 1960). The popular paper *Expressen*, however, thought that the study left much unsaid concerning the political role of television (*Expressen* 7 October 1960).

The newspapers also regularly reported on the dissemination of television in society. The launch of colour TV in the US was presented by the Danish quality *Berlingske Tidende* (9 October 1960), which concluded, with reference to the Danish industry, that there was still a long way to go before that technology is in everyday use. In Finland, a small news report in *Helsingin Sanomat* told that the number of TV licences exceeded 900,000 in Sweden (*HS* 9 October 1960). As reported by the popular paper *Ilta-Sanomat* next day, the corresponding figure was only 72,000 in Finland, but the number was rapidly growing (*IS* 10 October 1960). Further comments of the growth were not given.

By 1970, television had become a nationwide medium in terms of distribution and use in all Nordic countries. Television now dominated radio in the newspapers' reporting, and it had become a taken-for-granted element of society and culture. In particular, its political role was emphasized and, as a result, television itself was politicized and became a forum of political controversies, as well as of value and moral conflicts. Politically, television was accused of representing a left-wing bias; socially and culturally it was seen to promote values and norms which threatened the national culture and the domestic way of life. These kinds of controversies around television, and broadcasting more generally, were particularly strong in Finland, which experienced an extremely rapid social change towards urbanization in the 1960s. The Finnish parliamentary elections in 1970 are often characterized as 'the YLE elections' referring to the important role of the national broadcasting company YLE as a major issue of political conflict (Hujanen 1995; Salokangas 1997).

A look into the newspapers of the first October week of 1970 to a large extent confirms the above kind of general picture. Both in Finland and Sweden there are political controversies around TV. The chairman of the Finnish YLE's administrative council wanted to close down the TV theatre, which was strongly criticized as a 'political decision'. Both the quality paper *Helsingin Sanomat* and the popular *Ilta-Sanomat* devoted a lot of space to the debate (8 October 1970). The Finnish controversy spilled over to Sweden, and *Dagens Nyheter* reported on the threat to the Finnish TV theatre (*DN* 8 October 1970). But also, on the same day, an example of a Swedish TV controversy could be observed. Under the headline 'Left lining against shareholders', a representative for a company handling shares accused a TV1 programme of a partisan presentation of the share market (*DN* 8 October 1970; for other aspects of the debate see *DN* 6 and 11 October 1970). Another reaction is recorded in the popular *Expressen*, where the programme was regarded as a 'funny theatre satire on shares' (*Expressen* 7 October 1970).

The accusation of a left-wing bias of television was also taken up by the Danish quality paper *Berlingske Tidende,* which reported on a study of how the citizens perceived the main newscast (TVA) on television. The headline 'Every fourth person thinks that the TVA is biased' focused on the criticism of television news, but the attached table showed that 33 percent of the audience thought that TVA is not biased and 42 percent had no opinion. Later the same week there were two new controversies reported in the Swedish papers: a preview of a theatre performance on the development of Northern Sweden, and the TV coverage of the so-called Vietnam Tribunal (or Russell Tribunal) in Stockholm. Both were positively regarded in the TV commentary in *Dagens Nyheter* (*DN* 9 October 1960), but were later to create some of the most intense debates on Swedish TV programming (Djerf-Pierre and Weibull 2001). In Denmark, the popular *Ekstrabladet* (5 October 1970) hinted that the biases in broadcasting were of a recurrent character in the headline: 'The radio goes to the police again', reporting on a clergyman who had gone to the police because Danish Radio had permitted a singer to perform a 'blasphemous' song.'

As the discussion on individual programmes shows, television was a source of political and value conflicts. At the same time, its growing importance as a political medium was hardly questioned. An exception is offered by a conflict in Finland, which concerned the delivery of election results in two municipalities which voted for eventual unification. A news report in *Helsingin Sanomat* accused television of slowing down the counting of election results in the two municipalities (*HS* 7 October 1970). According to the news report, television and radio were favoured in the timing of the delivery of the results. The report made fun of the way television influenced the counting of results – mistakes were made because election officials were forced to rehearse the filming. The next day, *Helsingin Sanomat* commented on the news in an editorial with a headline 'Rehearsed News' (*HS* 8 October 1970). The editorial recommended ironically that television news started using 'a candid camera' – it does not require any rehearsals and does not interrupt the news event itself. The TV reporters' letter to the editor (*HS* 9 October 1970) concluded that blaming television for everything is so common a mode today that it is already out of mode.

In Finland the political controversy over broadcasting, and particularly over television, led to the birth of citizens' movements that played an important role in the formation of public opinion in the 1970 election. These movements also remained active after the election, but then died out gradually in the course of the 1970s. Most of them were loosely affiliated to political parties, but a few represented a conservative 'moral panic' without a clear party affiliation. The resignation of the chairman of an organization of the latter category was reported by both of the Finnish newspapers of the sample (*IS* 9 October 1970, *HS* 11 October 1970). The quality paper *Helsingin Sanomat* noted also the founding of a new movement called the Labour Movement's Radio and Television Association (*HS* 8 October 1970), which, according to *Helsingin Sanomat*, wanted to promote the independence of public broadcasting from the pressure of the economic power elite.

Conclusions

In her discussion on the early reception of American television, Spigel (1990) notes that popular discourses on television are a product of the modern imagination, a part of the history of ideas about communication technology. According to Spigel, the telegraph, telephone, movies, and radio were all received with a mixture of utopian hope and dystopian fear (cf. Boddy 1998; Jensen 1990). This kind of modern imagination has not been less common on the European side of the Atlantic. In fact, the typical public control of broadcasting in Europe has been motivated by the kind of dystopian fears about dysfunctional effects of electronic media, which Spigel refers to.

Judging on the basis of our newspaper sample from 1960, the public reception of early television was more positive than critical. As hinted by Salmi (1992) on the basis of the Finnish experience, a reason for such an attitude might be that, although television as technology was new, the medium itself had already been a subject of popular imagination for a couple of decades. Among sources for popular imagination one should not only include the printed press but also American movies and comics like Donald Duck. So, at the introduction of television, people were already aware of what the new 'visual radio' was about. One may also suppose that the enormous rise in the popularity of cinema, parallel to the launch of television, created positive expectations about the audiovisuality of television.

Technically, television still had a major problem of credibility in 1960. The broader contexts of credibility are well illustrated in a cartoon in *Helsingin Sanomat* (*HS* 7 October 1960) which comments on the technical failures of early television. The cartoon, drawn by the acronym Kari who later became a kind of political institution in Finnish public life, depicted a small person with a big hat, the known symbol of the cartoonist himself, watching television. On the television screen one could see a text up side down 'We are sorry for a technical failure.' Text in relation to the picture commented: 'Within the so-called culture, radio and television are hardly anything else than a kind of "technical failure."' The cartoon expressed the typical suspicion of the political and cultural elite to television as mass culture. But one should notice that, although the cartoon visually dealt with television, the comment of the text referred to both radio and television. In other words, a distinction was drawn in relation to broadcasting as a whole, a kind of Gutenbergian comment on the electronic sublime of the broadcast media.

But it is noteworthy that technical problems of reception did not hinder the rapid spread of television. As we have demonstrated, by 1970 television started dominating over radio in the newspaper coverage of broadcast media. Television became a taken-for-granted dimension of everyday life which affected the volume and structure of television coverage, particularly in the popular newspapers. The growth of television into the dominant national medium made it subject to political controversy, which is in striking contrast with the early positive reception. The conflicting views concerned, first of all, the content of television – the way individual programmes dealt with social problems and with so-called reality in general. Another area of conflicting views was the nature of television as a public institution, and its bureaucratic nature and waste of public funds.

In 1960, television as a social phenomenon was a matter of what could be characterized as externalized reporting, treating the new technology and its contents in a diversified, or even straggling way. In ten years, from 1960 to 1970, TV coverage became internalized: it found its character, both in form and content.

References

Andersson, Ulrika (2003) *Fokus på TV. Artiklar om TV i Dagens Nyheter och Expressen 1960–2000*, Department of Journalism and Mass Communication, Göteborg University.

Barnouw, Erik (1977) *Tube of Plenty. The evolution of american television*, New York & Oxford: Oxford University Press.

Bastiansen, Henrik (2003) *Partipolitiske pressestrategier overfor NRK-fjernsynets valgsendninger 1965*, Paper presented at the 16th Nordic Conference for Media and Communication Research, Kristiansand, Norway.

Boddy, William (1994) 'Archaelogies of electronic vision and the gendered spectator', *Screen*, 35(2), p. 105.

Boddy, William (1998) 'The beginning of American Television', in A. Smith (ed.) *Television: An international history*, Oxford, New York: Oxford University Press.

Brooks, Tim, and Earle Marsh, (1988) *The complete directory to prime time Network TV shows, 1946–present*, 4th edition, New York: Ballantine.

Dahl, Hans Fredrik & Bastiansen, Henrik G. (1999) *Over til Oslo. NRK som monopol 1945–1981*, Oslo: J W Cappelens forlag.

Djerf-Pierre, Monika & Weibull, Lennart (2001) *Spegla granska tolka. Aktualitetsjournalistik i svensk radio och TV under 1900–talet*, Stockholm: Prisma.

Eco, Umberto (1984) *Semiologia quotidiana*, Milan: Gruppo Editoriale Fabbri-Bompiana.

Edin, Anna (2000) *Den förestälda publiken. Programpolitik, publikbilder och tilltalsformer i svensk public service-television*, Eslöv: Symposion.

Ellis, John (1992) *Visible fictions*, London & New York: Routledge.

Ellis, John (2000) *Seeing things: Television in the age of uncertainty*, London: Tauris.

Endén, Rauno, (ed.) (1996) *Yleisradio 1926–1996: A history of broadcasting in Finland*, Helsinki: Finnish Historical Society.

Graf, Heike (1997) *Fernsehen als gemeinschaftsstiftende Instanz?: Fernsehen und Alltag in den Anfangsjahren von Sveriges Radio*, Berlin: Humboldt Universität.

Hadenius, Stig (1998) *Kampen om monopolet*, Stockholm: Prisma.

Hellman, Heikki (1999) *From companions to competitors: the changing broadcasting markets and television programming in Finland*, Tampere: University of Tampere, Acta Universitatis Tamperensis 652.

Hujanen, Taisto (1995) 'Political versus cultural in critical broadcasting research and policy: A reevaluation of the Finnish radical experiment in broadcasting in the late 1960s', in John A. Lent (ed.) *A different road taken*, Boulder: Westview Press.

Hujanen, Taisto (2002) *The power of schedule: Programme management in the transformation of Finnish public service television*, Tampere: Tampere University Press.

Hujanen, Taisto (2005) 'Implications for public service broadcasters', Chapter 3, in Robert Picard & Allan Brown (eds.) *Digital terrestrial television in Europe*, London: Lawrence Erlbaum.

Jensen, Joli (1990) *Redeeming modernity: Contradictions in media criticism*, Newbury Park: Sage.

Jensen, Klaus Bruhn (1993) 'The Past in the future: Problems and potentials of historical reception studies', *Journal of Communication*, 43(4), pp. 20–28.

Jensen, Klaus Bruhn (1997) *Dansk Mediehistorie 1–3*, Köpenhamn: Samlerens forlag.

Jensen, Klaus Bruhn, Agger, Gunhild & Drotner, Kirsten (eds.) (1997) *Dansk mediehistorie*, Volume 2, Köpenhamn: Samlerens forlag.

Johansson, Anngreth & Törnqvist, Tobias (2002) *TV i pressen 1965–1971. En kvantitativ innehållsanalys av hur pressen uppmärksammade televisionen i slutet av sextio- och början av sjuttiotalet*, Department of Journalism and Mass Communication, Göteborg University.

Kress, Gunther (2001) *Multimodal discourse: The modes and media of contemporary communication*, London: Arnold.

Kortti, Jukka (2003) *Modernisaatiomurroksen kaupalliset merkit: 60-luvun suomalainen televisiomainonta* [The commercial signs of modernization: The Finnish TV advertising in the 1960's], Helsinki: SKS.

Kytömäki, Juha, Nirkko, Juha & Suoninen, Annikka (eds.) (2003) *Yksi päivä mediaa* [One day of media], Helsinki: SKS.

Lehtonen, Mikko (2001) 'On no man's land. Theses on intermediality', *Nordicom Review*, 22(1), pp. 71–83.

Mintz, Lawrence (1985)'Standup comedy as social and cultural mediation.' *American Quarterly*, 37 (Spring 1985), pp. 71–80.

Ruoho, Iiris (2001) *Utility drama. Making of and talking about the serial drama in Finland*, Tampere: Tampere University Press.

Salmi, Hannu (1992) '"Pyhäkoulujen kilpailija'" vai '"kokoava keskipiste"'? Suomalaista televisio-keskustelua 1940- ja 50-luvuilla' ['"Competitor of sunday schools" or "Centre point of togetherness"? Finnish Discussion on TV in the 1940s and 1950s], *Lähikuva*, 1(1992), pp. 28–37.

Salokangas, Raimo (1997) Finlands rundradio i ett föränderligt samhälle 1949–1996, in *Rundradion 1926–1996. Rundradions historia i Finland*, Helsingfors: Rundradion AB/Yleisradio Oy.

Silvo, Ismo (1988) *Valta, kenttä, kertomus: Televisiopolitiikan tulkinnat* [Power, field, narratives: Interpretations of television policy], Helsinki: YLE, Research and Training, Publication 2/1988.

Spigel, Lynn (1990) 'Television in the family circle: The popular reception of a new medium', in Patricia Mellencamp (ed.), *Logics of television*, Bloomington and Indianapolis: Indiana University Press.

Spigel, Lynn (1992) *Make room for TV: Television and the family ideal in post-war America*, Chicago: Chicago University Press.

Sterling, Christopher H. & Kittross, John M. (1990) *Stay tuned: A concise history of American broadcasting*, Belmont, CA: Wadsworth Publishing Company.

Tiedge, James T. & Ksobiech, Kenneth J. (1987) 'Counterprogramming primetime network television', *Journal of Broadcasting & Electronic Media*, 31(1), pp. 41–55.

Van Zoonen, Lisbeth & Wieten, Jan (1994) '"It wasn't exactly a miracle": The arrival of television in Dutch family life', *Media, Culture & Society*, 16(4), pp. 641–660.

Chapter 5

Televisualization of the Popular Press: An Eye-catching Trend of the Late Twentieth Century's Media

Juha Herkman
University of Helsinki

There has been a lot of discussion of so-called visualization of culture, at least since the late twentieth century. Visualization was one of the main arguments, for example, in theories of postmodernism between the 1970s and the 1980s, especially in France. Jean Baudrillard and Jean-François Lyotard established the point of view that we had moved into a culture where images had taken the place of 'reality'. Baudrillard's famous ideas of 'hyperreal' and culture of 'simulations' suggested that there is no more any substance or 'truth' behind the images but images themselves constitute 'the truth' or 'hyperreal' world. As Martin Jay (1993: 544) puts it: 'We are no longer even in front of a mirror, but rather stare with fascination at a screen reflecting nothing outside it.'

The stance in relation to visualization has varied from highly pessimistic to more optimistic views. Guy Debord – a leader of the avant-garde movement the Situationist International (*L'Internationale Situationniste*) – for example, published in 1967 a book entitled *La Société du Spectacle* ('The Society of the Spectacle') in which he argued that, in late capitalist societies, people's lives are determined by mediated images that produce alienated socioeconomic relations and 'the false objectification of the producers'. Debord's ideas were part of Marxist criticism of the 1960s and are reminiscent of the Frankfurt School's theory of 'false consciousness' and the culture industry. It can be said that Debord translated Horkheimer and Adorno's ([1947]1972) theory of the culture industry into terms of vision and images. But as Adorno and Horkheimer had their counterpart in Walter Benjamin ([1934]2008), who did not have so pessimistic a view of cultural reproduction industries, so Debord had his counterpart in Baudrillard, who did not judge the loss of substance or 'truth' in visualized world of 'hyperreal world of simulation'. For Debord, the 'society of spectacle' was a threat constructed by corporate capitalism, for Baudrillard, the 'society of simulation' was merely an ironic condition that has to be taken as it was: visualization has to be accepted without pessimism because, according to Baudrillardian cynicism, there is no return to some authentic reality behind the 'simulacra' – the term borrowed from Plato's doctrine of ideas and means 'a copy without an original.'

Whatever the stance to so-called postmodernism has been, the idea of cultural visualization has not usually been denied. Even more sociological theorists have admitted that there has occurred some kind of transition from discursive, or coded, forms of signification to more figural or pictorial representations during the late twentieth century (e.g. Lash 1990). The natural reason for this was an invasion of visual media – cinema, television, video, the Internet – during the twentieth century.

There is also empirical research that supports the visualization thesis, even though quite differing results have also been revealed (e.g. Connell 1998: 18–19). It is true that *all* kinds of communication forms – aural, textual, visual – have been spread and diversified by digital networks, especially since the 1990s, but in the long run it is also possible to find a transition towards visual forms and technologies of communication. An historical analysis of newspapers, for example, has shown that the relationship between textual and pictorial representation has radically changed during the last hundred and fifty years. Kevin Barnhurst and John Nerone reveal in their impressive empirical study on history of news forms that the number of front-page items and stories has declined about 500 per cent between 1885 and 1985 and the mean number of words has halved during the same period. At the same time other indicators of layout – columns, headlines, typography, images – changed towards trends of modern visual design. The most rapid changes were seen in the late twentieth century. (Barnhurst & Nerone 2001: 194–202.) This is why Barnhurst and Nerone argue that the late modern newspaper (newspapers in the 'postmodern era') 'became a designer's newspaper' (ibid: 211).

As Barnhurst and Nerone imply, the visual design has become one of the key elements – if not the key element – of late modern newspaper production. There have been several reasons for increasing the importance of visuals in print media: the most obvious of course, is the technical development which made it possible to design the layout in new ways. But there are many other reasons, some of them economic, societal and cultural. It is important to understand that visualization of the press is a part of long historical and cultural development, and that a single medium – for example a newspaper – is always related to other media and cultural tendencies of a particular context. Changes in newspaper design can therefore be seen 'as a result of a shift to new layout and printing technologies employing photographic and digital processes' and motivated by 'a fear that newspapers had lost the competition with other technologies, especially television' (Barnhurst & Nerone 2001: 190). But they can also be seen as a part of a 'longer emergence of the modern aesthetic that began at the end of the medieval world' (ibid: 191).

The problem in studying such phenomena as visualization empirically might be a tendency to focus on a single medium instead of a larger view of contemporary media and culture within media research. Yet, there has been a growing trend toward convergence of media technology, forms and economics side by side with the visualization of the late modern media (see, for example, Murdock 2000). Because of media convergence, intermedial relations will be more and more important and should be taken seriously by media researchers (see Lehtonen 2001). Intermediality has also been a central aspect of visualization.

Thus we need to research visualization in a way that takes into account more precisely its historicity and intermedial relations. This is what I am trying to do by introducing a concept of 'televisualization'. By televisualization I mean a certain kind of visualization that was realized largely in European popular newspapers during the late twentieth century. So, in short, televisualization refers mainly to television's impact on the popular press of the 1990s, but it also pinpoints the economics and technologies of visualization as a whole. Television has therefore really been *tele*-visual in its impact on visual culture.

In this chapter I will first define the concept of televisualization and consider how it relates to other concepts. Secondly, I will analyse the various implications that televisualization has had on the popular press. This is based on my empirical research on the Finnish popular press as well as on the RHACNA analysis, discussed in this volume. Thirdly, I will consider televisualization as a general phenomenon of late modern culture and link it to discussions on tabloidization and commercialization of the media. The key question is to understand televisualization as a historically- and contextually-specific form of visualization that is based on certain intermedial relations in a certain cultural and economical context of the late twentieth century.

What is televisualization?

At the beginning of the 1990s, media researchers reported on significant changes in US television structure during the previous decade. The US television market was formerly governed by three national networks but, in the 1980s, an invasion of commercial satellite and cable channels radically challenged their position (see Dahlgren 1995: 48–49). Jay G. Blumler (1991: 194–200) writes about the 'multichannel revolution' that intensified competition, fragmented audiences, heightened the uncertainty of audience response, increased scheduling and put a higher premium on programme promotion. This 'revolution' created a new television marketplace with a new 'image of the capricious audience member, who has grown up with multichannel television, become accustomed to its style, enjoys riffling through its many offerings, and incessantly grazes across the dial in search of even more entrancing viewing pastures' (Blumler 1991: 198; see also Avery 1993).

John Thornton Caldwell called this phenomenon 'televisuality'. According to Caldwell (1995: 4–11) televisuality consists of multiple levels. On the one hand, televisuality is a question of style: television became more self-conscious and self-reflexive in style. Television had begun to develop its own visual effects from, and to reform, the Hollywood style that had formerly set standards for all audio-visual representations. On the other hand, televisuality was a question of the television industry. It was a mode of production that had an impact on programming and the construction of audiences. The very base of televisuality lay in the economic crisis that was created by the new television marketplace; even 'the stylistic excess can be seen as one way that mainstream television attempted to deal with the growing threat and eventual success of cable' (Caldwell 1995: 11).

Even though there are remarkable differences between US and European television traditions, many researchers would agree that Caldwell's ideas of televisuality would also suit, at least to some degree, the European context of the 1990s (see Dahlgren 1995: 49, 54–7). It was the Italian historian and semiotician Umberto Eco (1984) who wrote in the 1980s about 'neo-television' that had challenged traditional 'paleo-television'.[1] 'Paleo-television' was a modern project in the sense that its main focus was journalistic: to inform citizens and represent the world to the audience as opposed to 'neo-television', which is postmodern in the sense that its main focus is to represent itself; 'neo-television' is more interested in itself than the world outside.

In many European countries, the new television marketplace was created not by cable or satellite television but by national commercial channels that challenged public service broadcasting (PSB), even if cable and satellite channels have more recently increased their penetration in a 'deregulated' European television market (Richeri 2004: 178, 180–1). As a result, there has been an increasing competition between PSB and commercial television in Europe. In some countries this competition began to restructure the television market in the 1980s, but in other countries – for example in the Nordic Countries and in Eastern Europe – it did not really happen, for historical reasons, before the 1990s. Competition has also meant a completely new kind of ideology for PSB in these countries. As Taisto Hujanen (2002: 24) puts it: 'Increased channel competition is linked with a major transformation process in public service television that can be described as a change from broadcasting as a national institution to a cultural industry.'

There has been a great tension between traditional PSB values and commercial values in the new European television market. Jay G. Blumler wrote, in 1991, that

> policy makers in most West European societies have been pursuing, in different ways, a twin-track approach: on the one hand, opening the doors to more competition, commercialism, and channel abundance; on the other hand, devising safeguards to protect societal and broadcasting values thought vulnerable to the pressures these will unleash. (Blumler 1991: 212)

In spite of this 'twin-track' tension, televisuality has reached European television as styles and production modes. Video-graphics, digital effects, interactivity, self-reflexivity and real-life programming have also become common stylistics of contemporary television in Europe (see Caldwell 1995). Scheduling, programme planning and promotion are an integral part of the contemporary European television industry (see Ellis 2000; Hujanen 2002).

The so called 'television crisis', then, was mainly financial, and it has been linked to the increase of competition in the new television market as well as to the expensive development of digital television technology (see Richeri 2004: 181nn). But in spite of financial crises it is undeniable that television was the medium of the 1990s. In many European countries people spent most of their mass-media-use in front of the television set. Even in Finland, where print media flourished and people read more books, newspapers and magazines than almost anywhere in the world, the average reading time was four to five times less than the average television-watching time per day during the 1990s (Finnish Mass Media 2002). In spite of the 'digital revolution' and increased use of the Internet and mobile communication technologies, Edward Herman and Robert McChesney (1997: 2) wrote in 1997 that 'in our view TV is the defining medium of the age, and it provides the basis for an integrated global commercial media market.'

The popularity of television and changes in its styles and structures at the same time encourage us to consider its relation to other media; especially interesting has been television's relation to the press. As Taisto Hujanen and Lennart Weibull demonstrate elsewhere in this volume, newspapers have constituted an important framework for television from the very beginning of regular TV-broadcasting. It was the press that powerfully framed the meanings of television programmes in the 1960s and the 1970s. Even in the late 1980s and the early 1990s, comparisons were made between the new styles and forms of television and the evening tabloids (see Dahlgren 1995: 60).

In spite of this, during the 1980s and especially the 1990s, causality in relations between television and the press turned backwards, or – at least – it became more complex and multidimensional. This is true particularly with the popular press that established a kind of symbiosis with television during the late twentieth century; publicity for television programmes, celebrities and issues became central for the popular press and vice versa; television and the popular press began to feed each other. A good example of this can be seen in Jenni Ukkonen's (2000) research on writings about *Bold and Beautiful*, the first American daytime-soap on Finnish television. When it was first launched at the Finnish audience in 1992, newspapers and magazines published stories that were concerned about the attractiveness of this kind of 'rubbish' and possible consequences of 'Americanism' for the national culture. But after a couple of years, the stories were quite different: they discussed characters, plots and the actors of *Bold and Beautiful* as if they were the most important theme for the paper. Ukkonen writes, that 'the press tried to benefit from the popularity of *Bold and Beautiful* and courted potential readers by publishing a lot and often material that was linked to the serial' (Ukkonen 2000: 258).

As a leading medium of the era, television penetrated to every level of culture and set standards for mass communication and entertainment. The common view is that it was television that had great effect on the newspapers for their visual design (see Barnhurst & Nerone 2001: 190). Because television, after the Second World War, anchored itself to family and home, it also achieved a kind of 'normal' status as a mass medium of everyday life (e.g. Dahlgren 1995: 48; see also Silverstone 1994). During the 1980s and the 1990s this 'normality' was also achieved by commercial television in Europe, where television had formerly been institutionalized mostly by public service broadcasting and therefore as somehow opposite to commercial media.

My thesis is, then, that television began powerfully to impact as a cultural and communication form on other media in the 1980s and especially in the 1990s. I call this impact 'televisualization'. It is clear that much of those debates on postmodernism and visualization can actually be linked to television as a master medium of late modern culture – even though television had not been explicitly mentioned in those debates. It was precisely television that highlighted the surface, the image and the visuality in late twentieth-century Europe.

Implications of televisualization on popular press

Because the examples in this discussion are from research on the popular Finnish papers *Ilta-Sanomat* ('Evening Post') and *Iltalehti* ('Evening Paper'), their national context has to be kept in mind but, in spite of this, they still serve to highlight some general tendencies of intermedial relations between television and the press. I will also compare the examples to the RHACNA analysis and therefore to a larger European context (*Ilta-Sanomat* was one of the papers analysed in RHACNA).

Even though *Ilta-Sanomat* and *Iltalehti* are tabloid in size and their content is full of scandals, entertainment and sports, they can be defined as (semi-serious) popular newspapers (see Sparks 2000: 15). There are no US-type supermarket tabloids or tabloids like the British *Sun* and the *Daily Mirror* or the German *Bild-Zeitung* in Finland. This has been true also in Sweden and Norway (see Eide 1997: 174). Jostein Gripsrud (1992: 85) argues that there is no specifically 'intellectual' newspaper in Sweden and Norway, and intellectuals therefore read the same papers as 'ordinary folk'. The general level of education in Scandinavia is high and this can be seen reflected in the popular papers. However, *Ilta-Sanomat* and *Iltalehti* are sold six days a week in shopping malls, supermarkets, bars, cafés, kiosks and gas stations with striking ad-posters and front pages. Because of this there are many tabloid-like features in their form and content (cf. Eide 1997: 181).[2]

I examined *Ilta-Sanomat* and *Iltalehti* between 1996 and 2001 because there were some significant changes in the Finnish media structure during the period: a new national commercial television channel Four (Nelonen) was launched in 1997 and – connected to that – the commercial media was concentrated into two cross-media corporations. One, SanomaWSOY, owned both *Ilta-Sanomat* and channel Four, the other, Alma Media, owned *Iltalehti* and the most popular television channel in Finland, MTV3, which was launched in 1993.[3]

Televisualization of popular papers consists, then, of changes in their content, form and economics. I therefore suggest four levels in televisualization of popular press: (1) changes in quantity of TV-related material, (2) changes in quality of TV-related material, (3) changes in visual forms of the popular papers, and (4) organizational, technological and economic changes in relation to intermediality of television and the press.

1) An increase in quantity of TV-related material

The first implication of televisualization is obvious: the increase of television-related material – stories, news, issues, celebrities, images – in both papers. This kind of material almost doubled in the papers during the last five years of the 1990s: while television was mentioned in 13–14 stories per paper in 1996, in 2001 it was mentioned in 25 stories per paper. The increase of TV issues in pictures, from 10 to 21, was even more evident during the same period (see Figure 1). The increase of TV-related material was seen in every section

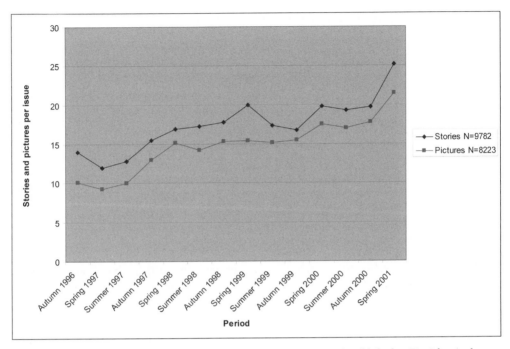

Figure 1: TV-related materials (stories and pictures in an average paper) published in Finnish popular papers *Ilta-Sanomat* and *Iltalehti* during autumn 1996 and spring 2001.

of the papers, but it was most obvious on front pages, entertainment pages, TV pages and advertisements.

The RHACNA analysis also showed that the volume of television pages increased remarkably during the 1980s and the 1990s, especially in Scandinavian popular papers and in the Turkish *Milliyet* and Czech *DNES*. In the French (*Le Parisien*) and especially in the German (*Bild-Zeitung*) popular press, there was not the same rate of increase in the volume of TV-related pages but, comparing a share of editorial volume in different sections of the papers, it is clear that the amount of TV-related material increased radically in every European popular paper included in the RHACNA analysis between 1960 and 2000.[4] The increase is naturally linked to the spread of television at the same time in many countries but change in the 1990s was so radical that, at least in Finland, it can be explained only by deeper changes in media structure.

2) Changing quality of TV-related materials: promotion

In addition to quantitative changes there were also qualitative changes in television material in the popular papers. Probably because much of TV-related material was published on the front pages and in the entertainment sections, the main themes of them were scandals, rumour and gossip about television celebrities and personalities or particular TV programmes. It was certainly this combination of human-interest stories, scandals and television that received a lot of attention on front- and entertainment pages. The RHACNA analysis showed that the Scandinavian popular papers in particular preferred popular culture and celebrities for their front-page stories at the very end of the twentieth century.

Popular papers are sold by their front pages and by ad-posters. It is therefore understandable that scandals and famous personalities are used for their sales. Because television was the major medium of the 1990s, it was especially profitable to pick up the celebrities and scandals made popular by television for the front pages. That papers use television for their sales is not a new phenomenon; as Graham Murdock shows elsewhere in this book, television celebrities received a lot attention in the British tabloids as early as the 1960s. There is a significant historical variation of intermediality between television and the press in European countries, even though it is evident that, during the 1990s, the quantity and the quality of television material changed radically in many countries' popular papers.

One reason for the changes is that television has come to use the newspapers for promotion more intentionally than hitherto. It is common that the run of a television serial will begin with dramatic or even 'scandalous' episodes that will guarantee the interest of the popular press, as it did with *Ally McBeal* at the beginning of the autumn season, 1999, on Finnish television, when Ally had wild spontaneous sex inside the automatic car cleaner in the first episode and kissed a girl in the second. Papers also continuously published stories about the most popular TV celebrities' personal problems, such as about Calista Flockhart's (Ally McBeal) alleged anorexia and boy friend candidates or about the drug problems of Robert Downey (Ally McBeal's fiancé). Production companies and channels have nothing against this kind of publicity; on a contrary, they often promote these stories.

Television channels make efforts to promote their programmes and celebrities in ways that have previously been more common with the cinema's star system (see Ellis, 1992). This promotion is easier nowadays because of cross-media corporations that link the different media – television, radio, magazines, newspapers, the Internet – financially and organizationally to each other. My research showed that in Finland SanomaWSOY's interest was to promote channel Four in *Ilta-Sanomat* and Alma Media's interest was to promote MTV3 in *Iltalehti* – where channels and tabloids were parts of the same corporations.

3) A transformation of televisual forms to newspapers

Side by side with televisual *content* there has been an increasing tendency in popular papers to also benefit from televisual *form*. Serialization is maybe one of the most traditional and characteristic feature of television form (e.g. Williams 1975; Fiske 1987; Ellis 1992; Creeber 2001). Popular papers also often construct dramatic serials through, for example, their front-page headlines and even by the news. The target in serialization is a chain of stories that constructs a dramatic narrative which tempts the readers to buy the paper day after day, as long as the drama continues – or is continued by the media.

Figure 2: A frame-capture from CNN-News published in *Ilta-Sanomat* on 23 May 2005: 'Saddam is the kindest father on the earth'.

As Barnhurts and Nerone (2001: 3) note, '[a newspaper] form includes the things that are traditionally labelled layout and design and typography; but it also includes habits of illustration, genres of reportage, and schemes of departmentalization.' Televisualization concerns the newspaper form as a whole. There has been an increasing trend for popular papers to use the serial form through pictorial representation. Photo-collections are not a new journalistic invention, but there is an increasing tendency towards a televisual-style narrative form in those collections.

Popular press 'photos' have recently quite often been captured from television (see Figure 2) or taken by mobile phone cameras. During the 1990s, using digital technology, frame-captures became easier than ever before, but there are also cultural and ontological dimensions in using them. Frame-captures printed on porous paper are not very good in quality, and their composition is not usually the best possible for newspaper. The main function of frame-captures, then, is to illustrate stories when it would be impossible to get photos any other way – and it is a 'must' to have visuals in the age of televisualization. Because television, the medium of the era, 'was always there', it has been possible to find TV images on almost every subject: frame-capture constructs 'a real-time' or 'being there' effect through the status of television. Quite often there is a logo of the TV channel – CNN, BBC, Fox, etc. – which guarantees the authenticity of the image. In this respect, frame-captures are more modern than postmodern; they really appeal to trust in authentic reality or 'truth' behind the televisual image.

4) Intermedial economics and technology

Frame-captures are just one example of technological convergence: digital technology made it possible to circulate the same material very easily in different mediums (see, for example, Küng et al. 1999; Sauter 1999). As the television image is also usually shot digitally, the circulation of the TV image is no problem to media companies – especially if the television image is also transmitted via the Internet. So, convergence encourages companies to make cross-media productions and therefore the conglomerization of the media by horizontal cross-media ownership (see Mosco: 175–177).

The core idea of convergence is to reduce costs by distributing the same digitally-produced material in different media forms. This has meant radical organizational reforms in many commercial and PSB companies. It has also changed journalistic practices and working environments in many respects (e.g. Cottle & Ashton 1999). Emphasis is often placed on the digital technology in convergence debates but, as Robert Hassan (2000: 21) notes, 'the convergence of these technologies has been the result of the social and cultural struggles that take place within the political economy of capitalist competition.'

In the converging media market the key word used by corporations has been synergy, which is attained by cross-production and cross-promotion (Croteau & Hoynes: 113–136). *Ilta-Sanomat* and *Iltalehti*, for example, have had several cross-productions with the television channel of the corporation. The most popular themes in these cross-productions have been popular culture (music videos and hit-lists), leisure time (special themes for women) and sports (ice hockey and soccer), i.e. mainly entertainment, but there has also been remarkable intermedial cooperation in news production (e.g. financial and sports news). TV channels have also shown many reality-television programmes that have been promoted largely by the companies' popular papers. Televisualization, then, has its economic base in a very material sense.

Televisualization as a cultural phenomenon

As the examples above show, televisualization has been a specific form of visualization that came about in the late twentieth century and was framed by technological and economic changes of late modern culture, where the mass media was restructured by convergence, commercialization and corporatization tendencies. Televisualization has also been part of so called 'remediation', where media forms established to one medium are (digitally) transported to another medium (see Bolter & Grusin 2000). Has televisualization, then, been a good or a bad thing, and what will its future be in the twenty-first century?

As discussion on postmodernism has shown, there is a great variation of valuations on 'the real nature' of it; those who think that we need to, at least to some degree, trust in ideas of Enlightenment criticize the moral vacuum of postmodernism; those who think that there is no return to the modern project of Enlightenment see postmodernism in a more positive, sometimes even liberating, manner as a possibility for the 'free nomadic subject'. A similar juxtaposition of valuations also applies to visualization and televisualization.

Sociologist Pierre Bourdieu, for example, was keen to criticize television's negative impact on culture. In his *Sur la télévision* ([1996]1998), Bourdieu claimed that television as a cultural form is 'a threat to democracy' because of its extremely commercialized nature, connected to its institutional practices and aesthetic forms that support mainly cultural 'fast-food' and 'fast-thinkers' who prevent important rational debates of the political public sphere. But there are others who have not been as concerned about television as a cultural form (see Corner 1995, 1999). According to Peter Dahlgren, for example, the role of television as a mass medium is different from that of the press: 'for more analytic forms of knowledge, we simply must rely on printed (albeit digitalized) media…On the other hand, television is exceptional in its ability to mobilize affective involvement and convey the amorphous entity called implicit social knowledge' (Dahlgren 1995: 58–9). Glen Creeber thinks that the television serial is an especially great form for historical narratives, because 'in attempting to dramatize the personal dimensions of this "ontological event", the audience is slowly and carefully forced to make sense of history, not as rhetoric but as discursive practice, not as knowledge but as private experience'(Creeber 2001: 446). Whether this is true or not, it is important to keep in mind that every medium has multiple functions that cannot be reduced, for example, to a simple and uniform relation to a civic society.

Differing opinions about television can be compared to debates on so-called tabloidization that was also a popular theme in the 1990s (see Sparks & Tulloch 2000). Even though the term tabloid primarily refers to a size of newspaper (half of broadsheet), tabloidization debates refer more the form of journalism. Colin Sparks argues that the tabloid form concerns television as well as newspapers and has two major features: 'it devotes relatively little attention to politics, economics, and society and relatively much to diversions like sports, scandal, and popular entertainment; it devotes relatively much attention to the personal and private lives of people, both celebrities and ordinary people, and relatively little to political processes, economic developments, and social changes.' Tabloidization, then, means that 'content marked by these features of sensational entertainment is becoming more common and driving out the serious journalism of the past'; it means 'a shift…away from news and information toward an emphasis on entertainment' (Sparks 2000: 10–11; see also Sparks 1998; Connell 1998).

There are many similarities between the definitions of tabloidization and televisualization. The popularity of television celebrities and their personal problems or scandals as top headline issues is one of them; the use of visuals is another. Jostein Gripsrud reminds us that 'a very important feature [of the tabloid form] is also the principles of layout, the visual design of each page; tabloids have large, preferably dramatic or dramatized photos, and large, more or less dramatic or dramatized headings' (Gripsrud 1992: 86). A tendency towards storytelling and emplotment has also been linked to popular journalism as a feature distinguishing it from so-called quality journalism (see Dahlgren 1992; Connell 1998). Thus, television as a general source of media content and form could – at least to some degree – be linked to tabloidization.

But as Gripsrud notes elsewhere (2000: 285), '"tabloidisation" is a tabloid term, more of a journalistic buzzword than a scholarly concept'. A difference in the results of various research projects confirms that there is no unitary empirical evidence about some universal tabloidization process:

> Overall, the empirical evidence…suggests that there is no simple and uniform process of tabloidisation going on everywhere. On the contrary, there is much room for debate about exactly what features of the media constitute tabloid form and content, and the success of such innovations depends upon prevailing local circumstances. A trend toward the tabloid that might be marked in one country or one medium may be absent or even reversed in other places or in other media. (Sparks 2000: 42)

It is also questionable if every feature of so-called tabloidization is bad for the public sphere. Some researchers have stressed that, for example, personalization of complex societal or economical questions – i.e. that those questions are represented through some known persona and his or her individual problems – might be a better solution for the public than an abstract argumentation of 'pure facts' (see, for example, Macdonald 1998; Tomlinson 1997).

What is evident, however, is that a stance on tabloidization varies from researcher to researcher, according to how he or she relates him- or herself to the idea of the Habermasian political public sphere as a key structure of a civic society (see Gripsrud 1992; Macdonald 1998). The tabloidization debates have been so intense precisely because there are many who see that tabloids are 'a threat to the proper workings of democracy and provide the fuel for dangerous populist flames' (Sparks 2000: 25). But there are also others who think that, on the contrary, the tabloid form supports democracy because it creates an alternative to the official or hegemonic truth of so-called quality journalism that is governed by power elites of society. The greatest enthusiast for this point of view has been John Fiske (1992) who has claimed that, because the political public sphere is constructed by the power-bloc, it is the popular that makes it possible for the subordinated to resist its power; sensationalism and the excessiveness of the tabloid form challenges a stability of societal power relations supported by rational and 'objective' quality journalism.

It is certainly true that the tabloid style is not a new invention. The first known tabloid papers were published more than a hundred years ago (Gripsrud 2000: 289), and some researchers see that the model of a human-interest story, which is at the heart of tabloid journalism, 'was not invented by the modern newspaper out of nothing, but was an industrial form for the circulation of gossip' (Sparks 2000: 19). Actually John Hartley thinks that it was this scandalous popular or tabloid journalism that transformed the power of monarchy for the public during the French Revolution in the late eighteenth century:

Just as the illicit pre-revolutionary press in France inevitably focused on the gossip, glances, affairs, scandals, sexuality, potency and sexual performances of Queen Marie Antoinette (proto-Di) and King Louis XVI (a proper Charlie), so the contemporary popular media are actually quite right, in straightforwardly political as well as more broadly anthropological terms, to insist on foregrounding the bodies, sexuality and infidelities of those who constitutionally don't represent but *are* the legitimacy of the state. (Hartley 1996: 11–12)

It was this popular journalism and popular readership of the French Revolution that, according to Hartley, created the 'mediasphere' that constitutes the core of democracy (ibid: 13).

However, since the French Revolution, the 'mediasphere' has faced remarkable technological, economical and cultural changes, and a direct comparison of popular presses of these two contexts does not seem so brilliant an idea: Charles and Diana certainly had a different relation to the power, the state and the citizens in 1990s Great Britain from Marie Antoinette and Louis XVI in 1780s France. It might even be that in the contemporary global commercialized mediasphere, which is governed by cross-national media corporations rather than national governments or states, the popular sphere has a hegemonic or dominating role compared to the rational bourgeois public sphere that was identified with a strong nation state of the eighteenth and the nineteenth centuries. In spite of this 'triumphing' popular mediasphere, we have not seen radical changes in power relations of societal groups or nations during the 1990s (cf. Dahlgren 1995). But as Colin Sparks (1998: 5–6) notes, the Habermasian public sphere is also a normative utopia: '…no such media exist in the world today, and never have existed in the past.' Another question, then, is whether 'the normative concept is essential as a standard against which we may measure the actual practice of particular media system', as Sparks suggests (ibid.).

In my view, tabloidization debates concentrate too much on the ideals of journalism and forget the political, economic and historical contexts that always frame journalist practices. Tabloidization debates are determined by the simple opposition of tabloid and quality journalism, where tabloid is often used 'as a rhetorical antithesis against what normal, "good" journalism can define itself' (Dahlgren, 1992: 8). Ian Connell (1998) demonstrates that, at least in Britain, the dichotomy between news discourse and tabloid discourse has been so strong that even in the most popular tabloid papers the news has remained quite clearly separated from entertaining discourses and based on traditional news values and criteria.

The concept of televisualization is one way of overcoming this juxtaposition. Televisualization is a more analytical concept which demonstrates that there are always multiple cultural continuities and discontinuities at the same time in the 'mediasphere'. It highlights that television became a central subject for the late twentieth century's popular press as a source and a topic, in both news and entertainment genres. On the one hand, televisualization is most explicitly a representative of a 'postmodern visualization process', where visual styles, forms and celebrities made popular by television circulate the 'simulacra' of the popular mediasphere. On the other hand televisualization is ontologically connected to very modern ideas of 'truth', and therefore to the political public sphere by appealing to 'authenticity' of the television image in news practices. The concept is also modern in a sense that it relies more on one medium than others even though, at the same time, it highlights intermedial relations.

Televisualization emphasizes the political, economic and technological aspects of media in the context of cultural visualization. It was not a coincidence that televisualization took place in late-twentieth-century Europe, where deregulation politics and technological convergence challenged national media structures. It is no coincidence, either, that global computer networks, the invasion of mobile technology, as well as the fragmentation of audiences by cable and digital television, all challenge television as *the* medium of the age in the twenty-first century. What happens to televisualization, then, if there is no more mainstream television at all in the future (see Richeri 2004)? However, the new millennium has started with an intensive televisualization process. Televisual forms have occupied new information technologies by YouTube, mobile-TV and other applications. Television schedules determine many great national and international events, and some critics have even argued that American television schedules had an impact on the scheduling of US military operations in the Iraq war. Therefore, televisualization of culture is not over yet, even though the new generation of social media and digital networks seriously challenge the status of television.

Notes

1. In Italy PSB changed radically in the early 1980s (see Richeri 1986).
2. In Finland the most 'vulgar' and populist publications are not newspapers but popular periodicals, whose sales have increased rapidly in the beginning of the twenty-first century. At the same time the level of education has not dropped – quite the contrary. So taste cannot be determined solely by the level of education. It is more likely a question of whether education and other institutions, like family and the media, promote traditional 'high' cultural tastes and values or not.
3. Alma Media sold its broadcasting division to Swedish Bonnier and Proventus in 2005.
4. The sample of RHACNA is quite small and its reliability in measuring this kind of phenomena is limited, but it supports in some respect my thesis on televisualization in its quantitative level.

References

Avery, Robert (1993) *Public service broadcasting in a multichannel environment: The history and survival of an ideal,* New York: Longman.

Barnhurst, Kevin G. & John Nerone (2001) *The form of news: A history*, New York: The Guilford Press.

Baudrillard, Jean (1988) *Selected Writings,* (ed. Mark Poster) Stanford CA: Stanford University Press.

Benjamin, Walter ([1934]2008) *The work of art in the age of its mechanical reproducibility, and other writings on media*, Cambridge, London: Belknap Press of Harvard University Press.

Blumler, Jay G. (1991) 'The new television marketplace: Imperatives, implications, issues', in James Curran & Michael Gurevitch (eds.) *Mass media and society*, London: Edward Arnold, pp. 194–215.

Bolter, Jay David & Grusin, Richard (2000) *Remediation: Understanding new media*, Cambridge, Massachusetts: The MIT Press.

Bourdieu, Pierre (1998) *On Television and Journalism*, London: Pluto.

Caldwell, John T. (1995) *Televisuality: Style, crisis and authority in American television*, New Brunswick, New Jersey: Rutgers University Press.

Connell, Ian (1998) 'Mistaken identities: Tabloid and broadsheet news discourse', *The Public Javnost,* 5 (1998): 3, pp. 11–31.

Corner, John (1995) *Television form and public address*, London: Arnold.

Corner, John (1999) Review of Bourdieu's *On television and journalism, European Journal of Communication,* 14 (1999): 2, pp. 251–53.

Cottle, Simon & Ashton, Mark (1999) 'From BBC newsroom to BBC news centre: On changing technology and journalist practices', *Convergence: The Journal of Research into New Media Technologies*, 5 (1999): 3, pp. 22–43.

Creeber, Glen (2001) '"Taking our personal lives seriously": Intimacy, continuity and memory in the television drama serial', *Media, Culture & Society*, 23 (2001): 4, pp. 239–455.

Croteau, David & William Hoynes (2001) *The business of media: Corporate media and the public interest*, London: Pine Forge Press.

Dahlgren, Peter (1992) 'Introduction', in Peter Dahlgren & Colin Sparks (eds.) *Journalism and Popular Culture,* London: Sage, pp. 1–23.

Dahlgren, Peter (1995) *Television and the public sphere: Citizenship, democracy and the media,* London: Sage.

Dahlgren, Peter & Sparks, Colin (eds.) (1992) *Journalism and popular culture*, London: Sage.

Debord, Guy ([1967]1983) *Society of the spectacle*, Detroit: Black & Red.

Eco, Umberto (1984) *Semiologia quotidiana*, Milan: Gruppo Editoriale Fabbri-Bompiana.

Eide, Martin (1997) 'A new kind of newspaper? Understanding a popularisation process', *Media, Culture & Society*, 19 (1997): 2, pp. 173–82.

Ellis, John (1992) *Visible Fiction: Cinema, television, video*, London: Routledge.

Ellis, John (2000) 'Scheduling: the last creative act in television? *Media, Culture & Society*, 22 (2000): 1, pp. 25–38.

Finnish Mass Media (2002) Tilastokeskus: Helsinki.

Fiske, John (1992) 'Popularity and the Politics of Information', in Peter Dahlgren & Colin Sparks (eds.) *Journalism and Popular Culture*, London: Sage, pp. 45–63.

Fiske, John (1987) *Television culture*, London: Routledge.

Gripsrud, Jostein (2000) 'Tabloidization, popular journalism, and democracy', in Colin Sparks & John Tulloch (eds.) *Tabloid tales: Global debates over media standards,* Lanham: Rowman & Littlefield, pp. 285–300.

Gripsrud, Jostein (1992) 'The Aesthetics and politics of melodrama', in Peter Dahlgren & Colin Sparks (eds.) *Journalism and Popular Culture*, London: Sage, pp. 84–95.

Hartley, John (1996) *Popular reality: Journalism, modernity, popular culture*, London: Arnold.

Hassan, Robert (2000) 'The space economy of convergence', *Convergence: The Journal of Research into New Media Technologies*, 6 (2000): 4, pp. 18–35.

Herman, Edward & McChesney, Robert (1997) *The global media: The new missionaries of global capitalism*, London: Cassell.

Horkheimer, Max & Adorno, Theodor W. ([1947]1972) *Dialectic of Enlightenment*, New York: Seabury.

Hujanen, Taisto (2002) *The power of schedule*, Tampere: Tampere University Press.

Jay, Martin (1993) *Downcast eyes: The denigration of vision in twentieth-century French thought*, Berkeley: University of California Press.

Küng, Lucy, Kröll, Anna-Martina, Ripken, Bettina & Walker, Marcel (1999) 'Impact of the Digital Revolution on the Media and Communications Industries', *The Public Javnost*, 6 (1999): 3, pp. 29–48.

Lash, Scott (1990) *Sociology of Postmodernism*, London: Routledge.

Lehtonen, Mikko (2001) 'On no man's land. Theses on intermediality', *Nordicom Review*, 22 (2001): 1, pp. 71–83.

Macdonald, Myra (1998) 'Personalisation in current affairs journalism', *The Public Javnost*, 5 (1998): 3, 109–26.

Mosco, Vincent (1996) *The political economy of communication: Rethinking and renewal*, London: Sage.

Murdock, Graham (2000) 'Digital futures: European television in the age of convergence', in Jan Wieten, Graham Murdock & Peter Dahlgren (eds.) *Television across Europe: A comparative introduction*, London: Sage, pp. 35–58.

Richeri, Giuseppe (1986) 'Television from service to business', in Phillip Drummond & Richard Paterson (eds.) *Television in transition*, London: British Film Institute, pp. 21–35.

Richeri, Giuseppe (2004) 'Broadcasting and the market. The case of public television', in Andrew Calabrese & Colin Sparks (eds.) *Toward political economy of culture: Capitalism and communication in the twenty-first century*, Rowman & Littlefield: Lanham, pp. 178–93.

Sauter, Wolf (1999) 'Regulation for convergence: Arguments for a constitutional approach', in Christopher T. Marsden & Stefaan G. Verhulst (eds.) *Convergence in European digital TV regulation*, London: Blackstone Press Ltd, pp. 65–98

Silverstone, Roger (1994) *Television and everyday life*, London: Routledge.

Sparks, Colin (1998) 'Introduction', *The Public Javnost*, 5 (1998): 3, pp. 5–10.

Sparks, Colin (2000) 'Introduction: The panic over tabloid news', in Colin Sparks & John Tulloch (eds.) *Tabloid tales: Global debates over media standards*, Lanham: Rowman & Littlefield, pp. 1–42.

Sparks, Colin & John Tulloch (eds.) (2000) *Tabloid Tales: Global Debates over Media Standards*, Lanham: Rowman & Littlefield.

Tomlinson, John (1997) '"And besides, the wench is dead": Scandals and the globalization of communication', in James Lull & Stephen Hinerman (eds.) *Media scandals: Morality and desire in the popular culture marketplace,* Cambridge: Polity Press, pp. 65–84.

Ukkonen, Jenni (2000) 'Juonittelut kirjoitetaan kilteiksi', in Anu Koivunen, Susanna Paasonen, & Mari Pajala (eds.) *Populaarin lumo – mediat ja arki*, Turku: Turun yliopisto, pp. 255–72.

Williams, Raymond (1975) *Television: Technology and cultural form*, New York: Schocken Books.

Part IV

Policies

Chapter 6

British Media and Regulatory Change: The Antinomies of Policy

John Corner
University of Leeds

I n this chapter, I want to examine some of the more significant changes to the organization
of the media as public institutions that have occurred in Britain over the last four
decades, the period of the RHACNA survey.

In looking across the sweep of change since the 1960s, it is useful to see a broad (and familiar)
play-off between what we might call the 'public frame' and the 'market frame' occurring
in the organization and practice of the media.[1] These two frames are not comprehensively
incompatible (indeed part of the recent story of British and other European broadcasting
is the attempt to achieve a degree of harmony between them) but their different values and
imperatives regularly produce confusion and a certain degree of incoherence both in the
working perspectives of the media and the ways in which these perspectives are debated. Hence
my title's indication of antinomy – of the presence of paradox and a sometimes hidden, but often
deep and active, set of tensions. One obvious route towards responding to this at the policy
level is through regulatory review and regulatory change. As Golding and Van Snippenburg
(1995) suggest in their useful exploration of regulatory questions in the context of public
attitudes across Europe,[2] such change has covered attempts to legislate and re-legislate both
for the funding of the media, the organization of the media and for their practices and output.
Quite a lot of what I have to say here has to do with regulatory measures and their contexts
across these three connected but different dimensions. The double character of regulation as
both 'negative', a means of constraint, and 'positive', a means of securing the space for certain
kinds of opportunity and the exercise of rights, emerges at several points and is, of course,
a key theme in the climate of dispute surrounding the very idea of 'regulation' (and of 'deregulation', now the more dynamic term in many contexts). Golding and Snippenburg (1995)
see this as a central contradiction underlying many current regulatory initiatives, confounding
attempts both at arguing for further intervention and arguing for less. The tension between
economic and more broadly political and cultural implications is identified as a key factor
here, providing governments with 'good' reasons for not intervening directly in markets, but
at the same time with 'good' reasons, variously democratic or otherwise, for ensuring that
content is under some framing legislation and scrutiny.

The liberal model and the public sphere idea: A context for regulation

In thinking about the relationship that should exist between media systems and political
systems, the precepts of a 'liberal model' are often referred to both by those within the

media industries and policy-forming elites. This model features strongly in discussion of the newspaper press, although its limitations, both in theory and in practice, are well established (Splichal, 2002, provides a detailed intellectual history and Baker, 2002, a comprehensive review of the relations to economics, political theory and legislative practice). Briefly, the liberal model asserts the necessity of the 'freedom of the press' to ensure independence from the state and the consequent ability to perform the political task, for the good of the public, of exposing and criticizing abuses and errors in state affairs. As many commentators have pointed out, this model of how the press should work is grounded in a politics where the threat of the state to the popular good is seen to greatly outweigh threats issuing from elsewhere, notably the corporate sector. Its use of an eighteenth-century version of bourgeois market freedom to offset the potential for (feudal/royal) state control does not transfer easily to a situation in which corporate growth and corporate strategy pose at least equally significant threats to civil liberties. To say this is not at all to underestimate the continuing power of state management of information in the strategic furtherance of elite interests in many countries (sometimes in alliance with corporate groupings), or to neglect the recent history of those countries in which this power was both comprehensive and coercively enforced.

The model also works with a sense of freedom that is almost entirely negative rather than enabling (it is 'freedom from' rather than 'freedom to'). As Splichal (2002) eloquently argues, the effect in practice of emphasizing 'press freedom' has often been to defend private ownership rights and to displace attention from the more general communicative liberty and rights of citizens themselves.

As in many other countries of Europe, a tradition of the press as institutionalized primarily within the 'market frame' (whatever public obligations are recognized and honoured from this private setting) has been joined in Britain since the 1920s by a tradition of broadcasting as a sector institutionalized within the 'public frame' (often perceived as effectively the 'State frame', although British radio and television have only indirectly justified this description).

Many commentators from across Europe have noted how the key idea here, that of 'public service broadcasting', has been put under pressure and made subject to revision and redefinition in the last two decades. This has been caused by the rapidly changing nature of the technology of distribution, the profusion of channels that this allows, and the increasing corporate attractiveness of broadcasting as an area for profitable development as part of a broader market push into home entertainment and leisure. It has also been encouraged, in the last few years, by the shift to a home-entertainment pattern increasingly using other than conventional broadcasting resources, including web platforms. In the last three decades, these opportunities have coincided, in Britain, with a retreat of government (first Conservative from 1979 and then, from 1997, Labour) from many areas of public expenditure and an encouragement of commercial development through de-regulatory and liberalizing policies designed to replace older institutional controls with light touch, oversight bodies.

Continuing problems with the public performance of both press and broadcasting have been recognized. But any critical sense of an 'under-regulated' newspaper industry has found it especially hard to gain ground in a context where the view of an 'over-regulated' broadcasting sector has been supported by successive governments and where all the media in general have been perceived more strongly as *business* operations, requiring a degree of unfettered space to develop and sustain profitability in the (healthy) context of vigorous competition. The longstanding problem of how to advance beyond the protocols of the liberal model of the press ('freedom from') so as to achieve an improved range and quality of communicative practice ('freedom to') has had to contend with the success of neo-liberalism as a way of organizing the economy and of reforming parts of it (like broadcasting) that previously worked within terms broadly cognate with the positive civic imperatives of the 'public' idea.[3]

Media structures and public values

Since the arrival of broadcasting in the 1920s, the media system in Britain has, therefore, essentially been split between a lightly-regulated and privately-owned newspaper press and a more tightly-regulated broadcasting sector with a commitment to public accountability and with a level of state funding supporting the core functions of the BBC.

The BBC was formed as a public company and then a corporation in 1922 (see Briggs 1961), following a debate that had considered and finally rejected commercial alternatives, some of which were close to the Free Press model, in favour of a system giving greater national coherence (and national control). Its 'Public Service' ethos, not always realized in practice, has been formative, albeit in revised forms, on all developments in British broadcasting through to the 1990s, but is now seriously in question, as I have already indicated, through the further opening-up of broadcasting as a market sector with strong internal competition, and strengthening external competition from non-broadcast options.

The continuing problems with newspapers' performance of their public role have been the familiar ones of unbalanced political profile (see Curran and Seaton, 2003, Part 1, for the history of this skew, and Hallin and Mancini, 2004, for a useful comparison between Britain and the United States). The situation follows from a largely conservative private ownership, the established priority of gaining advertising revenue and a shift towards concentration which destroys plurality of provision. These problems have been compounded by a general shift towards entertainment, leisure and lifestyle as key areas of newspaper identity and performance.

The single greatest change in the recent history of the British media was undoubtedly that which occurred in broadcasting in 1954.[4] The passing of the 1954 Television Act allowed commercial networks to broadcast in competition with the BBC, which continued to be funded by the Treasury (through a licence fee system). The act was passed only after a long and often intensive debate about what the political and cultural consequences were of admitting private ownership into the broadcasting sphere and thus breaking the monopoly of a national corporation. The documents surrounding this period, and the language and assumptions at work in many contributions to the debate, provide a continuingly valuable prism through which to perceive the nature of the wider and later arguments about the media and the public sphere in Britain (Briggs, 1995, provides detailed citation). There was, on one side, a range of arguments about the benefits of constraint and limited choice, the effective control of the quality of supply, and the regulation of the relationship between television and the project of national social and cultural development. If television were to fulfil its democratic promise, so the argument went, it needed to continue to be a nationalized concern.

However, a strengthening economic imperative – the encouragement of corporate growth and profit – was in conflict with this view. Drawing selectively on elements of the 'liberal model', it was also able to point precisely to the undemocratic character of present arrangements and the need to introduce a degree of choice into people's use of what had quickly become the major means of home entertainment. This dual character of television, as both an agency of public knowledge and a provider of diversion and amusement, made argument about it distinctive from that about the press. Even though the popular press, too, had for a long time fulfilled an entertainment function, its defining function was still seen as the provision of varieties of news.

Some of the problems come through in a remark made in support of commercial television by the Conservative MP, Mr Selwyn Lloyd:

> I am not attracted by the idea of compulsory uplift achieved by 'the brute force of monopoly', to use Lord Reith's phrase. If people are to be trusted with the franchise, surely they should be able to decide for themselves whether they want to be educated or entertained in the evening. (Home Office 1951: 205)

The quote presents some of the elements that would be heard in many disputes to follow. The restriction of choice is undemocratic, and the market offers a way to extend choice. In this context, it is not surprising that those in favour of commercial services often claimed to be wanting 'to set television free' or to introduce 'people's television' and that the official name chosen to describe the new services when the Act was passed was 'independent' not 'commercial'. A version of the liberal idea, with its links between democratic rights and market freedoms against state control, was being selectively applied to a medium whose initial terms of national development had been otherwise.

However, this 'liberalization' was in fact only partial, whatever the ambitions of many who supported it. It was subject to considerable regulatory constraints, some of which disappointed those poised to enter the new television market (Briggs, 1995, provides a close account, within their political context, of the key points around which compromise was reached). First of all, commercial broadcasting was set up as a regional rather than a national venture, so there was no direct competitor in size and reach to the BBC (this 'control' was partly undercut by the networking agreements that quickly developed between the regional companies). Secondly, sponsorship was barred and commercial revenue had to be obtained through the 'spot' method of grouping together advertisements within brief interruptions in programming (which, with a nice sense for the contradictory, were described as 'natural breaks'). This measure had the effect of putting some distance between programme-making itself and the companies who were paying for the service through their advertising. Thirdly, and most important of all, the new commercial services were to be regulated by a new public body, the Independent Television Authority. This would have responsibility for the maintenance of standards and it would require that broadcast schedules on the new services followed broad guidelines as to the mix and proportion of the programme elements. It, rather than the companies, would also own the means of transmission, the infrastructure of the new system.

Many proponents of commercial television had wanted the level of regulation to be no more than that exercised over the newspaper press, but here the 'liberal model' was subject to radical adaptation in order to get the Television Act through Parliament in a climate where a significant number of Labour and even Conservative MPs feared the consequences of too 'free' an approach.

Given their character as an experiment in a relatively new kind of combination of public control and private enterprise, it is not surprising that the precise form that the regulatory controls of the new Authority should take were strongly contested in their initial definition and became subsequently the subject of controversy when put into practice.

The first major public statement that there were problems with the way the regulation was working came in the Report of the Committee on Broadcasting 1960 (The Pilkington Report, Home Office, 1962). Among other things, this expressed dissatisfaction with the controls exerted over standards and taste in the new service. There was, it noted, a 'failure to realize the purposes of broadcasting'. The recommendation was radical. The Independent Television Authority itself should assume responsibility for planning programmes, which would then be made and sold to the Authority by the companies. It should also sell advertising time directly, cutting the companies out of any directly commercial connections and further distancing funding from the actual business of programme making.

These measures, in effect an attempt to carry out a degree of 'de-liberalization' of television in the name of the public interest, were bound to be rejected in a climate where a Conservative government was presiding over expanded commercial development in other spheres.

However, assessment here was further complicated by the ways in which commercial television had actually served to open up aspects of the 'public' character of broadcasting through programming policies that the BBC had neglected and might even have opposed. For despite its embedding in commercial profit and the fact that its advertising slots could be seen as 'propaganda for capitalism', a good proportion of the new system's programmes had engaged with popular, and often regional, issues in a way that constituted an expansion of the popular public sphere.[5] As well as a shift towards more regional accents and regional concerns, the very requirement to seek out and hold a popular audience gave television a new dynamic, and even a sense of dialogue, that is not adequately described simply as a cynical 'populism' (although there was some of that too). Many former critics of commercial services recognized this more positive and undeniably 'public' consequence and the kind of response it was receiving from the BBC, now under pressure to think more carefully about the audience in its programme design and scheduling. For instance, the news service of the commercial system (Independent Television News), the only authorized source of national supply for the new companies, was widely seen as working with levels of clarity, visual imagination and inquisitiveness, both in relation to domestic and to world events, that surpassed the BBC's practice at the time.

BBC radio broadcasting, later to be opened up to commercial competition at local level in the 1970s, had in fact already had its monopoly attacked through the success with British audiences of non-UK stations like Radio Luxembourg (from the 1930s, but with increasing power in the 1950s) and then the ship-based 'pirate stations', such as Radio Caroline, in the 1960s. The effect, comparable in some ways with developments in television, was to foster an audience demand for certain kinds of format, content and tone that the BBC quickly found itself then having to respond to for economic reasons. The BBC's launch of Radio One in 1967 was an attempt to win back, and then secure, a youth audience essentially formed by 'pirate' radio (see Briggs 1995 Section VI, subsection 4).

The next public marker of major shifts in the broadcasting sector came with the publication of the Report of the Committee on the Future of Broadcasting (The Annan Report, Home Office 1977a). This document placed broadcasting in a far more explicitly political and social context than the Pilkington Report, which had led strongly on issues of 'culture' and 'taste'. It also articulated a more profound sense of change as it reflected on the 15 years or so that separated it from the debates of the early 1960s.

Underneath many of its comments, a sense of the new plurality of the United Kingdom comes through. The undesirability of broadcasting attempting to fulfil its 'public' role by consciously setting out to shape national values is noted:

> We do not accept that it is part of the broadcasters' function to act as arbiters of morals or manners, or set themselves up as social engineers…Parliament is the place where national policies are devised and advocated. The broadcasters' duty is to see that the different policies which purport to solve our problems are given an airing…Nor should the broadcasters usurp the function of a multitude of individuals and organizations which try to persuade men and women how best to live their lives. (Home Office 1977a, para. 3.21)

The Annan report shows a sometimes nervous stand-off between this essentially passive model of public service broadcasting, in which the system acts merely as an enabling agency in response to perceived 'public' requirements, and the older, more active model in which a degree of responsibility is accepted for the character and quality of public debate, and broadcasting is seen as a central constituent of public life and culture as well as its primary information source. Something of this more active interpretation, broadcasting as constructing 'nation' rather than simply reflecting it, can be seen in a statement such as the following:

> At a time when people worry that society is fragmenting, broadcasting welds it together. It links people, gives the mass audience topics of conversation, makes them realise that, in experiencing similar emotions, they all belong to the same nation. (Home Office 1977a, para. 3.1)

So the audience is still regarded throughout the document as being made up of members of the 'public', or of 'publics'. The setting up of Channel 4 in 1981, as an exercise in increased diversity and plurality of viewpoint and cultural style, confirmed this commitment, even against the political tendencies that had set in with the arrival of a Conservative Government in 1979.

It was only in the mid-1980s that the idea of the audience as essentially 'consumers' began to appear in official publications. Underneath the political, social and cultural reasons for this development, the economic implications of new technology were clearly at work. New systems of distribution involving satellite and cable were changing the nature of the TV market, the way in which the idea of the audience would be framed and the consequent sense of the 'public' which television could afford to work with. To say this is not to be technologically determinist but to recognize the strong implications that a changing systemic infrastructure had for national principles that had, as we have seen, already been subject to questioning and contestation on other grounds.

One of the baldest statements of the new perspective, in whose terms broadcasting was located primarily within a set of market relationships and its 'public' dimension thereby displaced, came with the Peacock Report of 1989. Significantly, this was called upon to look specifically at the *funding* of television rather than to reflect upon the more general role of the medium in national life in the way that previous reports had done. Its views can be gauged from the following comment:

> British broadcasting should move towards a sophisticated market system based on consumer sovereignty. That is a system which recognises that viewers and listeners are the best ultimate judges of their own interest which they can best satisfy if they have the option of purchasing the broadcasting services they require from as many alternative sources of supply as possible. (Home Office 1986, para. 592)

Here, there are echoes of the terms used to advance the cause of commercial television over 40 years earlier, but the language of 'choice', individual satisfaction and consumer rights has become more confident and more prominent. The very idea of 'public broadcasting' is being questioned (and along with it, the continuation of the BBC's funding through the licence fee system).[6] The ideological framework for a de-regulatory drive around 'consumer sovereignty' is being established.

The shift to deregulation in the context of expanded channel-availability via digital cable and satellite provision continued through the turn of the century, despite the 1997 return of a Labour government to power. The Independent Television Commission succeeded the Independent Broadcasting Authority in 1991 as the regulating body for private sector television, with a commitment to a 'light-touch' regulation more compatible with market development. The 1996 Television Act 'liberalized' the rules on media cross-ownership, reducing the level of constraint on controlling interests in both television and newspapers and creating the opportunity for greater corporate consolidation in the media sector. A 'public interest' test was introduced, in which the liberal virtues of 'plurality and diversity' were ostensibly protected, along with controls on undue cross-media advantage and market distortion. However, the play-off between commitment to public values and the dynamics of the market frame had now swung decisively in favour of the latter, as some of my earlier quotations presaged. The Act also introduced the Broadcasting Standards Commission, a statutory body for standards and codes of practice across the entire field of broadcasting.

Among the many problems that the new economics and culture of broadcasting brings for public sphere structure and practice is that of a fragmentation of the national audience into a range of much smaller, taste-related groupings, finding their television across a dispersed choice of channel permutations. The continuing strength of the two main terrestrial channels in Britain (BBC1 and ITV1), particularly as providers of news services and documentary output, delayed a major impact of this kind for some years. However, the growth of channels and, more recently, the development of new kinds of online home entertainment is undoubtedly 'privatizing' television not only at the level of the ownership pattern within the industry[7] but also at the level of the medium's identity within home and everyday life.

This transition is further strengthened in the latest regulatory change to affect British broadcasting. Following the Communications Act of 2002, the functions of five separate regulatory bodies, including the Independent Television Commission and the Broadcasting Standards Commission, have been merged into the 'Office of Communication' (www.ofcom.org.uk).[8] This body follows the broad model of 'oversight' bodies set up to monitor the performance of once publicly-owned services that have now been privatized. The stated regulatory mission of Ofcom was to 'further the interests of citizen-consumers' (a hyphenated phrasing that still appears in its documents). This involved, among other things, measures that would 'support the need for innovators, creators and investors to flourish'. The idea of the 'citizen-consumer' in such an official statement is significant. The supposed harmonies or balances indicated by the term seem, despite intentions, to suggest an unresolved argument. If earlier drafts of this text had simply used the category of 'citizen' and then later modified it, we might be tempted towards a certain reading of the priorities encoded in the duality. In fact, the indications are that previous drafts had used the category of 'consumer' extensively (in this respect, following the approach advocated by Peacock), suggesting rather different priorities. However, even in these circumstances, the public frame can be seen still to be exerting its modifying influence, albeit in this case at the level of legislative intent rather than corporate practice.

What of the British press across the same broad period? Here, the history is of course very different and less 'busy', as I indicated earlier. The starting point is the market setting, with diversity the supposed outcome of multiple outlets, and quality a product of competition. Recognition of the negative political consequences of the national newspaper system, including those that follow from ownership concentration, has been a point frequently aired in official commentary on press structures and functions. For instance, in the report of the 1977 Report of the Royal Commission on the Press (The McGregor Report, Home Office 1977b),[9] it was noted as a point of consensus among those who gave evidence that the press 'should neither be subject to state control nor left entirely to the unregulated forces of the market' (ibid: 12). The same report also noted the need for 'boundaries' to be set to self-defined 'press freedoms' and considered the possibility of forms of subsidy to offset the consequences of market imbalances in provision (ibid: 2, 3). However, what it did *not* do is give any clear guidelines as to the precise level and kind of regulation to be applied to the market, the points at which boundaries on ownership freedoms could be drawn and the procedures which a subsidy model might follow. Despite there being no shortage of recognition of a problem, then, it is clear that hesitation, caution and plain fear (economic and political) have characterized British approaches to the question of how to square a vigorously commercial and self-righteous press with public values and political equity. Intervention at the level of *structure* has been tentative and gestural at best. I return to this question at the end of the chapter but for a clear and comprehensive review of the situation as it has developed, see Curran and Seaton (2003).

In Britain since the 1960s, the newspaper market has been in a period of contraction and consolidation around fewer owning groups.[10] Shifts in production technology during the 1970s strengthened the position of owners in relation to the print unions, and also allowed a greater flexibility in page layout, photographic use and multi-site printing (with its consequences for regional and European editions). Rupert Murdoch was a central figure in the reconfiguring of the British press as a more aggressive kind of business venture, but the managers of other press groups followed his 'retreat from Fleet Street', which ushered in new attitudes not only to production but to the organization of journalism and to editorial policy in respect of competition and a more volatile advertising market. The traditional problem of a press largely hostile to Labour politics was partly reconfigured in the late 1990s when a Labour government was elected on economic and social policies that were insufficiently different from those of Conservatism to provoke the kinds of press attack that earlier Labour politicians had often had to accept. Indeed, part of what was often seen as Labour's high levels of anxiety about the television reporting of politics, particularly that by the BBC, can be explained by the extent to which it routinely found itself faced by a hostile press.

Another important change since the 1960s is the extent to which, in relation to their different markets, newspapers have greatly extended their coverage of lifestyle, leisure and popular culture, including show business and celebrity culture. They have developed a 'magazine' identity pushing out well beyond their news pages into a range of supplements (a tendency identified clearly in the RHACNA data).

A number of issues, to do mainly with privacy, harassment and right of reply, but also including questions of accuracy, led to the setting up in 1991 of the Press Complaints Commission (www.pcc.org.uk) as a public body charged with ensuring as far as it could that British newspapers kept to a code of good practice. It replaced the long-running regulatory body, the Press Council, which was widely judged to have failed to monitor standards closely enough, and to lack authority and impartiality (largely by being too close to the industry itself in membership and attitude). It was also seen to have failed to show that responsiveness to public complaints that the new body took up as one of its main commitments. In fact, within three years, the Press Complaints Commission itself came under scrutiny, with a House of Commons Committee recommending that it be toughened into a Press Commission with a Press Ombudsman, holding direct powers to impose fines within a more developed legal framework. Predictably, however, the newspapers themselves attacked the report as an encroachment upon press freedom and, faced with this broad industrial opposition, the government backed off, introducing only improved rights to claim damages through civil law where there had been an invasion of privacy not justified by the 'public interest'. Just a few years later, the coverage of Princess Diana's death caused a further furore about press conduct and a new Code of Practice was introduced, providing more detailed specification of the standards required. However, no significant move away from the established and relatively comfortable climate of 'self-regulation' has been achieved, even with the introduction of the new bodies and codes (although see McQuail, 2003, for a more positive review of self-regulation and its continuing potential).

British media and the culture of the 'public'

Across the last three to four decades, the strongest continuing tendency in the structure and organization of the British media has been towards a more comprehensive placing within the 'market frame'. For broadcasting, this has occurred against the background of an initially strong public model, one that survived in revised form even after the introduction of commercial television services. In the newspaper industry, of course, the 'market frame' has been the established one for discussing the issue of 'freedom of the press'. The idea of 'self-regulation' (of the industry, by the industry) has been powerful and attempts to impose a stronger element of 'public' accountability upon press practices have mostly been unsuccessful, even allowing for the improved performance of the Press Complaints Commission in monitoring questions of ethics.

As I suggested, the impact of commercial provision upon British television is not usefully seen as a straightforward reduction in the scope and quality of the public sphere. In many ways, the new sensitivity towards a wider range of perspectives, and the extension of notions of the national popular, brought with them an enhancement of the culture of the public sphere, whatever the commodified terms upon which this was achieved. It encouraged the shift away from a politics of deference and encouraged a number of imaginative attempts to 'make the serious popular', particularly within news and documentary formats.[11] It introduced a more demotic voice to broadcasting, a voice constituted both by the broadcasters themselves and those they accessed. This complicates any simple antagonistic relationship between what I have called 'market' and 'public' frames and further indicates the public benefits that institutions within the market frame can confer within certain settings.

As well as reflecting and reinforcing broader social change, broadcasting and the press also contributed to the growing character of politics as an arena of 'celebrity' and of 'scandal' (with the *Sun* and the *Daily Mirror* dominating this kind of coverage, but with a much wider take-up in broadsheet and broadcast news). In part, this growth was a consequence of the extent to which clear ideological divisions and conflicts of policy had been displaced by an emphasis on political personality, style and presentation (see, for example, the discussions around this in Corner and Pels 2003). The election of a Labour Government in 1997 brought with it a new, more robust and energetically pro-active approach to media-political relations, one in which the management of the national news agenda in the government's favour was attempted by a number of strategies relatively unfamiliar in British politics, at least in their prominence and combination. An emerging 'Politics of Spin' was treated as a major, running story by broadcasting and the press from the late 1990s. Thus, an approach whose tactics were devised to win favourable coverage for the government ended up being portrayed as the biggest and defining political deficit of its period in office, culminating in the continuing dispute over the play-off between political propaganda and intelligence data prior to the Iraq war of 2003. It has further encouraged a shift towards cynicism and distance in the attitude of the public towards high politics, one for which both politicians and the media have blamed each other.

In conclusion

British media are now much more firmly located in the 'market frame' than was the case in the 1960s. Largely, this is due to the gradual weakening of the 'public frame' for broadcasting over the same period, a trend accelerating during the 1990s. The ending of the BBC monopoly that first introduced commercial television services in the 1950s carried with it an enrichment of many aspects of public culture at the same time as it provided the basis for the later repositioning of the audience as 'consumers' exercising 'choice'. Within this perspective, programmes themselves shifted towards a stronger commodity status despite the initially quite robust public regulation of the broadcasting market. As a range of new channels was introduced in the 1980s and 1990s, continuing through into the early 2000s, many of them available only through forms of subscription, 'the audience' could no longer be so easily regarded as a manifestation of the national public, with television a mode of civic address. Instead, a more differentiated market demographic was applied to channels, slots and programmes. Audiences were increasingly seen as taste groupings within a more individualized, or at least strongly sectored, perception of 'broadcasting' (the term itself becoming more open to question). Within this cultural regime, the public funding of the BBC as a dedicated public broadcaster, with adequate resources for growth and for handling inflation, continued to be the focus of political dispute and it remains a precarious arrangement today.

Over the same period, the press has been subject to greater consolidation and convergence in ownership and has variously been pushed towards greater supplementation of its news offer with a broader array of cultural and lifestyle contents. The claims of 'press freedom' and of the benefits of 'self regulation' have helped it survive a number of attempts to regulate its activities more directly, although revised forms of 'light-touch' public accountability have been introduced.

Foremost among the ways that have been proposed to counter this tendency has been the use of alternative sources for funding media, including emerging new media. Essentially, this has been an attempt to reposition, if only marginally, certain media functions more centrally within a public frame by reducing their direct dependency on commercial revenue. However, the current problems of getting commitment to new areas of public expenditure, even if this is only at the level of a contribution or of a partnership, continue to make such projects largely unrealizable. The further involvement of existing public broadcasters in the development of public space and resources on the Internet is another way in which some protection could be offered against further erosion. In a paper usefully reviewing the history of the corporate 'enclosure of the commons' in British communications, Graham Murdock pointed to the potential that the BBC had (and which it has since at least partially realized) in the performance of this role (Murdock, 2001). The apparent paradox that positive communicative freedom is most often the product of coherent and properly enforced regulation will perhaps need to be more widely acknowledged than hitherto for any significant progress of this kind.[12] The time-hallowed negative freedoms of the liberal model (to some extent reinforced by dominant perceptions of the way in which the Internet could work and might work) will have to be seen not only as insufficient but also as a serious block to the inclusive and effective use of contemporary media as agencies of continuity and development in public life. This will be a challenge to the political economy of a policy process that is already subject to internal contradictions in its attempt to extend the market frame at the very same time as it wishes to impose further controls over product and use. Retaining a broad European awareness here (one able to criticize as well as support EU formulations through comparative dialogue) will be a great help. The wider and continuing play-off between the dynamics of globalization and the sphere of desirable, and possible, self-determination by the nation-state will also clearly be a significant factor too.

The shift to a dominant model of media markets and media consumption is what is most immediately striking in the current situation, but this has brought gains as well as deficits. It has achieved more extensive terms of engagement between everyday life and politics than old models managed to do, whatever their unfulfilled potential here, and it is has displaced what in Britain was a system of routine deference (grounded in the deeper codes of social and cultural authority) towards the political establishment. The deficiencies of a system moving towards a greater commercial dependency are obvious. However, the 'thinning' of the older model of democratic culture that many of the new structures and practices have reflected, and in part helped bring about, can only be properly assessed against a complementary sense of the real limitations of past media practice and of past politics. In the discussion of current problems, a degree of pragmatism is greatly needed. This might help to provide a sense of what the practical possibilities really are for the optimum development of public knowledge and democratic debate in settings likely to be defined, for some years to come, by the shifting contours of a global market economy, and by coordinates of civic culture in which a citizen's identities and aspirations will partly be shaped by their concurrent behaviour in the role of consumer. Whatever the routes taken, 'optimum development' will certainly involve a commitment, continuingly controversial, to regulatory structures and processes.

Notes

1. By the use of the term 'frame' here I mean to indicate the primary set of operating imperatives within which an organization is set, its determining 'frame of reference' in strategic and localized practice. Dominance by the 'market frame' does not preclude an organization from pursuing public goals but it is likely to introduce a firm commercial logic to such pursuit. When an organization perceived to be located primarily within the 'public frame' (for instance, the BBC) moves beyond a certain point in orienting its policy towards competitive market advantage, it is likely to be questioned as to its priorities. The terms are indicative rather than categoric and both can connect variously with ideas about performance of 'public sphere' functions, as international debate about Habermas' influential concept indicates. McQuail (2003) uses the term 'frame' in a more limited way to explore usefully different approaches to media accountability.
2. The chapter offers a schematic indication of interventionist and liberal approaches across both 'content' and 'structure' dimensions. The data indicate the inconsistency of public opinion, its largely reactive nature in relation to policy initiatives and the way in which opinion around content is stronger than around questions of structure.
3. For a broad discussion of how ideas of 'public knowledge' are currently in tension with ideas of 'popular culture' see Corner (2009).
4. A recent, detailed discussion of the political and cultural context surrounding the introduction of commercial television and the subsequent period of dispute about regulation, funding and taste is to be found in Black (2005).
5. A sizeable audience was quickly achieved once transmissions were available nationally, although thereafter audience figures varied and comparison with the BBC was hindered by the fact that the methods used to measure audience size varied from those of the Corporation. For details on the debate about audience share in the early years, see Briggs (1995) Chapter 1, particular section 2 'People and Numbers'.
6. The BBC's funding through a licence fee paid by viewers is, of course, a cornerstone of the British notion of public service broadcasting, however far this principle might be seen to have extended beyond BBC provision. Not surprisingly, the fee, always the subject of political dispute, has become

increasingly contentious as the 'market frame' has strengthened its hold, supported by the options of new technology. In this situation, not only has the BBC had to demonstrate its continuing capacity to appeal to a wide audience, it has had to show that it does not seek to achieve this by offering a range of programming similar to that of its commercial competitors, thereby reducing its distinctive identity as a 'public' provider. Getting this balance right in the eyes of its critics, including many newspapers, has proved difficult and, on many occasions, impossible.

7. Recently, there has been an extensive merging of the major television companies as the economic and structural viability of the older model (regional companies feeding into a national network) has been dramatically reduced in the new conditions of production and distribution of home entertainment and within the new economy of advertising.

8. The remit, structure and performance of Ofcom have attracted recent academic as well as public commentary. Much of this turns on the perceived primacy of Ofcom's economic rather than civic perspective and therefore it indicates yet a further point in the complex inter-articulation, both in media institutions and in national regulatory policy, of what I have earlier referred to as the 'public' and 'market' frames. See particularly Sylvia Harvey (2006), Smith (2006) and Livingstone and Lunt (2007).

9. Published in the same year as the Annan Report, discussed above, this contributed to what then became a quite intensive period of speculation about the overall future of British media in the context of economic and social change.

10. Most commentators on the British press refer to this problem; see for instance Doyle (2002). A very large proportion of British newspapers, national and regional, is controlled by just a few major groups, among which are News International, Trinity Mirror and Northern and Shell. Rupert Murdoch (whose titles include *The Times* and *the Sun*) has almost legendary status as a powerful, politically strategic, proprietor but other owners have also been the centre of public attention, particularly Richmond Desmond of Northern and Shell (whose titles include the *Daily Mail*) when it was revealed that his portfolio also extends to a large number of 'soft porn' titles.

11. For a detailed account of the structures and practices involved in making current-affairs television for a popular audience, see Goddard, Corner and Richardson (2007).

12. A comparison with the current situation in the finance sector is interesting. For a limited period at least, 'regulation' is being perceived on both sides of the Atlantic as a tool of public interest working against the damage caused by private strategies. However, the 'crisis' in the finance sector achieved a widespread visibility and recognition that is unlikely to be paralleled by any negative tendencies occurring in the sectors of knowledge and the arts.

References

Baker, C. E. (2002) *Media, markets and democracy*, Cambridge and New York: Cambridge University Press.

Black, L. (2005) 'Whose finger on the button? British television and the politics of cultural control', *Historical Journal of Film, Radio and Television*, 25.4, pp. 547–75.

Briggs, A. (1961) *The history of broadcasting in the United Kingdom Vol 1: The birth of broadcasting*, Oxford: Oxford University Press.

Briggs, A. (1995) *The history of broadcasting in the United Kingdom Vol 5: Competition 1955–1974*, Oxford: Oxford University Press.

Corner, J. & D. Pels (eds.) (2003) *Media and the restyling of politics*, London: Sage.

Corner J. (2009) 'Public knowledge and popular culture: spaces and tensions', *Media, Culture and Society* 31.1, pp. 141–49.

Curran, J. & J. Seaton (2003) *Power without responsibility*, London: Routledge.

Doyle, G. (2002) *Media ownership*, London: Sage.

Goddard, Peter; Corner, John & Richardson, Kay *(2007) Public issue television: World in action, 1963–98,* Manchester: Manchester University Press.

Golding, P. & Van Snippenberg, L. (1995) 'Government, communications and the media', in O. Borre & E. Scarbrough, (eds.) *The Scope of Government*, Oxford: Oxford University Press, pp. 283–312.

Hallin, D. & P. Mancini (2004) *Comparing Media Systems,* Cambridge: Cambridge University Press.

Harvey, S. (2006). 'Ofcom's first year & neoliberalism's blind spot: attacking the culture of production', *Screen* 41.1, pp. 91–105.

Home Office (1951) *Report of the committee on broadcasting 1949* (Beveridge Report – Cmnd 8116), London: HMSO. (Minority Report submitted by Selwyn Lloyd).

Home Office (1962) *Report of the committee on broadcasting 1960* (Pilkington Report – Cmnd 1753), London: HMSO.

Home Office (1977a) *Report of the committee on the future of broadcasting* (Annan Report – Cmnd 6753), London: HMSO.

Home Office (1977b) *Report of the Royal Commission on the press* (McGregor Report – Cmnd 6810), London: HMSO.

Home Office (1986) *Report of the committee on financing the BBC* (Peacock Report – Cmnd 9824), London: HMSO.

Livingstone S. and Lunt P. (2007) 'Citizens and consumers: discursive debates during and after the Communication Act 2003', *Media, Culture and Society* 29.4, pp. 613–38.

McQuail, D. (2003) *Media accountability and freedom of publication*, Oxford: Oxford University Press.

Murdock, G. (2001) 'Against enclosure: Rethinking the cultural commons', in D. Morley & K. Robins *British cultural studies*, Oxford: Oxford University Press, pp. 443–60.

Smith, P. (2006) 'The politics of television policy: the making of Ofcom', *Media, Culture and Society* 28.6, pp. 929–40.

Splichal, S. (2002) *Principles of publicity and press freedom*, Lanham: Maryland, Rowman & Littlefield.

Chapter 7

French Media: Policy Regulation and the Public Sphere

Josiane Jouët
Université de Paris II (Panthéon-Assas)

This chapter aims to provide a synthetic overview of the major changes that have affected the French media and public sphere over the last five decades. The point of departure is the mediatized public sphere and its fundamental evolution from 1960 until the modern day. In 2009, TV viewers and radio listeners have gained access to dozens of private radio and television channels, which marks a sharp contrast with the very limited number of public broadcast media programmes that used to be the only option in the past. Moreover, the popularity of daily newspapers is declining while magazines are thriving and the Internet has recently become another extremely competitive mass medium.

The dramatic transformation of the French media system began in the 1980s when the breakup of the State monopoly over broadcasting was paralleled by the emergence of a neo-liberal economy, giving way to media concentrations and the development of marketing techniques. These changes have actually been encouraged by a number of public policies which have varied, depending on the makeup of the government. Nevertheless the media sphere remains a high locus of public debate and a major political concern, as new measures are regularly taken to regulate the role of media in the public sphere. A specific characteristic of the French scene is that media remain at the centre of a normative political discourse and public broadcast media are still quite active. However, most of the media sphere has now adopted the liberal model, catering to audiences of consumers by focusing more on leisure and entertainment than on public affairs and educational programmes.

Media policies and the democratization of culture

The relationship between media and the public sphere has always been a controversial field in France due to significant involvement of the state in controlling media until the early 1980s, and regulating media subsequently. The influential role of the State over broadcast media is actually embedded in the French conception of democracy, where the state is expected to broaden opportunities for the masses by enabling the development of their general culture and knowledge (Missika & Wolton 1983). The development of television in the 1960s was consequently seen as a major tool to accomplish this goal. Television was officially conferred a cultural and educational mission in the public service as part of a far-reaching policy that also encompassed, for example, the building of public theatres and cultural centres in poor neighbourhoods. While, since deregulation, television no longer broadcasts classical theatre plays at prime time, the general consensus is that the State should lead the way in promoting culture, thus explaining the recurrent conflicts about the role of public television. Similarly, there is a strong national consensus in backing the position of the French government, which took a very active role in the creation of the European policy imposing broadcast quotas to ensure that a minimum set of all programming would be European-made. While this policy is partly a measure to protect European and French audio-visual industries from American competition, it also reflects the conception that cultural goods are commodities of a special type that must benefit from special consideration in WTO agreements in order to preserve cultural diversity.

The major role played by the State in regulating the media has led to an enormous number of laws and administrative measures which make the French regulatory system the most complex in Europe aside from Italy. The intricacies of the regulatory system are still very constraining today. This is true both for public and private media, although the directives aim at maintaining a certain political and economic equilibrium in the media system that is increasingly jeopardized by the growth of the liberal economy.

The complex market of print media: dailies' decline vs. the magazines' rise

The general climate of distrust towards the media in France originates in the coverage of World War I and World War II, when media were strictly controlled and played a propaganda role that ruined their image as reliable sources of information. It is worth noting that the French newspaper readership was at the forefront in Europe in 1914 and that it has significantly dropped since then. At the end of World War II, the French government assumed strong regulatory functions of the media in reprisal for their cooperation with German invaders. Many newspapers were banned and strict measures were taken to protect the press against the power of big money interests by setting rules to prevent media concentration and to favour the pluralism of print media (Albert and Leteinturier 1999).

At the beginning of the twenty-first century, French print media are still very much subsidized by the State. As a result, the print media system does not really reflect market forces since without State subventions many publications would just disappear. The measures which were taken at the end of World War II (Ordonnance 1944) in order to spur the revival of the 'free press' remain to this day (Charon 1991). Newspapers and magazines are private enterprises, with a specific statute, that still benefit from several tax cuts and subventions for paper purchase, mailing and distributing costs, etc. All of the 4,435 publications registered have access to these advantages, which are also a way to compensate for the weakness of the advertising market in France in comparison to other European countries. However, this statute has encouraged corporatism, and the development of trade unions in manufacturing (e.g. printing and distribution) has often prevented the modernization of the press, as many publications only survive on State assistance due to meagre readership and advertising sales.

Undoubtedly, the system of subsidies to the press in France is the most elaborated and important in the world. Most subsidies are indirect as the state grants several measures that reduce the costs of the media firms, either by consenting to preferential postal tariffs or by limiting the burden of taxes. Finally, the amount of the subsidies or the form of the aid is independent of the political orientation of the titles. Nevertheless, the daily newspapers are more favoured than the periodicals (Le Floch & Sonnac 2000, Toussaint Desmoulins 2004). In order to remedy to the persistent decline of print media, the government organized, in 2008, a wide consultation of all the actors of the press, 'les Etats Généraux de la Presse,' which ended up in even more subsidies provided to print media, and especially to dailies.

A defining characteristic of the French daily newspapers is that, except for two of them – *L'Humanité*, the organ of the Communist Party, and *La Croix* linked to the Catholic Church – most newspapers are independent from any clear political alliance. However, most of them have an editorial stand that can be identified as more to the left or more to the right. Moreover, there is supremacy of regional daily papers covering local news over the national press that sticks to a somewhat narrower market. In 2007, there were only 3 national dailies with a circulation around 300,000 (*Le Parisien, Le Figaro and Le Monde*). Only 19 regional dailies have a circulation of over 100,000, the first being *Ouest France,* with a circulation of nearly 800,000, which largely surpasses the second, *Sud Ouest,* with nearly 320,000 (Balle 2007). This gloomy picture, which shows a decline of about 30 per cent in the circulation of dailies over the last two decades, is paralleled with the incursion of free dailies, such as *20 Minutes, Metro, Direct Matin, Direct Soir,* which are distributed in all urban centres and which reach an overall circulation of about 2 million. Nevertheless, national dailies like *Le Monde, Libération, and Le Figaro* are important opinion leaders in the press sector and more active in the public debate while some news magazines (*L'Express, Le Point, Le Nouvel Observateur*) can also position themselves as watchdogs of public affairs. Another distinction is that the popular tabloid press does not exist in France and even the non-elitist papers provide rather serious coverage on a variety of issues.

In comparison to the shrinking of the dailies' market, magazine and periodical sales are thriving. Between 1988 and 1998, the number of titles has grown by 20 per cent and there are about 250 new titles launched every year, many of which are quick to disappear. In 2007, there were nearly 3,500 magazine and periodical titles. The magazine market is very heterogeneous and caters to all types of audiences. Sales are at the highest in the following sectors: television, women, health, news, youth, and senior issues (Sonnac 2001). The reasons for the success of the magazine market are numerous: magazines have adjusted to societal change and use marketing techniques and audience studies to meet viewers' expectations. They cover a wide range of interests in the areas of leisure, sports, hobbies, science, etc. Moreover, they address a fragmented readership, as each segment of the audience seeks to find content that is treated at length and with a deeper analytical distance than, for instance, television or regional dailies. Magazines not only provide specialized information but also offer substantial advice and services (such as folders specifically designed to be clipped out and collected by readers) while maintaining a close link to their readership. Magazines feature a sophisticated combination of text and images (pictures, charts, etc.), that illustrate the aesthetic dimensions of their design. Further, they hire growing numbers of young designers specialized in digital graphic arts, and rely extensively on freelance journalists in order to reduce production costs. In fact, the main explanation for this success story is that magazines have so far managed to successfully adapt to the changing social and cultural nexus of French society (Charon 1999).

The juicy magazine market has led some daily newspaper corporations to invest in magazines. Ouest France corporation launched regional magazines while Le Monde corporation has invested in high standard magazines like *Courrier International* and *Le Monde Diplomatique*.

Even though many small press corporations still exist, this trend exemplifies how the print market has become more concentrated, as it is now dominated by 3 major groups that own several daily, weekly or monthly publications. Lagardère Media is by far the leading group with its full ownership or significant stock holdings in 56 titles. For instance, it fully owns dailies like *Nice Matin*, controls 25 per cent of *Le Parisien* and *Le Monde*, and also occupies a major role in the magazine sector (*Paris Match, Elle, Télé 7 Jours*). Prisma Presse, a French subsidiary of the leading European communication group Bertelsmann, is the second largest group in magazines and it publishes 20 titles like *Géo, Télé Loisirs, Gala, Voici, Femme Actuelle, Capital*. Mondadori is the third major press group and controls magazines like *Télé Star, Biba* and *Auto Plus*. Independent average corporations gravitate around these mastodons: Le Monde/La Vie group (*Le Monde Diplomatique, Télérama, etc.,*) Ouest France group and Bayard group, which is a main actor in the youth sector (Balle 2007).

The concentration of the newsprint, particularly in the national daily press and local daily press, is neither a recent nor a geographic phenomenon. This observation is found in many other European countries like England, Germany, Italy, Ireland, but also in the United States. In France, it is a regular subject of public debate since, if the press industry is concentrated into the hands of a few, it may lead to a restriction into the diversity and pluralism of opinions and as a consequence threaten democracy (Gabszewicz et al. 2001).

Furthermore, during the last decade print media have been challenged by the rise of the Internet, and they have all launched websites that allow them to reach a wider audience than the readership of the paper format. As an example, the circulation of the print version of *Le Monde* was 350,000 in 2008 while its website was consulted by nearly 5 million visitors in October 2008 alone (mediametrie.fr). At the same time, mainstream dailies and magazines have to compete with the news provided by the web portals and search engines like Google news, as well as by amateur news sites. According to a survey done by TNS-SOFRES (tns-sofres.com) in November 2007, 37 per cent of the French used the Internet, at least occasionally, to read news about local, national or international events. Another survey done by IPSOS found that this rate reached 74 per cent among regular Internet users in 2008 (ipsos.fr, profiling 2008). In sum, numerous questions are raised today about the survival of traditional print media because it faces a market crisis as it struggles to cater to the evolving habits of a population that is now more inclined to watch television than to read, and which relies increasingly on the Internet for news reporting.

The emergence of a hybrid market of broadcasting media

During the four decades of State ownership of broadcast media, the government's monopoly over radio was an illusion because French citizens could easily listen to radio from neighbouring countries, such as Radio Luxembourg, Radio Monte Carlo, and Europe 1, which broadcast from the borders and covered French news. However, it is the civic struggle for the liberation of the FM band waves which led to the deregulation of broadcasting. By the late 1970s dozens of illegal independent radio stations had started to broadcast. One of the first decisions taken by the French left when it came to power in 1981, after decades of rule by the right wing, was to pass the law that abrogated the State monopoly over radio and television on 29 July 1982. Independent, non-profit, radio stations were then authorized and hundreds of local and associative stations mushroomed and became a major locus of public and political debate. Most of these stations, in fact, could not make ends meet and when the right wing came back to power it allowed the creation of commercial radio networks. Though several associative radio stations are still in operation, the radio-wave liberalization has finally contributed to the domination of a few radio corporations like Fun Radio and NRJ that mainly broadcast music and commercials.

In 2008, there were 1,500 radio stations in France. Private radio stations attract the majority of the overall public, although public service stations maintain steady and rather substantial audience figures. State-owned Radio France has several stations (generalist stations like France Inter, or specialized stations like Radio France International, France Culture, France Musique, and Le Mouv', a new youth station). The French cultural elite considers the quality of Radio France programmes much higher than those of private radio stations, except for news coverage where Radio France must compete with the private generalist stations (i.e. RTL, Europe 1, RMC). Radio remains a central locus of the public sphere since it organizes daily controversial debates and opens up its air to the opinions of both experts in public affairs and ordinary listeners to a far greater extent than television.

The deregulation of television in 1982 was very controversial since it was the media which most attracted big corporations, not so much as a source of profit but as a source of societal influence in order to reinforce their public image. In fact, the privatization of television was initiated under the socialist government and started with the creation of Canal + (also known as Canal Plus), a broadcast TV channel requiring a monthly subscription. It was soon followed by the launching of two regular private television channels, which were allocated to big media groups, including the Italian Berlusconi conglomerate. In 1986, the right wing came back to power and the first public service TV channel, which had the biggest audience, was allotted to Bouygues, a powerful private entrepreneur in public works. It was the first time that in Europe a state had sold a public TV channel to private interests (Albert and Leteinturier 1999). This decision was perceived by the left and by a large majority of the population as a strong sign of the dismantling of the public service broadcasting system. Today, this private channel, TF1, is still under the control of Bouygues and it remains the leader in audience ratings. In the last twenty years, the ownership of other private TV channels has changed hands several times in a complex game depending on competition rules, financial intricacies, and political acquaintances.

In 2009, the French television system offered six TV broadcast channels (the private channels TF1 and M6 and four public service channels), the subscription-based TV broadcast channel *Canal +*, and over one hundred cable, satellite, and DTTV (Digital Terrestrial TV) channels. In 2008, 45 per cent of French households were equipped with DTTV, 25 per cent with satellite TV, 13 per cent with cable TV, and 17 per cent with IPTV.[1] In twenty years, the PAF (*Paysage Audiovisuel Français, i.e.* the French Audiovisual Landscape, as it is usually called) has radically changed from the only three public TV channels available at the beginning of the1980s; cable television was launched in 1982 and satellite TV in 1996. The TV market is highly concentrated. A few corporations – especially Bouygues, RTL (a subsidiary of Bertelsmann) and Lagardère – dominate and they have also invested in cable and satellite TV (Charon 2003). The same groups have also invested in DTTV when it was launched in 2005. Television is a strong sector for cross investments, and big corporations have concentrated their assets in the capital of several channels. Furthermore, they now have to face new competition from telecommunications and Internet operators (like Orange, linked to France Telecom), which are entering into the production and diffusion of TV and video media. Today, new marketing strategies have developed to offer TV programmes, like news or fiction, and other types of video content on different technological formats like on the Internet (IPTV) or mobile phone (Greffe & Sonnac 2008). The marketing of TV and video production is now based on the ATAWAD strategy (Any Time, Any Where, Any Device).

> The French audiovisual landscape is again experiencing a major shift that some commentators do not hesitate to describe as a revolution or even a big bang. Indeed, the technological mutations permit to multiply again the modes of diffusion and to increase the offer with digital terrestrial TV and IPTV, which transform in depth the modes of consumption and reception, with the appearance of Television On Demand (TVOD), Video On Demand (VOD), and mobile television. Diversity, Mobility, and Fragmentation of the offer and the audiences: the old audiovisual landscape is completely reconfigured. (Chauveau 2008: 25)

Regulatory rules and erratic media policies

The French media system is characterized by incoherent policies which combine a profusion of regulatory rules and political measures that are often contradictory. In 1982, the law which abrogated State monopoly over broadcast media created an independent supervisory body known as la Haute Autorité de la Communication Audiovisuelle, close to the model of the American Federal Communications Commission (FCC). This body was replaced by La Commission Nationale de la Communication et des Libertés when the political right came back to power in 1986. The re-election of the socialists led to its replacement by the Conseil Supérieur de l'Audiovisuel (CSA) in 1989, which is still in charge of regulating the media (Balle 2007). The CSA is composed of nine individuals[2] who are assisted by several technical committees. In order to ensure the independence of public media from government, the CSA elects the presidents of the public radio and television channels. It also assigns broadcasting licences to private companies after a round of auditions.

The permanent function of the CSA remains to watch over the strict application of the regulatory rules that apply to all radio and TV companies, especially in matters of advertising, content of programmes for sex and violence, and European quotas for broadcasting programmes of national and/or European origin. During electoral campaigns, the CSA examines that the airtime between all political parties is 'well balanced.' This authority has not only a key role in monitoring broadcast media it has also the power to sanction TV or radio stations that violate regulations by enjoining them to duly apply the rules and/or inflicting fines for non-compliance. Broadcast media complain extensively about the myriad rules they have to follow, but on the other hand the regulation is so complex that it gives way to many loopholes. Furthermore, the CSA has enacted rules to inform parents and protect youth by establishing a specific coding system of TV programmes according to their degree of violence and sex.

The French regulatory system takes place in a context of successive media policies that normally evolve as consequences of changes in government. It is noteworthy that it is the left that broke the state monopoly over broadcasting and encouraged the investment in television and the emergence of new private channels. It is reasonable to say that there is a certain disorder in French media policies, which is especially obvious in the management of public television. During the last four decades the financing of public TV was mixed: it got the revenue of the national tax paid by television set owners but it also received funding from advertising, which was allowed on public TV. In fact, public channels have been facing contradictory injunctions. On the one hand, they were supposed to broadcast programmes of public service interests and, on the other hand, they had to gather large audiences in order to attract advertisements on which they relied for almost half of their financing. This double bind created the conditions for 'an impossible mission.' In consequence, public service channels started in the 1980s to stray from the mission of advancing culture and education in an effort to target broader audiences by joining private TV in broadcasting popular game shows, talk shows, soaps, and action series. This evolution led to lots of complaints among the public TV professionals, members of the general public, and some politicians from both the left and right wings.

Another matter of recurrent public discussion is the extent of sex and violence in broadcast media. In 2002, a controversial report stated that there was a lot of sex and violence on

TV (mainly on private channels and pay TV) and that open air programmes devoted to youth on private radio stations were obscene (Kriegel 2002). The findings of the report were denounced by media professionals as unsubstantiated due to gross exaggerations. Though some excess did actually exist – especially on certain youth radio stations that were subsequently enjoined to monitor their programmes more rigorously – pornography as such is only available on subscription TV. As far as violence is concerned, it is rather less present in programmes devoted to children than it used to be, but rampant violence of many kinds is part of many TV programmes targeting all audiences. In the end, the outrage caused by the 2002 report precluded the government from making reforms, while, in addition, the European Commission held that existing French regulations were already very strict and sufficient enough to protect the young.

The role of public television in society is an important matter of public debate and questions about its financing and its programming were consistently raised in Parliament. Many parliamentary commissions examined the situation of public television and the question of whether public television should be similar to private television. On the one hand, the fact that public channels imitate private TV and compete overtly on the market was a way to ensure that it keeps a sufficient part of the popular audience which would then not drift to commercial TV and, as such, this policy has been rather successful. On the other hand, public channels have always offered more quality programmes than private television (e.g. documentaries and literary programmes), although they are not broadcast at prime time anymore but late in the evening. In fact, it is when the right came back to government in 2002 that the issue was clearly formulated by another commission, which concluded that public television should be significantly distinct from private television (Clément 2002) and engage in the production of higher quality cultural programmes (Schwarz 2003; Copé 2008).[3]

However, the reinforcement of the public service mission of television did not really occur until the end of 2008, when a law was introduced in Parliament to forbid advertisements on public TV. The government forged a complex mechanism, according to which the loss of advertising revenues for public TV would be compensated by several types of taxes on private TV channels as well as on mobile phone operators and Internet providers. Furthermore, the law stipulates that all public TV channels are now merged in a common body (France Television) under the supervision of a President appointed by the Council of Ministers. The debate caused uproar on all sides. While many circles commended this initiative, this law was also interpreted as a political manoeuvre meant to have large audiences flock to private stations by lowering competition in the market. Furthermore, the employees of public TV went on strike in fear that public television would not get the promised resources and would soon decline. They also resisted the appointment of the President of France Television by the State, which was perceived as a loss of editorial independence and as a return to the State's political control over television before the deregulation of the 80s. The debate went on for weeks and many intellectuals expressed their views mainly in the printed press. However, the law was finally adopted in March 2009.[4]

This rapid overview of the dynamics of deregulation and re-regulation in France shows that, despite the fact that the broadcasting media system is now opened to private entrepreneurship, the State still plays a significant role in monitoring the media. Mass media remain a hot political issue. Regulatory policies are subject to continuous change and still depend on the composition of government and on the relationship that media establish with political entities.

The evolution of the mediatized public sphere

The mediatization of culture and politics is an international phenomenon which is also a trend in French society. Television has now become the leading entertainment media since deregulation, as it doubled, all at once, the number of channels and the number of recreational popular programmes. Even though cultural programmes are still available on a daily basis – mostly on public channels and more rarely on private channels – the best audience ratings are for popular programmes. The programmes that rely on public participation, such as games and talk shows, are now numerous on all channels. Many shows ask viewers to participate by voting on air by dialling (non-toll free) calls to TV stations. Participatory shows have high audience ratings in France, as large numbers of viewers are eager to be seen on television and display aspects of their personality and intimate life (Mehl 1996). This evolution is a source of extensive controversy in France, not only among academics but also among journalists and some politicians concerned by this phenomenon. Opinions can also split sharply among the general public. Many viewers are absolutely fond of these shows, which they find very exciting. Others have a profound aversion to what they perceive as voyeurism and decadence.

Numerous scientific articles and books have been published on the emergence of a new form of public sphere that distracts people from engaging in issues of general interest about the res publica with trivial issues about daily life. This analysis points out that these programmes are a reflection of the growing trend towards individualism and of rampaging market values that encourage people to sell themselves on TV in the prospect of becoming heroes for a day and gaining easy rewards in forms of money, travel, etc. On the other hand, this societal change can also be interpreted as an extended form of democratization. Television is the medium catering most to popular culture and remains the only way for ordinary people to make themselves heard and to participate in the public arena, because of their general exclusion from decision-making circles (Macé 1993). Many of these programmes are, nonetheless, criticized for their low character.

The introduction of reality TV in France, at a somewhat later time than other Western countries, has caused much uproar and galvanized a major national debate. When *Big Brother* (in France called *Loft Story*) began to be broadcast in 2001 it led to an instantaneous public forum. All groups – politicians, legislators, media professionals, intellectuals, the Church and other associations – expressed their point of view, and usually their concern about the arrival of what they deemed Trash TV to definitely eradicate the remaining cultural forms of television (Jost 2002). France is the only country in the world where reality TV was the *primary issue* in public affairs for about two months due to heavy involvement of the nation's elite. This unique phenomenon illustrates that, despite the fact that private channels are free enterprises, television remains a social institution and a matter of public concern. This momentum of rhetoric did not prevent the development of reality TV in France, as all types of international Reality-TV shows have now been aired in France, many of them among the top audience ratings. Strong objections still remain about what is considered the demagogical role of television and the way it is controlled by audience figures for the sake of profit at the expense of culture and public interest.

Although a few programmes focusing on national and international issues remain (mainly on public TV), discussion of these issues is essentially led in the national press and on radio, which provide much more detailed information and analysis. If national dailies are the best source for international news, all media also cover the latter. Europe is, however, not a regular item in news and is only widely featured when major events take place, like the transition to the Euro, the expansion of the European Union to Eastern European countries or the European constitution. Whereas some critics of the European Union can be heard, the editorial policy of most media leans towards a pro-European stand.

Overall, only a minority of the French population pays regular attention to public debates, while the majority contents itself with listening to radio bulletins or TV news. Today, television is still the primary source of information for the French. Watching the 8 o'clock evening news on TF1 and France 2 has actually been compared to a 'modern ritual mass' by numerous observers and as a source of 'common knowledge' shared by the majority of citizens. Nevertheless, whereas TV news coverage attempts to provide balanced coverage of national and foreign news, its does not provide a highlighting and critical interpretation of issues. The gap between 'informed elites' and 'entertained majorities,' mentioned by Peter Dahlgren in his chapter in this volume, exists in France as in other countries. However, one cannot say that it is widening since it has always been a structural component of French society, while at the same time, television has considerably broadened the outlook of ordinary people, such as by exposing them to several dimensions of world politics. However, the audience's behaviour is rapidly evolving and TV viewers are now inclined to watch news and other programmes offered by cable, satellite TV, DTTV or web-TV. As a result, the audience of the generalist broadcast channels has started to erode, as the market share of thematic channels rose to 36 per cent of the TV audience in June 2007.[5] The growing fragmentation of publics has become a major component of the French media scene.

Journalism as a new public issue

Since the 1990s journalism has itself been at the core of public debate due to the emergence of several instances of disregard for ethics that lowered the trust of the audience towards news coverage (Lemieux 2000). Under the intense pressure of increased media competition, some journalists have reported false news without duly verifying sources, while others have made up stories and have allegedly been co-opted in exchange for free travel from big corporations, juicy contracts to supervise corporate board meetings, etc.

The main public concern in this matter remains collusion between journalists and the powerful oligarchy in the field of politics, as well as business and culture. The degree of dependence between media and decision makers has been investigated by several academics (Neveu 2001), but more attention was paid to Pierre Bourdieu's famous manifesto *Sur la télévision* (Bourdieu 1996) denouncing the way journalists contribute to maintain the interests of the establishment. In fact, this question is a recurrent theme of public debate in a country whose early journalistic practices did not rely extensively on the reporting of facts, as in Anglo-Saxon countries, but on official news commented, interpreted, and critiqued by journalists. Coverage by French journalists has become more fact-oriented since then, although commentary has maintained a strong importance, especially in print media.

Print and television journalism are separate fields which lead to distinct career tracks, except for a handful of famous journalists of the elite who have become media 'stars': they are usually columnists in major papers or radio stations and they are invited as guests or commentators in political TV programmes. Print journalists consider that the press remains the 'noble field' and that it is less subject to catering to sensationalism than television.

Some journalists have become active participants in the public debate over media's societal purpose while monitoring violations to the ethics of the profession. Public TV has initiated weekly programmes which screen reports subject to ethical infringements. These reports are criticized, live, by media experts and by concerned viewers while journalists are asked to answer. It has also created a system of ombudsmen, called in France mediators, as did several papers. Questions were raised as to whether it was opportune to revise the ethical code of professional journalism set in 1918 and revised in 1938, but there was no consensus and a few media decided to reinforce it by adopting a home-made deontological chart. Controversies also emerged about the creation of a professional judiciary order, ordre des journalistes, which would be entitled to give sanctions to journalists who disregard professional ethics. No consensus was found, and the position was clearly that journalism should keep the present system of self-regulation and avoid specific jurisdictions which could lead to political interference with the independence of the press (Rieffel & Watine 2002). In sum, all the debates have contributed to a form of meta-journalism where journalists themselves animate a public debate where opinions of media critics and citizens are heard, but this forum often turns into a process of self-justification as journalists impute the breach in ethics to the media system. This debate has not been vain and many journalists have become more respectful of professional ethics and aware of their social responsibility. Today, in the present context of the rise of amateur journalism on independent news websites, accredited journalists put an even stronger accent on the importance of professional norms as they try to defend the integrity and the privileges of their profession.

Media as a core of societal change

The last three decades were a period of dramatic change in French society as a whole. The values of free entrepreneurship and liberalism have permeated all strata of society. The ensuing trend towards concentration and international partnership in the ownership of media is analogous to comparable evolutions in other economic sectors. Media have contributed to the spread of capitalistic values, especially with the rise of the Internet, and money-making as an end in itself is less frowned upon by society than it used to be in the past. Concomitantly, the public sphere has shifted away from traditional political issues into a whole array of daily-life matters that parallel the rise of individualism and the emergence of ephemeral new TV stars.

Daily newspapers have expanded their coverage to popular culture, leisure, and modern lifestyles in order to attract young readers who, according to empirical studies, are losing interest in reading articles thoroughly and even more about formal news politics (Spitz 2004). This evolution is, as previously explained, even more striking in television. If the main generalist TV channels still attract the vast majority of viewers, the drift towards specialized channels on cable and satellite has started, thus attesting to a growing fragmentation of the audience. It is comparable in that regard to what has already taken place on FM radios and in print media with the success of specialized magazines. Media are more and more used as tools to satisfy private centres of interest.

Media must also deal with an obvious generation gap, as patterns of consumption by the young differ greatly from the forms of media uses by older generations. Due to the abundance of media generated by deregulation, young people are able to select what caters most to their interests: youth radio stations, TV series and films, reality TV, specialist magazines on leisure activities (e.g. video games, sports, etc.) and social network websites. While their use of the Internet is mostly geared towards leisure and communication with their peers, they still tend to follow news headlines and read a few selected articles (Barbier-Bouvet 2001). They usually disregard traditional politics, which is seen as the domain of greedy and corrupt politicians. Surveys show that most of the young are in favour of the European Union (Tns-Sofres surveys 2003–2004), though they do not pay much interest to the intricacies of its policies. Their withdrawal from the traditional political sphere does not, however, mean that they are not at all concerned with public affairs, especially environmental and humanitarian issues.

At the beginning of the twenty-first century media are faced with questions about the role they are going to play in a context of profound social and economic change. While the French have become more accepting of liberal values, they remain very much attached to the democratic principles of equal access to public services (e.g. education, health care, etc.) and fair redistribution of wealth. As globalization and neo-liberalism infiltrate national economic structures, the foundations of the Welfare State are slowly crumbling. In this regard, the enlargement of the EU is a particularly sensitive topic. The media have the potential to either instigate a withdrawal on nationalistic and xenophobic attitudes or, conversely, favour the opening up to the vision of a dynamic, multicultural, and prosperous Europe.

In conclusion, this longitudinal overview of the role of French media politics in the public sphere shows that while the State no longer has the same dominant impact on the media sphere it had in the past, its influence has not vanished. The State still has a crucial role in maintaining the pluralism of print media, encouraging the production of national TV programmes and ensuring the airing of French and European programmes according to EU regulations. Over the last four decades, the media market has extended considerably and media have become the core of the cultural and the political public spheres. The mediatization of the public sphere has not only encompassed the commercialization of all forms of cultural and sporting entertainment but also formal political affairs, as well as all types of social movements in France. As such, media have probably contributed to widening the scope of the audience over the complexity of national and foreign public issues, even though the dramatization and trivialization of current affairs in dominant media, mainly television, have concomitantly led to a deterioration of normative debate. At a time when patterns of democracy are evolving, media are a locus of the tensions and contradictions at stake in the public space and are facing the challenge of fostering the emergence of still unknown new forms of democracy.

Notes

1. Conseil Supérieur de l'Audiovisuel. Les chiffres clés de l'audiovisuel français. Direction des Etudes et de la Prospective. March 2008
2. Three are designated by the Head of State, three by the President of the National Assembly, and three by the President of the Senate.
3. Commission pour une nouvelle télévision publique, présidée par Jean-François Copé, 2008. Website: www.premier-ministre.gouv.fr/chantiers/culture_851
4. Loi organique N°2009–257 du 5 mars 2009 relative à la nomination des présidents des sociétés France Television et Radio France.
5. Conseil Supérieur de l'Audiovisuel. Les chiffres clés de l'audiovisuel français. Direction des Etudes et de la Prospective. March 2008.

References

Albert, P. & Leteinturier. C. (1999) *Les médias dans le monde. Enjeux internationaux et diversités nationales*, Paris: Ellipses.

Balle, F. (2007) *Médias et Sociétés*, Paris: Montchrestien.

Barbier-Bouvet, J-F. (2001) 'Internet, lecture et culture de flux', *Esprit*, Décember 2001.

Bourdieu, P. (1996) *Sur la télévision; L'emprise du journalisme*, Paris: Liber-Raisons d'Agir.

Charon, J-M. (1991) *La presse en France de 1945 à nos jours*, Paris: Le Seuil.

Charon, J-M. (1999) *La presse magazine*, Paris: La Découverte, Repères.

Charon, J-M. (2003) *Les médias en France,* Paris: La Découverte.

Chauveau, A. (2009) 'La réforme de l'audiovisuel, La Documentation Française', *Regards sur l'Actualité*. N°347, pp. 15–25.

Clément, C. (2002) *La nuit et l'été: quelques propositions pour les quatre saisons*, Report submitted to M. Aillagon, Minister for culture and communication on an evaluation and analysis of proposals concerning the cultural offer of French Television, Paris : La Documentation Française.

Gabszewicz, J.; Laussel, D. & Sonnac, N. (2001) 'Press Advertising and the Ascent of the "Pensée Unique ?"', *European Economic Review*, 45, pp. 641–51.

Greffe, X. & Sonnac, N. (2008) *Culture Web*, Paris: Dalloz.

Jost, F. (2002) 'L'empire du loft, Paris, La dispute, Collection des mots sur les images', *Esprit*: 1.

Kriegel, B. (2002) *La violence à la télévision*, Report submitted to M. Aillagon, Minister for culture and communication, Paris: La Documentation Française.

Le Floch, P. & Sonnac, N. (2000) *Economie de la presse*, Paris: Editions La Découverte, collection Repères.

Lemieux, C. (2000) *Mauvaise presse, Une sociologie compréhensive du travail journalistique et de ses critiques*, Paris: Métailié.

Mace, E. (1993) 'La télévision du pauvre. La participation du public', *Hermès* N°11–12, Paris: Presses du CNRS.

Mehl, D. (1996) *La télévision de l'intimité*, Paris: Seuil.

Missika, J-L. & Wolton, D. (1983) *La folle du logis, La télévision dans les sociétés démocratiques*, Paris: Gallimard.

Neveu, E. (2001) *Sociologie du journalisme*, Paris: La Découverte, Repères.

Rieffel, R. & Watine, T. (eds.) (2002) *Les mutations du journalisme en France et au Québec*, Paris: Editons Panthéon-Assas.

Schwarz, A. (2003) *La production audiovisuelle française et son financement*, Report submitted to Minister for culture and communication, Paris: La Documentation Française.

Sonnac, N. (2001) L'économie des magazines, *Réseaux*, 19 (105).

Spitz, B. (2004) *Les jeunes et la lecture de la presse quotidienne d'information politique et générale*, Report submitted to Minister for culture and communication, Paris: La Documentation Française, 2004.

Tns-Sofres surveys 'Les jeunes et l'Europe' of 19 November 2003 & 12 May 2004, www.tns-sofres.com. Accessed 19 August 2009.

Toussaint Desmoulins, N. (2004) *L'économie des médias*, Paris: Presses Universitaires de France, n° 1701.

Chapter 8

Changing Media and Public Sphere in Turkey: The Role of the State, Market and the EU Candidacy

Mine Gencel Bek
Ankara University

Introduction

This chapter aims to trace the changing public sphere in Turkey by focusing mainly on the media as a 'structural' dimension of the public sphere, which defines the type and quality of public sphere (Dahlgren, this volume; Dahglren 1995). The 'structural dimension', which is related to the 'formal', institutional features of the public sphere, will here be given more priority than 'interactional' dimensions. This structural dimension involves such media-related issues as 'the media organizations and regulatory frameworks that include questions of ownership, financing, control', etc. as well as the legal framework which defines 'the freedoms of and constraints on communication' which makes this dimension connected with the political institutions (Dahlgren, this volume). The representational dimension will be touched upon with some examples from the Turkish media content. The six trends altering the mediascape of Western Europe, commercialization, concentration, deregulation, globalization, proliferation and digitalization (Dahlgren, this volume) are also valid for the Turkish media industry in the sense that Turkey is experiencing the advance of market forces and private enterprise, especially since the 1980s. Also, Turkey witnessed three military coups (1960, 1971 and 1980), the last of which was to facilitate the accumulation of capital for a neo-liberal course. This chapter will consider these changes, specifically focusing on Turkish media history and changes in the industry, by analysing the role of the state, market and EU candidacy. The 1990s mark the development of the EU in Europe (see Dahlgren, this volume) and the European Union is also now a key element in the Turkish public sphere, especially since the candidacy was approved in 1999. For Turkey, EU membership would have a big influence on political life, while, for the EU, Turkey's membership would be a turning point. This chapter, then, will focus on 'changing media' and public sphere in Turkey, whose membership also will be one of the elements of 'changing Europe'.

Historical background of the media in Turkey

It is always difficult to trace the changes chronologically and, at the same time, elaborate the context of particular moments, as Corner (2003) states in relation to the historiography of television. Another difficulty in writing a historical background is at what point to start. If the starting point in the history of the media in Turkey is taken as the establishment of the

Republic (rather than the Ottoman Empire), then the first thing to say is that the media were used in establishing and then modernizing the Republic of Turkey by the Kemalist elite. Mustafa Kemal Atatürk, the founder of the Republic of Turkey, published the newspaper *Hakimiyet-i Milliye* and established a news agency called Anadolu Ajansı in 1920. These were used in the independence movement against the Empire and occupier-states through the control of the news networks. After the establishment of the Republic, the media worked for modernization and for the establishment of the Kemalist ideology by disseminating Western values and ways of life (Karpat 1964; Heper & Demirel 1996; Oktay 1987). Radio, which started in 1927, had a very important function in the process of modernization and nationalist indoctrination. Radio broadcasts not only spread the political principles of the new regime, but also encouraged modernization in general through cultural expression in music, drama and other forms[1] (Karpat 1964). After 1922, the minority press (such as Armenian and Greek, also Turkish newspapers that were against the Republic and were supporters of the Caliphate or of socialism) disappeared. Some opponents were sent into exile abroad, some were imprisoned (Koloğlu 1994).

Until 1945, the press was controlled by the one-party government, the RPP (Republican People's Party) and became its instrument as a 'government-sponsored organization' (Karpat 1964: 272). One striking feature of this period is that some of the newspaper owners were members of the parliament, including Yunus Nadi, the owner of *Cumhuriyet*.[2] They were used by the government to legitimize the one-party regime with the public (Güvenir 1991). There were 40 journalists, media owners or senior columnists who worked as members of parliament in different periods until the death of Atatürk. After Atatürk, the largest number of members of the parliament was related to the military, and then journalism until 1957 (Kocabaşoğlu 1984).

Besides this close relationship between the press and the government there were some mechanisms that made the press dependent on the government, such as the distribution of official advertisements and paper supply. At that time there was a fall in circulation as a result of the adaptation to the Latin alphabet from Arabic in 1928. It is argued that this opened the way for government subsidies for the press (Koloğlu 1994). However, after a few years, the negative effect of the change of alphabet on press circulation diminished, and the circulation, to a great extent, rose again (Kocabaşoğlu 1984). In the 1950s and 1960s, after the creation of the multi-party system, newspapers gradually started to gain a 'mass' character by increasing their circulation (Karpat, 1964). This was compatible with the economic and cultural anticipation of the people in a 'free' environment (Oktay 1987).

Although the new Democratic Party (DP) government ended the one-party rule of the RPP, the period of the DP, 1950–1960, was not so different from the period of the RPP in terms of democracy. In the beginning, the new government seemed democratic. It enacted a new press law, which extended the limits of press freedom. However, the freedom did not last long. Since the government was not very successful in economic policy, discontents arose. The DP government would not tolerate the existence of criticism, and thus new legal arrangements were brought in to restrict press freedom. Furthermore, a committee of inquiry was authorized to suppress publications and arrest journalists who were 'dangerous to national security' (Karpat 1964: 280); during the period from 1955–1960, 867 journalists were imprisoned. Both parties, the RPP and the DP, used radio and news agencies as tools of their parties during their rule: in addition to legal pressures, the operation of an oppositional press was inhibited through the distribution of official advertisements; some newspapers were rewarded with official advertisements while others were punished (Koloğlu, 1994; Oktay 1987; Tunçay 1995).

The DP government ended with the military coup on 27 May 1960. Koloğlu argues that the dictatorial pressures of the DP on the press played an important role in leading the press to sympathize with the military. In fact, after the 1960 military coup, the MBK (National Unity Committee) members declared that they were influenced by the ideas in the press (Koloğlu 1994). In the editorial of 28 May 1960, one day after the military coup, Nadir Nadi, the owner of *Cumhuriyet* and an ex-MP, welcomed the army by criticizing the corrupt multi-party democratic system. He described the army as brave and welcomed its extraordinary responsibility to prevent the fratricidal quarrel that was going to explode (Kahraman 1996). The relatively free environment of the 1960s ended with the 1971 military intervention; the growing leftist movement of the 1970s was eroded by the 1980s military coup.

It is quite interesting that the press for the 1980 military coup used similar words to those of 1960. On the 14 September 1980, two days after the military coup, the editorial in *Milliyet* was entitled 'the success of 12 September military coup is a requirement' (Karaca 1995: 236–240). During the rule of the military government in the 1980s, the press was given directives by the military officers on how to write the news. The control continued using various methods such as legal restrictions, written or oral requests and personal meetings. Self-censorship of the press was also a much greater issue. On the first anniversary of the military coup, there were headlines which described the environment as peaceful and as happy days of unity, and which thanked the army for their liberation of the state (Tartanoğlu 1994).

Despite the fact that the 1980 coup produced severe reduction of freedom, Heper makes a very optimistic evaluation. For him, the military's system of ethics created 'a new kind of Turk' who plays the role of 'citizen' in the political system, not the role of 'subject'. In addition, this new system is based on 'participation, and tolerance towards others' opinions' (Heper, 1985: 147). Furthermore, in a rather mystical way, he states that the

> ...post-1980 military in Turkey did not wish to impose upon society a closed system of thought and believed in the inherent capacity of the people. (Heper, 1985: 152)

Moreover, Heper claims that the military had been trying 'to create a political environment in which, through multiple confrontations of civil societal groups, a dynamic consensus may be possible' (ibid: 151). Therefore, the military in Turkey 'has aimed at a democratic reconsolidation rather than a regime breakdown' with the interventions (ibid: 151).

It is difficult to understand how citizenship, political participation and democracy can be spoken of in relation to the 'post-1980 military regime' which removed the channels of representation (Sayarı 1992: 32), ended all political activities and organizations, and brought severe restrictions on the freedom of expression. Executions of prisoners under 18 years of age were carried out. The human rights violations record reached its peak in the history of the country. As Gülalp states, the 1980 coup was the worst one in terms of destruction of freedoms. It brought a 'complete breakdown of all forms of democracy' (Gülalp 1985: 329).

There are differing views about the MP government. Ayata classifies these views into two different groups. According to the first view, the MP is the extension of the military in integrating the Turkish economy into world markets. From this perspective, the MP is seen as 'essentially conservative and supported by the religious and nationalist groups, an executive committee of the Turkish bourgeoisie, and a reflection of the rise of the new right in Turkey' (Ayata, 1993: 33). There is strong evidence to evaluate the situation from the first perspective.[3] The second group considers the MP as the only party which was 'opposed to the military' (Göle 1994: 217), or more cautiously as the party which 'had distanced itself from the military more than had the other parties that competed in the 1983 general elections' (Heper 1994: 197). It should be mentioned here that the general elections were very restrictive; as a result of the bans on some politicians, the range of parties was not wide. As Ayata states, this group evaluates the MP as 'the "initiator" of liberal revolutions'. According to this perspective, the MP is considered to be 'antibureaucratic, pluralist, modern and able to bring together a coalition including a wide range of ideological groups' (Ayata, 1993: 33).

Although it contains people who have different interests with changing emphases and priorities, the second group draws a parallel between economic liberalism and political liberalism. Those who focus on the economy prioritize the successes of the liberal economic policies, mainly the Stabilization Programme, while those who are more interested in the political dimensions celebrate the differences in the 'strengthening civil society' of post-1980 Turkey as an extension of the liberal economy.

Göle, similarly to Heper, celebrates the 'autonomization' of civil society after the coup in the 1980s: 'the liberal discourse, which was rediscovered and became fashionable after 1983, developed simultaneously with market economy.'

Women, ecologists, veiled students, and homosexuals and transsexuals appeared on the political scene and brought to the agenda themes such as environmental protection, female identity, and individual freedom… (Göle 1994: 217–18).

Göle also notes 'the development of liberal, Muslim and leftist movements' in the autonomized civil society of post-1983 (Göle 1994: 215). First of all, there are many omissions from this list. The Kurds, as the largest ethnic group of Turkey, is one of these. Their absence prevents us making such optimistic evaluations. Göle's claim that the leftist movements developed is very inappropriate after the 1980 coup which paralysed the left. In fact, all the elements mentioned here should be put in context and understood within that environment rather than putting them in a list in order to demonstrate the evidence for the civil society.

Religion in Turkey cannot be understood only as 'the return of the repressed' (Robins 1996: 72) from Kemalist secularism, which was seen at the beginning of this chapter. Islam was used by the 1980 military as the Turkish-Islamic synthesis which had been created by a group of intellectuals in the 1970s (Birtek et al. 1993: 195–196) in order to 'create a secure ground for the liberal restructuring of economic life' (Keyman 1995: 111–12), more particularly, as an antidote to the left. This is not to argue that all Islamic movements are the outcome of that, nor is it to ignore the differences in Islamic movements. However, the impact of the coup on the development of Islam should not be underestimated. Currently the situation is changing with differing hegemonic struggles. The main emphasis here is that the context should be considered and examined when the autonomy or the simultaneity of the differences are declared. In addition, it should be considered that the elements of the civil society are also tools for the dominant block to maintain their hegemony against the existing 'enemy' in differing conditions. This is important not only to explain Islam but also the Islamic sect Alawites. It is true that there is an Alawite identity which is protected, changed and re-shaped according to the differing conditions by Alawites themselves. This identity was visible in the 1980s. However, at the same time, it is true that Alawite culture as a moderate and more secular one is emphasized against radical Islam as a guarantee of secularism by Kemalists or as the guaranteed voter for the social democrat parties.

The issue of prime importance is that there has been no policy change for the benefit of Alawites, such as their representation in the public religious bodies or the use of the state budget for the needs of Alawite communities. Despite the claim that the Alawite culture has appeared, Sunni Islam is still the one which is taught in schools, Sunni festivals are celebrated on public TV, mosques for Sunni Muslims are built with the taxes from all citizens.

When all the groups in Göle's list are examined, it is clear that not just Alawites but the others also have brought no policy change and, besides that, homosexuals and transsexuals are still subject to ongoing police violence and abuse. Ecologists are welcomed as long as they do not go beyond certain limits and become a potential to harm economic interests. Women's marches or demonstrations are stopped when they are considered to be a threat, whereas more Kemalist-dominated women's movements are encouraged to protect the system against enemies such as the Islamists. This is not meant to deny their struggles, or the potential for change, but to draw attention to the need to be aware of the strong state, and of the strategies of the dominant bloc before they are evaluated as the sign of an active civil society. If we do not do this, we may end up celebrating the appearance of these different social and political groups and their manipulation by the dominant groups for their own interests, rather than changes brought about for their benefit.

Groc evaluates the period of 1980–1990 as a conflict between the press and the new Motherland Party[4] (MP) government, which put pressures on the press with the transformation from Kemalism to liberalism. The government's aim, Groc believes, was to 'reduce the critical influence of a mainstream lobbying group which had formed around Kemalist traditions'

(Groc 1994: 200). It is true that (not only directly through the pressures, but also through the increasing logic of competition) the developments which were encouraged by the MP government, such as technological modernization and competition for advertisements, made the newspapers more vulnerable to the pressures from the government and resulted in an economic crisis (Koloğlu 1994). However, Groc's descriptions of the Özal government as distancing itself from the earlier military rule, and some definitions attributed to Özal, such as being 'the reformer of the old order, who aimed to liberate social, political, and economic life from the weight of the state, from which society had long suffered' (Groc 1994: 204), are misleading. Although there were tensions between the government and the press, I would argue that, when Groc explains press criticism in the 1990s against the MP and Özal as evidence of the Kemalist tendencies of the press, he ignores the fact that many policies of the MP did not work, which provoked a strong reaction from the public. The press, then, could not ignore such popular discontent if it was to be popular.

Changing media and public sphere in the 1990s

In the 1990s, some important changes were witnessed in the media scene. The biggest change, the end of the monopoly of TRT (Turkish Radio-Television) on broadcasting in 1990, was facilitated by Turgut Özal, the Prime Minister of the period, in accordance with the neo-liberal economic path being followed.[5]

The character of Turkish public television

TRT started television broadcasting in 1968. The state control of TRT broadcasts has always been an issue, with the government applying a variety of control mechanisms. After autonomy ended with a legal change following the military intervention in 1971, TRT became more open to government intervention. Following the 1980 military coup, TRT has its third former military officer as director general (Aziz 1993: 55). After 1990 the TRT's situation became financially harder, especially following the introduction of private channels. The public indifference when the deductions from electricity bills, which made up 70 per cent of TRT's income, ended in February 2003 demonstrated once again that the TRT did not have popular support. Even though this lack of support is related to the increasing neo-liberal assumptions, one should also recognize the fact that it is related to TRT not being a real public service channel; not reflecting the diversity of the society: 'TRT has operated according to an authoritarian state broadcasting model rather than a public service model' (Aksoy & Robins 1997: 81). It is 'the medium for the official definition and interpretation of the central Kemalist bureaucracy' (Şahin & Aksoy 1993: 32). TRT news is an indicator of the politically statist structure (Gencel Bek 2004), with the order of the news like state protocol: firstly the Prime Minister, the government, then the main opposition party and then others.

The situation has been a source of criticism by the opposition parties in all periods, but since TRT does not have an autonomous structure, it cannot fully determine its content.

It is certainly impossible to ignore the changes that the private media have brought about. From the outset, the range of the ideological debate in the private media has been widened and different forms of popular culture, which are not found in TRT,[6] have been included; other identities have been included, which Alankuş (1995) calls a 'pluralisation of identities'. In the news on private television channels audiences have seen crowds in the streets taking part in demonstrations. Şahin and Aksoy explain the transformation of the media as technological change and globalization. The commercial channels, according to them, brought the expansion of the range of the ideological debate, dissolution of the official dogmas and the relativization of Turkish culture (Şahin & Aksoy 1993: 34–5).

However, I will argue that the problem here is that the absence of an understanding of public, public service broadcasting, and the absence of civil rights makes the private sector seem as if it were more democratic than it really is. Although there is nothing wrong in describing the state and state broadcasting as official or totalitarian, automatically attributing to private broadcasting characteristics such as freedom or diversity is misleading.

Development of the media industry: concentration, commercialization and competition

There are many reasons why we should be cautious about the private media in terms of democracy. Firstly, private media is concentrated and, at the same time, conglomerated by media owners involved in other businesses or holdings involving the media sector. The media institutions, which were initially family-owned press institutions, have expanded to cover all spheres of the media sector and have enlarged their activities further by becoming involved in other businesses. Secondly, these holdings have started to enter the media sector and thus new media moguls are born. As a result of this, the smaller-scaled media of the earlier periods, when the newspapers were principally family-owned, completely changed; although they also had other businesses outside the media sector, these were far more limited in scale and range compared to the current situation. They increased their basis by establishing shares with holdings that own large financial institutions and banks.

The new holdings have companies which extend beyond the national boundaries. All of these groups have tended to expand towards different sections of the media industry, including newspapers, magazines, television, publishing, news agencies, distribution and marketing. Since the beginning of the 1990s it has also been observed that media groups and the holdings which have entered the media sector have also expanded towards the new media and telecommunications, and have established partnerships with global companies in these areas.[7] Therefore, instead of talking about different media in Turkey specifically, this chapter will mainly consider media groups in general. Currently,[8] Doğan, Merkez and Çukurova are the biggest media groups controlling the majority of media industry in Turkey. The conglomerates use their media to promote their other businesses, products and services, which reduces their advertising expenses. There is a big increase in the number of advertising companies, their foreign partners, and in the space devoted to advertisements in the media.

Advertising also can have an effect on the diversity of media content: Demirkent (1995) indicates the level of control of the media over the advertising agents by stating that big media groups put the advertising agents in a difficult position by intervening in their work, by making requests or sometimes by threat, such as creating false news about products advertised in the other newspapers (ibid: 149–50). The reverse also occurs: some news may not be written so as not to prejudice the relationship with a company that advertises in the newspaper (ibid: 124). That some issues may be raised while others are played down, or disappear, would not appear to be democratic as it threatens the diversity of, and access to, information.

As a result of the main motive of maximizing profit, the big media groups are in ferocious competition, often involving promotion campaigns that almost bring about a new understanding that, in buying a newspaper, you actually buy it to get something rather than just to read it. The promotion[9] war that started between the media groups[10] in 1993 illustrates the degree of competition between the media groups. It was advocated by the media as a new way to increase circulation and since then they have been involved in very intense competition to sell more and to get more advertising.

Although promotion campaigns were presented as a way to increase circulation, it did not guarantee keeping the circulation at a high level. As soon as a promotion campaign finishes in one newspaper, the readers gained through that campaign stop buying that newspaper. The promotion campaigns have reached the point where they are no longer aimed at gaining new readers but at preventing the loss of existing readers (Görgülü 1991: 95). The newspapers have tended to lose their reliability as a result of their quarrels about promotion, and the ongoing advertisements that attack the other group's newspapers and the readers have started to perceive the newspapers as providers of products rather than as purveyors of news. *Cumhuriyet*, which does not run promotion campaigns, had an advertisement on TV with the slogan '*Cumhuriyet*: It only gives the newspaper.'

These commercial, conglomerated structures have limits, shortcomings and dangers for democracy, as seen in their use of the media as a weapon against their rivals (Sönmez 1996: 76). In fact, many examples of this situation have been witnessed; media groups have used, or threatened to use, their media against each other.[11]

The media alliance for national interests and the media-state relations

The optimistic evaluations of the private television channels mentioned at the beginning of this chapter found their reflection in the press with the emergence of the *Sabah* newspaper in 1985. *Sabah* is a popular newspaper that describes the three necessary elements of its first page as being interesting, amusing, and sexually provoking (Münir 1993).

Aksoy and Robins argue that the low circulation has led the newspaper industry to accept state credits from the government. According to them, making the newspaper more popular can increase the circulation, and *Sabah* succeeded in that. *Sabah,* they state:

> was not part of the national media elite, and had not been compromised by drawing on state financial support. This afforded the newspaper a valuable peripheral perspective that allowed it to challenge the limits of the 'official' culture. (Aksoy & Robins 1997: 84)

This might have been the case initially but later it has been seen that neither high circulation nor *Sabah* being new, and not part of the media elite, could prevent it asking for state credits. Thus, *Sabah* is no different from the other newspapers in terms of its relationship with the government. The authors give examples of these challenges to the limits of the official culture, such as *Sabah's* decision to publish the newspaper on religious holidays,[12] or printing a photograph of President Demirel in his swimming costume. Although these developments are new, they are indeed indications of the sensationalism of the newspaper. These examples seem too weak to draw the conclusions that *Sabah* 'broke the taboos'; that 'it began to show Turkey as it "really" was', and 'it articulated the perspective of those who had been marginalised in Turkish society' (Aksoy & Robins. 1997: 84). *Sabah* in a way illustrates that politically-critical content of the media decreased to great extent while the infotaining and tabloidizing content, which underestimates and trivializes politics, increased. In fact, after 1960 there has been an increase in the popular culture theme, which can be seen even on the front page of newspapers in 2000 (see RHACNA discussion, this volume). All these can be related to the increase of commercial TV channels, and the tendency of newspapers to become similar to TV.

The private media in Turkey generally have close relationships with the state; they incorporate elements from the official ideology, and different media groups ally when the issue is the 'national interest': when there was a conflict the between the Turkish army and PKK (Kurdistan Workers Party), the issue was reduced to a military problem. The way *Sabah* covered the Kurdish issue was not so different from the other mainstream newspapers: the 'success' stories of the military were printed with headlines such as 'spring cleaning'. The legal party, which mainly focused on the Kurdish issue, was targeted and framed as being an extension of the PKK. The policies of the newspapers on the Kurdish issue might be explained by the existence of legal pressures over this subject, rather than it being just voluntary self-censorship.[13.] However, apart from the Kurdish issue, it is possible to see other cases in which the media work for, and even ally themselves with, national interests.

Done for profit through the alliances in advertisement and distribution, the competing newspapers of the two different media groups, *Sabah, Hürriyet* and *Milliyet,* formed a coalition on news coverage when the issue was about 'national interests' or 'national security'. The common declaration made by the media editors after the economic stabilization programme was a good example. It shows how the so-called watchdog supports the government on national interests. The common declaration of the two media groups with the title 'An

Invitation to the Nation! Come on Turkey! We Will Win This War', which was published in *Sabah*, *Hürriyet* and *Milliyet* on 22 April 1994, aimed to support the government's economic stabilization programme announced at the beginning of the month, using official and nationalist discourse, which is mainly based on conspiracy theory. It was talked about in the name of the country by emphasizing that the interests of the country as a whole should come before the interests of individuals or institutions. The term 'interests of the country' again could have been used by the military in wartime. The state was not seen as being for the people; rather people were seen as existing for the benefit of the state, advising the citizens to think: 'What can I do for my country?' It was emphasized that all people are the same: the fate of all people is common. This idea echoed the principle of populism in Kemalism. The media appeared to be above everything. The citizens were advised to think, the universities, intellectuals, and teachers were allowed to discuss, but thinking *was* restricted: it should be *for* Turkey. Young people were warned against the provocations of those who try to exploit the sensitive situation of the country. The declaration also demanded sacrifices without mentioning what these sacrifices might be; it was just implied that some things would be good for the country. The writers of the declaration, the media elite of the two big groups, considered themselves not only as followers of national mobilization, but as the creators, the vanguard and defenders of it.

The extract below is another example of the media protecting national interests: some journalists went to an island called Kardak and planted a Turkish flag as a reply to the Greeks planting the flag of Greece in 1996. It produced another crisis in the already-tense relations between Turkey and Greece. Whether the island belongs to Turkey or Greece is not the issue for this chapter, but the important thing is the attitude of the Turkish media during these discussions and their defence of the action of planting a Turkish flag. The editor-in-chief of Hürriyet, Ertuğrul Özkök, advocated that action in an interview not as an 'abuse' but as 'reflex of citizenship':

Question: You are of the opinion, Turkey first, journalism later. Does journalism not mean impartiality, though it is difficult?

Answer: Being a journalist in Turkey is not the same thing as being a journalist in America. There is such geography around you that you cannot understand this if you do not carry a responsibility to maintain the existence of this country. Journalists are not the citizens of the world. There is no such thing! There is no one who lives on the moon, whose passport is not stamped with any country…The owner of this newspaper pays me to find the events that others can not follow, every day. It is a forest. If you are not the best, you go…I can show the most impartial attitude, pretend to be impartial, in the world. See how it makes the most biased news against Turkey. I am a Turkish journalist. You cannot expect the journalists in Turkey to be Supermen and adopt the journalism ethics of other parts of the world. There is Syria at your door. There are Iran, Iraq, Armenia, Greece. There is a circle around you. A Turkish diplomat is not the same as a Portuguese diplomat. He/she has a meal and a nice invitation and sleeps at the end of a nice day. For Turkish diplomats, crypts work until the morning. (Aktüel, 14 March 1996)

This extract again contains nationalism and conspiracy. At the same time, it shows the media acting like a government even at the expense of such values of professional journalism as impartiality. The first example was the outcome of a very planned and organized act of the two media groups to support the policies of the government, whereas this one is of a spontaneous reaction. They are both nationalist. That the media's owner is not the state does not mean that the media is completely separate from the state. On the contrary, there is a close relationship between the state and the private media.

Since civil rights and freedom have been limited and damaged mainly by the military coups and the following 'civilian' governments with a military perspective: the state has had a role in banning, censoring and restricting the media. What should be mentioned here is that it is the radical media that suffer more from the legal and illegal power[14] of the state whereas, for the mainstream media, self-censorship is an issue more related to financial worries, and, moreover, they can use the discourse of press freedom even though the issue is only of protecting commercial interests. For example, after the elections, which brought the coalition government lead by Necmettin Erbakan (the Welfare Party) and Tansu Çiller (the True Path Party), Erbakan stated that they would restrict the promotion and opportunities for the payment for big media companies from public funds. The media refer to this as war and censorship. The Doğan Group in particular reacted strongly to this and Erbakan was labelled as the enemy of the media and democracy.[15] After a month, the law to restrict promotion was vetoed by the president.

Sönmez summarizes the economic relationship between the state and media very well: according to him, the state has power over the media through the price of paper, official advertisements, cheap credit from the state banks, the advertising budget of the state institutions, investment promotions, and, probably peculiar to Turkey, through hidden payments from the Prime Ministry as an incentive or punishment (Sönmez 1996: 77). What happened between 1990 and 1994, when TRT's monopoly was broken by 'delegalization' (rather than 'deregulation)' (Şahin & Aksoy 1993: 34), illustrates these close connections between the media and the state. This four-year period, before the new legal arrangement allowing the creation of private TV stations came into force, saw the actual start of commercial broadcasting. The fact that the regulation was so delayed is worth considering: commercial channels made regular use of lobby activity, using their close connection to government, and exploited this situation in which there was no legal obligation upon them (Kaya 1994: 397). As Aksoy states, this four-year period without rules was sufficient for the private media companies to gain time to settle down. The new Radio and TV Law obliged the private channels, which receive a national allowance from the RTÜK (Radio-Television Supreme Council), to extend their transmissions to at least 70 per cent of the country.

Changes in legal regulations, the effects of the EU candidacy in the 2000s

Legal regulations are important to show 'the freedoms of and constraints of communication' that demonstrate the type and quality of public sphere. As has been shown, this freedom has been contested in Turkey during the 1990s, but Turkey's EU candidacy has changed the perspective.

Concerning the principles of broadcasting in the earlier law on communication, İrvan (1999: 264–5) argues that what is intended to be protected by this law is the official state, ideology and the big companies. Furthermore, the principles, which aim to protect social life – such as protecting against unfair competition – are not applied in practice. In 2002 changes were made to the broadcasting law but it is reasonable to conclude that İrvan's argument is still valid.[16] The new RTÜK law (no: 4676) of 7 June 2001 was vetoed by the President Ahmet Necdet Sezer just eleven days later. The law, that had attracted reaction from many actors who agreed with the President, was approved for the second time by the Parliament (202 MPs voted for, while 87 'Islamic' Saadet Party MPs voted against). The President then sent the law to the Constitution Court, claiming that some of the clauses were unconstitutional. The Court annulled some clauses including the one on the composition of RTÜK. Following the Parliament amendment of the Constitution, a new RTÜK board was appointed.

The regulation of the media involves different, competing, interests: media owners who wish to protect their property; audiences, with their demands of access; civil society organizations wishing to access media to express and disseminate their opinions; society's interest in realizing a public interest function; and government, which protects citizens' rights and the right to address its opinions to them (Splichal, 1999: 298). When we look at the process of preparing the law, it is seen that the interests of government and media owners, again, become dominant while the ideas of other actors[17] are not sufficiently sought. The neglect of 'structural' or 'external' pluralism in terms of the plurality of actors affects 'internal' pluralism to a great extent in terms of content pluralism, programme quality and diversity, and the existence of different views (for theoretical discussions see Ward 2001; Porter 1993) .

The Situation described by İrvan about the issue of 'application' of the law and regulations still continues: when we look at the penalties given by the Radio-Television Supreme Council (RTÜK) during the years 1994–2002, it is seen that RTÜK explains that these *irticacı*, (a word which implies 'radical Islamist'), and 'separatist' channels constituted 94 per cent of all channels that were penalized (Özdiker 2002), which shows the narrow range of the official ideology. It is possible to argue that the principles of broadcasting protect the state: RTÜK controls mostly content and the channels which are 'against the state' are punished according to this control. On the other hand, on the negative outcome of market mechanisms, 'structural' reflections are not taken into consideration as much as ones related to content. The basic task of RTÜK (now the duty of Telecommunication Institution), frequency allocation, has not been implemented for years, while frequencies are being used freely by the big media groups' TV channels. RTÜK does not do much in terms of either protecting pluralism or struggling against concentrated media; its control of the advertising rules has been especially criticized: RTÜK gets 5 per cent from advertisement income, accepted silently in by consensus of the media, already winners of the game through non-payment for frequencies (Atabek 1999: 256). The problem is, as Pekman (2001a: 344–46) points out, advertisements transmitted without obeying the rules also violate consumer rights.

As seen above, the position of TRT is also different from public service broadcasting in many European countries. All these show that media systems develop in a parallelism with political systems and differ according to the dynamics of each country's specific history, conditions and social change (Kaya 1985). The source of difference, according to Erol Mutlu, (1999) is political culture. Bülent Çaplı explains this as the 'professional culture' of broadcasters, which shows whether media professionals are weak and, therefore, defer to the state or the media owners (Çaplı 2001). The question of how this professional culture is related to changing times can be answered by both the political culture and the political economic structure. It seems meaningless to talk about resistance when we remember that media professionals in Turkey are not members of the trade union because of pressure from media owners.

The differences between media policies in Turkey and European countries are explained broadly by both the determinacy of political culture and political-economic structure (Kejanlıoğlu et.al. 2001: 138). However, the same authors argue that to change the rules and their application in accordance with the international regulations, or harmonizing RTÜK with those of the European countries, is not meaningful because in Europe commercialization is prioritized over freedom of communication. Even though the author of this chapter does not take the European Union as an ideal model, and does not believe that harmonizing with Europe can solve all the problems, it is claimed here that EU will have positive effects on media policy in Turkey which, as a candidate, is in the process of harmonization.

The European Union has had effects on politics more broadly in Turkey, which will eventually affect media policies. The EU, with the 'culture and tradition of law' (Çelebi 2002: 49) in accordance with the European Human Rights Convention, the European Union Basic Rights Charter, the EU Copenhagen Criteria, and the Amsterdam Treaty, has a democratizing effect on political culture and communication in Turkey through the legal changes made in order to be considered as a member of the EU.

The adaptation process has contributed to the reduction of the power of the post-1980 military coup's state-centred legacy, at least in the legal regulations. It is obvious that the democratization of politics also affects the media. There have been many improvements in freedom of thought and expression and organization; in the protection of human rights and in gender inequality, following the enactment of the first and second series of adoption law (İlkiz 2003).

The law (4771) enacted on 3 August, 2002, in accordance with the third series of adoption laws, is one of the most important steps in terms of realizing the Copenhagen criteria (ibid: 59). The abolition of capital punishment has been one of the least-expected developments, both in Turkey and the European Union. There have also been developments in 'strengthening the legal guarantees of freedom of thought and expression' in accordance with the European Human Rights Convention (ibid: 60). Furthermore, it also abolished the law which banned broadcasting in different languages and dialects. As Timisi (2003) argues, that was a big challenge to the definition of national identity, until then constituted in official discourse.[18] Some EU-supported research and training projects and local, alternative, media initiatives can also be evaluated positively, with their role of strengthening civil society and the public sphere (see Gencel Bek 2003).

Conclusion

In this chapter, an attempt has been made to draw a map of the media and public sphere in Turkey. To summarize the two decades: 1960 was a year of only print press and radio, whereas the year of 1980 had TRT public service broadcasting, which started on air at the end of the 1960s. In the year 2000, we see a proliferation of commercial radio and TV stations which started in 1990. Aksop's (2003) categorization of the media industry is a very helpful attempt to understand the historical changes: until the 1950s, the form of production in journalism was based on artisan-like production without professionally-segmented division of labour and each person participated in different levels of production. The factory-like form of production has since become dominant. The 1980s brought industrialization and professionalization, led by the vision of globalization: we start to talk about the *media* rather than the *press*.

This chapter has underlined the dominant discourse that has been developed, especially since the 1980s, in Turkey that the private sector, thus also the private media, is democratic. Attributing all positive and democratizing characteristics to the private sector, by representing the issue as the dichotomy of state and media, has been a strategy used frequently by the private media in recent times. Private broadcasting, which started in the 1990s, can be seen as a cause of this idealization since it is more diverse than, and different from, state broadcasting. Thus, in comparison with the TRT channels, they have been called champions of democracy. Another source is the strong state that has violated basic civil rights. In this environment, it is rational to claim freedom from the state, even if this has been done for commercial interests. The large media groups have used the discourse of press freedom even when their economic profits are under threat as a result of the regulations of the state. The discourse of press freedom is very common and powerful in Turkey in an environment in which the citizens cannot fully exercise their rights and freedoms because of the strong state. The strong state prevents the development of the understanding of citizenship and the 'public', e.g. public interest, public communication and, in some sense, contributes to this view of the market as a democratic alternative.

Thus, the absence of the understanding of public, and public service broadcasting, and the weakness of civil rights can make the private sector seem as if it were democratic. Although there is nothing wrong in describing the state and state broadcasting as official or totalitarian, automatically attributing to private broadcasting characteristics such as freedom or diversity is worrying.

There are many reasons why we should be cautious about the private media in terms of democracy. The private media can threaten democracy with their concentrated and conglomerated structure. Involvement in other businesses can lead media owners to promote these by using the media: limiting the issues that would be news, or distorting them as a result of their commercial interests. The media conglomerates aggregate their power for maximizing their commercial profit through advertisements, and other strategies of competition, as can be seen from the examples given. The main motive of the private media institutions is maximizing profit, which has a potential for the restriction of information.

The private media has a close relationship with the state, despite the media professionals' claim that, as the media is strong through its own financial resources such as advertisements, it is independent of the state. In fact, they can unify their power for the national interest or for the government, which may be explained by the general situation of the private sector in Turkey: they were created and developed by the state, and partly because of that, they did not challenge the state. Since the private media was subject to economic reward or punishment by the government, it reported news in a partisan way, championing one candidate, party or programme. Big media groups get hidden payments from the government, in addition to the common economic support mechanisms such as official advertisement credits from state banks, and investment promotions. The return for these payments is support for the government, political party or political candidates, and the embracing of the government's policy or even the military view when the issue is of national interest.

Showing the limits and the dangers of both the state and the market is a starting point for creating the conditions for democratic communication. What needs to be done to create democratic communication in Turkey is to change the restrictive legal structure, to end the legal and illegal power of the state over civil rights, and to transform state broadcasting into public service broadcasting. In addition to these actions, it is necessary to curb the concentrating and conglomerating power of the media.

It seems that the Turkey's EU membership will at least contribute to the first necessity – changing the state-centred legal structure and limiting the state power in politics – even though the EU has not yet had any effect on the second necessity – curbing the irresponsible power of the market. Without that, it will be a partial improvement since freedom of communication is not only guaranteed through the absence of negative dimension, i.e. the freedom from the state, but also through the existence of conditions for freedom. If we remember the unbalanced income distribution, and the statistics showing unequal access to resources, computer and Internet, and if it is accepted that freedom can only be achieved together with equality, it is possible to say that there is still no public policy prospect which targets a fair redistribution of resources at national, regional and global levels.

Notes

1. In the mid 1930s, Turkish music was banned on the radio. The ban lasted almost two years. Education about classical Turkish music was also banned. Özbek suggests that, since the tradition was considered as backward in accordance with the ideology of modernization, the new Republic wanted to disassociate itself from the Ottoman culture completely. She argues that this ban was an indicator of the preference of a new path which is based on Western values (Özbek 1991: 146).

2. Yunus Nadi, MP and businessman, established *Cumhuriyet* in 1924 to struggle against the Caliphate supporters and Republic enemies (*Cumhuriyet* means Republic in Turkish). Kemalism, especially with the principle of secularism, gives *Cumhuriyet* its character (Karaca 1994).

3. For example, the stabilization programme, which will be discussed below, was actually brought before the MP government, but could not be applied until it was guaranteed by the military. Özal, the leader of the MP, was the ex-chairman of one of the leading employers' unions, The Union of Metal Goods Industrialist (MESS), top level manager of Sabancı Holding and the designer of the stabilisation programme in the State Central Planning (DPT). In fact, business groups complained about high wages and this was another issue addressed in the Stabilisation Programme. It was also included by General Kenan Evren in his first speech to the public following the military coup in 1980.

4. MP won a majority of 212 Assembly seats in the November 1983 elections, increasing its representation to 237 in the elections of September, 1986 and remained as the ruling party until it was replaced by the TPP in November, 1991.

5. It was in fact Ozal himself who showed the way for private broadcasting. He mentioned that although it was not legal to set up private television channels on Turkish soil because of the Constitution, broadcasting from abroad is not illegal. Following his explanation in late 1989, Magic Box started broadcasting from Germany (Şahin & Aksoy 1993, p. 33). Thus, the first private television channel, Magic Box was owned by Uzanlar and Ahmet Özal, who is the son of Turgut Özal.

6. The effects of the private media on TRT have not led TRT to broaden its perspective, but instead what Murdock calls 'commercialising the public sector' (Murdock 1990: 11) by 'making the success in the market place the major criterion for judging the performance of all communications' (Murdock and Golding 1989: 180). As the TRT director general states, TRT aims to increase its rating and advertising income in order to compete with the private channels. He mentions that TRT news should contain all ideas and parties equally, but adds that they have a responsibility to work on behalf of the state. The problems with TRT news, according to him, are that it is too long, and the presenters are too serious (see *Ekonomist*, 7 .6. 1998, pp. 74–76). It seems TRT is comparing itself with the private media, but what has been arrived at as a conclusion is not a need to transform the state channel into a public service channel, but rather to commercialize it with some changes in appearance.

7. The Doğan group co-operated with Time-Warner in 1999 and established CNN Türk news channel. The same group also signed agreements with Nortel Networks, Compaq and Microsoft on the sector of Internet network and expanded to new media. The Doğuş group signed agreement with MSNBC interactive (composed of Microsoft and General Electric NBC News). Digi-Türk as a product of the Doğan-Çukurova partnership signed a technical infrastructure investment agreement with Philips. As Doğan group directors mentioned during their purchase of 51% of Çevik family's Turkish Daily News, this means another step taken in order not be left outside the globalization trend for the group. In 2006, we witnessed more foreign capital investment such as

Murdoch buying the TV channel TGRT and Axel-Springer purchasing some shares of Doğan TV company.

8. Since this chapter was first written in 2004 it did not include the developments which took place in the last few years. It should be mentioned here that Sabah and ATV group were purchased in 2008 by the Çalık group which is close to the AKP and 'Anatolian-peripheral capital', whose manager in fact is the son-in-law of Prime Minister Tayyip Erdoğan. It is possible to talk about the rise of the pro-AKP media during the AKP rule.

9. Generally everybody who collects the coupons from the newspapers for a certain period, such as a few weeks, months or a year, can obtain the product through the distribution agents of the newspapers. The big prizes can be organized through draws. Or, sometimes readers have to pay extra payments in order to claim the product.

10. The campaign was started by *Sabah* at the suggestion of the owner, Dinç Bilgin, at the end of 1992. The Meydan Larousse encyclopaedia promotion increased *Sabah's* circulation while adversely affecting that of the other newspapers, especially *Hürriyet* and *Milliyet*. They also arranged similar promotion campaigns by claiming that the encyclopaedia they were offering had better paper quality. The war continued with the Doğan and Bilgin groups promoting their newspapers very aggressively and attacking each other on their TV channels.

11. For example, Doğan Group's magazine called EP Ekonomi Politika published an investigation on 28.3.1993 about Kemal Uzan who is the owner of Star TV, a banker, and a tradesman. The magazine gave information on how Uzan became rich with the support of the state during the MP (Motherland Party) government in a corrupt way. Kahraman states that the day the magazine was published, Uzan made contact with Aydın Doğan who is the owner of the magazine, and threatened him with using Star TV against the Doğan group. Then, the directives were given by Aydın Doğan to collect all the magazines in the market. The editor of the magazines, and the journalist who carried out the investigation and wrote in the magazine were dismissed (Kahraman, 1996, p. 256). This shows how the owners can use their media as weapons against each other, and by doing so, how they can limit the media content. In fact, Cem Uzan from Uzan group participated in the last elections as a candidate from Genç Party. By using their newspaper Star and their TV channel Star, they carried a campaign against the current AKP government and Doğan media group.

12. These days were holiday for the journalists. In addition, the Turkish Journalists Association used to publish newspapers on these days and use the income for the association. This challenge by Sabah can be explained more in terms of its ambition as a newspaper to compete with the other well-established newspapers

13. Kahraman (1996, pp 275–276, 347–348) traces the policy of the media on the Kurdish issue. He states that when Demirel was the Prime Minister, he asked for support from the press for three months until the struggle with the PKK was over. The support meant not writing anything except the official announcements. The press obeyed. Later, Demirel asked for another six months of full support from the press. After that, there was no need to ask, he argues, because the press had become like a voluntary guard. Press support has been seen as one of the most important elements of total war by the MGK (The National Security Council). The task of the press was described as maintaining the psychological war in the name of the state. According to this, the press was expected to publish only the information provided by the state. There was not to be any research or interviews in the press. The psychological war would be intensive, using just official information. MGK declared that the number of deaths reported amongst the PKK was to be increased in the press.

14. For the regular reports, see www.bianet.org.
15. Also, an alliance has been witnessed: their worries over profits were linked with the secular worries of the Kemalist social democrat parties (see *Milliyet*,7.7.1996, 8.7.1996, 13.8.1996).
16. For the law numbered 4756 see *Resmi Gazete*, 21.05.2002, no: 24761.
17. Especially local media and Internet organizations tried to reach the public in different ways: (BİA,www.bianet.org, 13.4.2002, 26.4.2002, 27.4.2002).
18. Timisi (2003) also evaluates the process of preparing a new directive by RTÜK on this issue and warns against the tendency of granting this right in the local area rather than nationwide. If it is not extended nationwide, as she points out, locality will be described as a common geography rather than common language. Therefore, people who do not live in the same area, but live in different regions of the country, will be unable to use that freedom of broadcasting in their native language, which could only be used by the communities inhabiting in the same region.

References

Aksop, G. (2003) *Türk Medya Sektöründe Mülkiyet ve Kontrol İlişkileri (1980-2003)*, unpublished Ph.D thesis, Ankara Üniversitesi, Sosyal Bilimler Enstitüsü.

Aksoy, A. (1995) 'TV'lerde Taş Devri', *Ekonomik Forum*, Kasım, pp. 16-20.

Aksoy A. & Robins K. (1997) 'Peripheral vision': Cultural industries and cultural identities in Turkey', *Paragraph*, Vol. 20, No.1, pp. 75-100.

Alankuş, S. (1995) TR'de medya, hegemonya ve ötekinin temsili', *Toplum ve Bilim*, no: 67, pp. 76-110.

Atabek, Ü. (1999) 'Üst Kurul'un Yap(a)madıklarına Eleştiri', *İletişim*, 1, pp. 253-261.

Ayata, Ayşe (1993): 'Ideology, Social Bases, and Organizational Structure of the Post – 1980 Political Parties' in (eds.) A. Eralp, M. Tünay & B. Yeşilada, *Political and Socioeconomic Transformation of Turkey*, pp. 31-49.

Aziz, A. (1993) 'TRT-Siyasal Yapı İlişkisi: Dünü, Bugünü, Yarını', *İletişim Fakültesi Yıllığı*, Ankara Üniversitesi, pp. 45-61,

Birtek Faruk & Toprak Binnaz (1993): 'The Conflictual Agendas of Neo-Liberal Reconstruction and the rise of Islamic Politics in Turkey: the Hazards of Rewriting Modernity', *Praxis International*, Vol. 13 No. 2., pp. 192-212.

Corner, J. (2003) 'Finding data, reading patterns, telling stories: Issues in the historiography of television', *Media, Culture and Society*, vol. 25, no. 2, pp. 273-280.

Çaplı, B. (2001) *Televizyon ve Siyasal Sistem*, Ankara: İmge.

Çelebi, A. (2002) *Avrupa: Halkların Siyasal Birliği*, Istanbul: Metis.

Dahlgren, P. (1995) *Television and the public sphere*, London: Sage.

Demirkent, N. (1995) *Medya medya*, İstanbul: Dünya.

Erel, N. & A. Bilge. (1995) *Tansu Çiller'in Siyaset Romanı*, 3rd.edn., Ankara: Bilgi.

Gencel Bek, M. (2003) 'Küreselleşme, Ulus-Devlet ve İletişim: Avrupa Birliği'nin Türkiye'deki İletişim Politikalarına Etkisi Üzerine Bir Değerlendirme', in Mine Gencel Bek, (ed.) *Küreselleşme, İletişim Endüstrileri ve Kimlikler, Avrupa Birliği ve Türkiye'de İletişim Politikaları*, Ankara: Ümit, pp. 237-86.

Gencel Bek, Mine (2004): 'Research note: Tabloidization of news media', *European Journal of Communication*, 19 (3): 371-86.

Göle, Nilüfer *(1994)*: 'Toward An Autonomization of Politics and Civil Society in Turkey', *in* M. Heper, A. Evin, (eds.) *Politics in The Third Turkish Republic*, San Francisco-Oxford: Westview Press Boulder p. 213-23.

Görgülü, G. (1991) *Basında Ekonomik Bağımlılık ve Tekelleşme,* Istanbul: TGC Pub.

Groc, G. (1994) 'Journalists as champions of participatory democracy' in M.Heper & A.Evin (eds.) *Politics in the Third Turkish Republic,* San Fransisco & Oxford: Westview Press, pp.199–210.

Gülalp, Haldun (1985): 'Patterns of Capital Accumulation and State-Society Relations in Turkey' *Journal of Contemporary Asia,* Vol.15, No.3, pp. 329–348.

Güvenir, M. (1991) *İkinci Dünya Savaşında Türk Basını,* İstanbul: Gazeteciler Cemiyeti.

Heper, Metin (1985): *The State Tradition in Turkey,* Walkington: The Ethoen Press.

Heper, Metin (1994): 'Turgut Özal's Presidency: Crisis and the Glimmerings of Consensus', in M. Heper & A. Evin (eds.) *Politics in the Third Turkish Republic,* San Francisco, Oxford, Boulder: Westview Press, p. 187–99.

Heper, M. & T. Demirel (1996) 'The press and the consolidation of democracy in Turkey', *Middle Eastern Studies,* Vol.33, No.2, pp. 109–23.

İlkiz, F., (2003) 'Yakın Tarihimizde İktidarların Basına Yaklaşımı', in Doğan Tılıç (ed.) *Türkiye'de Gazetecilik,* Ankara: ÇGD pp. 37–63.

İrvan, S. (1999) 'Radyo Televizyon Yasası ve Yayın İlkeleri', *İletişim,* 1, pp. 262–67.

Kahraman, A. (1996) *Cici Basının Sefalet ve Rezaleti,* İstanbul: Tüm Zamanlar Pub.

Karaca, E. (1994) *Cumhuriyet Olayı,* İstanbul: Altın kitaplar yay.

Karpat, H. K. (1964) 'Turkey', in R.Deward. D.A.Rustow (eds.), *Political Modernization in Japan and Turkey,* Princeton: Princeton University Press, pp. 255–82.

Kaya Raşit (1985): Kitle İletişim Sistemleri. Ankara, Teori.

Kaya, R. (1994) 'A fait-accompli: Transformation of media structures in Turkey', *METU Studies in Development,* 21: 3, pp. 383–404.

Kejanlıoğlu, B., Adaklı G. & Çelenk S. (2001) 'Yayıncılıkta Düzenleyici Kurullar ve RTÜK', in Beybin Kejanlıoğlu, Sevilay Çelenk & Gülseren Adaklı, (eds.) *Medya Politikalar,* Ankara: İmge, pp. 93–144.

Keyman Fuat (1995): 'On the Relation Between Global Modernity and Nationalism: The Crisis of Hegemony and Rise of (Islamic) Identity in Turkey' *New Perspectives on Turkey, Vol* 13, pp. 93–120.

Kocabaşoğlu, U. (1984) 'Türkiye'de Basın: 1919-1938 Dönemi Basınına Toplu Bakış', *Basın 80-84,* ÇGD yay, pp. 37–89.

Koloğlu, O. (1994) *Osmanlı'dan Günümüze Türkiye'de Basın,* 2nd. edn, İstanbul: İletişim.

Murdock, G. (1990) 'Redrawing the map of the communications industries: Concentration and ownership in the era of privatization', in M. Ferguson (ed.), *Public communication, The new imperatives,* London: Sage, pp. 1–15.

Murdock, G. & Golding, P.(1989) 'Information poverty and political inequality: Citizenship in the age of privatised communications', *Journal of Communication,* 39: 3, pp. 180–195.

Mutlu, E. (1999) *Televizyon ve Toplum,* Ankara, TRT.

Münir, M. (1993) *Sabah Olayı, Sabah ve Dinç Bilgin'in Öyküsü,* İstanbul: Altın Kitaplar Pub.

Oktay, A. (1987) *Toplumsal Değişme ve Basın,* İstanbul, BFS.

Özbek, M. (1991) *Popüler Kültür ve Orhan Gencebay Arabeski,* İstanbul: İletişim.

Özdiker, C. (2002) 'Basın, Temiz Toplum ve "Medya Terörü" üzerine', *RTÜK İletişim,* Mart-Nisan, pp. 10–12.

Pekman, C. (2001) 'Kararan Ekranlardan Görünmeyenler', *Yıllık 1999, Özel sayı: Sinema ve Televizyon,* A.Ü.İLEF, pp. 335–51.

Porter E. Michael (1990): *The Competitive Advantage of Nations,* London, Macmillan pub.

Robins Kevin (1996): 'Interrupting Identities, Turkey/Europe, in S. Hall, P. du Gay (eds.) *Questions of Cultural Identity,* London: Sage, pp. 61–86.

Sönmez, M. (1996) 'Türk Medya Sektöründe Yoğunlaşma ve Sonuçları', *Birikim:* Aralık, pp. 76–87.

Splichal, S. (1999) *Public opinion, developments and controversies in the twentieth century*, Lanham, Boulder, New York, Oxford: Rowman & Littlefield.

Şahin, H. & Aksoy, A. (1993) 'Global media and cultural ıdentity in Turkey', *Journal of Communication*, 43: 2, pp. 31–42.

Sayarı Sabri (1992): 'Politics and Economic Policy-Making in Turkey, 1980–1988', in *Economics and Politics of Turkish Liberalization*, (eds.) T. Nas, M. Odekan, London-Toronto, Associated University Press, pp. 26–43.

Tartanoğlu, A. (1994) *Baskın Basın'ın mı?* Ankara: ÇGD.

Timisi, N. (2003) 'Anadilde Yayın: Avrupa Birliği ve Türkiye' in Mine Gencel Bek (ed.) *Küreselleşme, İletişim Endüstrileri ve Kimlikler, Avrupa Birliği ve Türkiye'de İletişim Politikaları*, Ankara: Ümit, pp. 97–134.

Tunçay, M., (1995) 'Siyasal Tarih (1950–1960)', in Sina Akşin (ed.) *Çağdaş Türkiye* 4, 1908–1980 (4th edn), İstanbul, Cem Pub., pp. 177–84.

Ward, D. (2001) 'The democratic deficit and the European Union communication policy', *Javnost*, 8: 1, pp. 75–94.

Part V

Records of Cultural Change

Chapter 9

Reconsidering the Paradox of Parochialism and the Shrinking News Agenda

Daniel Biltereyst & Lieve Desmet
Ghent University

We still live and think very much as local and national citizens and not as the European and global citizens we are also slowly becoming. The rising gap between the A-team of globalisation, the global elites of politics, finance and media, and the B-team of ordinary national citizens is already very visible round this turn of a new millennium which will most certainly mean a rise in a virtual technological globalisation and a cultural and social globalisation in real time. (Bondebjerg 2001)

Introduction

In his classical *One day in the world's press* (1959), Wilbur Schramm argued that the amount and shape of foreign news is a good indicator for the state of the news media. Half a century later and after many more research projects, this might still be true. Witness the growing concerns and the public debate about the continuing bias on the coverage of foreign and international news, most notably on the coverage of military conflicts and interventions. The debate deals with questions on the supposed shrinking foreign and international news agenda, illustrating, so to say, a growing parochialism in our news media. It is about the fear that the ongoing globalization of public and private life is not reflected in the news. Critics even claim that the pervasive commercialization and popularization of the media lead to a decrease in hard, serious news – most notably a decrease in foreign and international news.[1]

This lament over the shrinking output of foreign and international news has been repeated over the last decade or so, not at least by leading journalists, concerned intellectuals, politicians and academics (e.g. Franklin 1997; Hallin 1996: 255; Utley 1997). In Britain, for instance, Anthony Sampson (1996, in Tumber, 1999) talked about a 'crisis at the heart of our media'. Writing about the British press and the broadsheets in particular, Sampson claimed that:

The most serious change in the broadsheet papers, I believe, has been the fading of serious foreign news. The world is disappearing out of sight. Foreign correspondents – those that remain – are discouraged from serious analysis…The retreat from the world is all the more worrying because the world since the Cold War has never been more important to follow, more exciting, fast-changing and relevant to Britain's future. (Sampson in Tumber 1999: 204)

Referring to US media, John Tomlinson (1999: 171) mentioned a similar paradox, indicating that as 'the technological capacity and sophistication of the global media expand, news coverage of foreign events on television seems to be shrinking.' Another notorious critic is Claude Moisy (1997), the former AFP general manager, who talked about an 'inescapable paradox'. The paradox referred to the situation where the 'amazing increase in the capacity to produce and distribute news from distant lands has been met by an obvious decrease in consumption' (p. 79). For Moisy, 'this is certainly true for the United States, but it appears that the same phenomenon exists, to some degree, in most developed societies' (p. 79).

In this age of hyper-commercialism (McChesney 2004) and infotainment (Thussu 2007), the "packaging and selling of news and arguably the nature of news reported" has led to the rise of soft news and consumer journalism (Harrison 2006: 15), leading to a decline in the amount and quality of foreign news reporting "especially about and from the developing world" (Thussu 2004: 47). The paradox on the narrowed news agenda with considerably less foreign/international news has become a classic argument for those who wish to prove dumbing-down tendencies in the media. The tendency towards journalistic parochialism is then often treated as a structural issue on how a hyper-commercial market conception of the media transforms vital 'hard news' into softer, more sensationalist formats. In this competitive media environment, most foreign or international news items are seen as too complex and expensive to cover. Only the very big foreign news items (e.g. the Gulf War, the US invasion of Iraq, the war in Afghanistan) survive, so critics claim. News media tend to address the audience more than ever as local or national consumers, detached from overall globalizing tendencies.

The news parochialism paradox throws up many other questions, including those on the (perceived) overall tendency in the West towards isolationism or the growing indifference to the world. The issue also fits into the debate about limits to the practices of globalization and the role of information and communication technologies (Biltereyst 2001; Tomlinson 1999), as well as into wider considerations upon the media's function in disseminating public knowledge. The news parochialism paradox (possibly) illustrates the declining potential for a free, democratic communication system, undermining the myth of the news media's central democratic functions of informing the citizen. It relates to the media's social responsibility and to the civic ideal of making it possible for citizens to have access to relevant information. From this perspective, news has been considered the 'lifeblood of our kind of culture' (Bird 1998), or as a central object of 'rational-critical debate within the realm of the public sphere', given the 'decisive role the news media play in establishing a discursive space' (Allan 1999: 4). It is seen as the common ground for informing citizens about what happens in society as well as about foreign cultures.

In this chapter we focus upon the validity of these alarming arguments on the shrinking foreign news output. First we describe some central issues in the study of foreign/international news research, followed by a discussion of the recent debate on the parochialism paradox. In the second, more empirical, part we rely upon some recent comparative research projects on the issue, including the European comparative and historical news analysis on which most chapters in this book are based. This chapter ultimately argues that the paradox should not be taken for granted too easily. Although there certainly are clear illustrations of a shrinking news agenda, we should not become infatuated by some idealizing nostalgia. More generally, we underline that more attention should be paid to the rapidly changing news media environment, which created new problems and opportunities as well. In this new information ecology, we must stay attentive and critical towards new forms of social exclusion, where the well-educated citizen, as well as a political and business elite is most willing to engage with and eventually pay for) a wider news media diet. Indicating that the shrinking news agenda might primarily refer to the more popular news media, the chapter ultimately links the paradox to wider questions on the growing information divide along education and cultural capital lines.

Foreign and international news, shrinking agenda and citizenship

International news research: from psychological warfare to the uninformed citizen

One of the strongest traditions in modern media and communication science is the study of the cross-border circulation of news and information. The tradition is intrinsically linked to the strategic use of mass communication and cross-border information technologies well before the Second World War (Simpson 1994). The practice of studying international and foreign news coverage goes back to, at least, the psychological and ideological warfare between the big European nations in the wake of the First World War and, afterwards, their ideological propaganda efforts during the inter-war period.

The research tradition is interesting because it deeply reflects the role of the media and information for changing power relations in geopolitical, military and wide political-economic terms. The different themes, touched by international and foreign news research, deals with some of the most central issues in communication research, notably those on the influence of the (mass) media in international diplomacy and military conflicts (propaganda, symbolic war, mass psychology). But research on foreign/international news was also related to other issues such as development, globalization and (what we are interested in here) the role of the media for informing democratic and cultural citizenship.

After the Second World War, growing east-west conflicts and their related international propaganda efforts again increased scholarly attention, while the discourse of world-wide modernization furthered research on the information flows between different people and nations (e.g. Zipf 1946). In the 1950 and 1960s, a growing amount of research, often inspired by UNESCO and other supranational institutions (e.g. Baechlin & Muller-Strauss 1951; IPI 1953; McNelly 1959; Schramm 1959; Unesco 1954), tried to understand the determinants in the international news flows and the bias in this type of news content. In one of the first huge international comparative research projects on the issue,[2] published half a century ago by the International Press Institute (IPI) (1953), the editors claimed that 'this study was undertaken because of the importance of foreign news not merely as 'news' but as information upon which the people of free countries base certain vital decisions' (1953: 3). From today's perspective, this IPI research project may seem highly Eurocentric in scope, but its results are still amazingly relevant. The report already referred to inadequacies in the coverage of foreign and international news items (p. 29); the 'natural bias of each correspondent' (p. 29); the 'spotty and incomplete' character, as well as the lack 'in continuity' and interpretation of foreign news (p. 33); and the influence of proximity as a news value in defining what is newsworthy (p. 67). Referring to the US situation, the report also throws up the question of the badly informed citizen:

> The average American reads very little of the foreign news published in his favourite newspaper. The level of his knowledge about important events abroad is low. He would not like to see national and local coverage reduced to allow his newspaper to print more foreign news. A major influence on his attitude toward international news is remoteness of foreign events from his own community and his daily life. Any increase in the attention he devotes to foreign news would appear to depend upon its being more closely related to the American scene. (IPI 1953: 57)

In the course of the 1960s and 1970s, the issue of studying international news content, sources and values, further developed in range and methodological sophistication. This increase was influenced by more critical questions on the biased coverage of Cold War conflicts (e.g. Galtung & Ruge 1965; Östgaard 1965) and by wider debates on the north-south dependency (e.g. Gerbner & Marvanyi 1977; Hester 1971; Masmoudi 1979). Several wide-scale, international comparative research projects tried to understand the dominance of Western Europe and North America (often indicated as the 'Centre') and their world news agencies, the under-representation of the Third World ('Periphery') and the overall bias in foreign news (e.g. dominance of politics, political figures, etc.). Researchers tried to understand this by looking at variables in the ownership of news exchange agencies, ownership of long distance telecommunication facilities, and concentration of wealth, technology and power in a few highly-developed nations (e.g. Sreberny-Mohammadi et al. 1984). Gate-keeper and news-value research tried to help understand news flows by addressing values such as the influence of regionalism, geographic or cultural proximity.

With the end of the Cold War, the collapse of the Soviet Union and the transformation of the communist bloc, the world map changed, not at least in a symbolic and cognitive sense (Sreberny-Mohammadi 1991; Wu 2000). Besides this new (geo)political constellation and the new world order, research on international news flows had also to take into account changes in technological and economic terms – both on the level of news production and distribution, as on the consumption/use/reception. More than ever, news became a commodity, given the overall liberalization and globalization of the news market, underlined by the gradual retreat of state interventions in the world of the big news agencies (e.g. TASS). Competition among the major news providers grew, while cost-effectiveness was a central concept on the managerial agenda. Ever since the end of the 1980s, the world of the traditional international news providers was dominated by a process of conglomeration and multimedia synergies – leading to a (completely western dominated) duopoly around AP and Reuters with huge interests in the production of words, images, photos, sounds, and so on. This process, however, was supplemented by the introduction of new technologies, not least digital Internet services, which revolutionized the news production and distribution market. New transnational news providers (e.g. CNN, Google) and practices (e.g. live reporting) came to the foreground, while the Internet became a special additional, but widely used source for news reporters and desk journalists.

Not only the world of the big international news providers changed. In this period, also wide-audience media such as television and newspaper companies were confronted by increased liberalization, competition and rationalization. Concentrating upon Western Europe, it is clear that these high concepts influenced foreign/international news coverage and choices. Audience maximalization was often translated into the intensification of proximity as a news value. In a competitive media landscape with commercially-driven mass communication, many foreign news items are seen as too complex, while proximity to the audience grows as a news value (Hjarvard 2000: 20). In the 1990s, new forms of presenting foreign news arose (e.g. news carousel system in television), while many news organizations cut into the costly network of correspondents and even seemed to limit their foreign news output.

A third level of wider changes, finally, deals with the reception or consumer side. The arrival of more television channels or the successful adoption of Internet services created in the 1990s a wider, completely new news ecology. Direct Internet access to digital news providers such as foreign digital newspapers seemed to dissolve geographical and temporal barriers in the consumption of news. This news environment opens up a nearly unlimited potential for news consumption.

These optimistic claims, however, have not been met with the actual audience's interest in foreign and international affairs. Besides the issue of the narrowing news agenda and the marginalization of 'the foreign' in the news media's output, there is a whole discourse on the uninterested and uninformed audience. This has been observed by several public opinion researches such as the regular surveys of the PEW Research for the People and the Press in the US (see also Tai & Chang 2002). This American survey reports how the American audience is interested in crime, local community news and health, while culture, the arts and, above all, international affairs are among the least interesting subjects. Even in its latest reports, published after 9/11, the PEW Research Center headlines that 'Americans lack background to follow international news' (Pew Research 2008: 38). The June 2002 report is quite depressing about the general audience's lack of interest in foreign news:

> The public's news habits have been largely unaffected by the Sept. 11 attacks and subsequent war on terrorism. Reported levels of reading, watching and listening to the news are not markedly different than in the spring of 2000. At best, a slightly larger percentage of

the public is expressing general interest in international and national news, but there is no evidence its appetite for international news extends much beyond terrorism and the Middle East...Traditionally, most Americans take only a passing interest in overseas developments, and the extraordinary events of the past year have done little to change that. Since 2000, there has been only a modest rise in the proportion of Americans who follow international news very closely from 14% to 21%. In addition, while slightly more say they pay close attention to overseas news most of the time (37% now, 33% in 2000), a solid 61% majority continues to follow international news only when something important happens. (Pew, Introduction and Section 111)

Besides the age variable, it seems that a crucial variable in interpreting audience interest is the education level:

Moreover, much of this increased interest has come among older, well-educated Americans groups that already showed disproportionately high interest in international news. More than a quarter of those age 50 and over (27%) say they follow international news very closely, up from 18% in 2000. College graduates are showing considerably more interest in overseas developments (33%, up from 21% in 2000). (ibid.)

To our knowledge, there are only very few examples of a similar systematic and longitudinal research effort in mapping out news audience preferences in other countries. Occasional studies, however, often go into a similar direction. In Belgium, for instance, research on news consumption indicates a positive correlation between a daily news consumption on the one hand, and education and age on the other hand (e.g. VRIND 2002: 122). A recent piece of research on foreign news consumption (Peeren & Biltereyst 2002: 83), which brings forward Bourdieu's notion of cultural capital, summarizes the importance of education and general cultural interest. The study makes a distinction between three groups, with on the two extremes a fairly large grouping of weakly-interested people with a middle- to lower-level of education. The other extreme is a rather small group of older, more highly-educated people. These analyses on the 'uninterested and badly informed' audience only reinforce the powerful lament over the state of the media's role in informing the citizen.

Hard claims about news parochialism

In his article 'Myths of the global information village', published in *Foreign Affairs* in the summer of 1997, Claude Moisy indicated how the major American newspapers and television stations had been cutting hard into their foreign news output. Moisy had been analysing the development of foreign news output ever since the 1970s. Due to commercial pressure and the reduced demand on the part of the audience, Moisy claimed, 'the share of foreign news in the US fell from 35 per cent to 23 per cent between 1970 and 1995, while the average length of those stories dropped from 1.7 minutes to 1.2 minutes' (Moisy 1997: 82). Moisy continued that 'while the American networks devoted on average more than 40 per cent of total news time to foreign items in the 1970s, that share had been cut to 13.5 per cent of news time by 1995.' Although this critical analysis only related to the major American television networks, it is clear that among the cable and satellite television stations, 'news programs in general – and foreign news in particular – seem to be disappearing in a flood of entertainment and niche-oriented channels' (ibid: 82).

What is interesting in Moisy's analysis is that he does not only blame un-responsible news media or the uninterested audience. For the influential former AFP chairman, the declining international and foreign news output is also due to the end of the Cold War, which has turned the world into a space which is increasingly more difficult to decipher. It had made an end at a 'user-friendly manicheism' (ibid: 81–83) in international news, while the convergent tendencies of globalization and localization reinforced the tendency to turn inward:

> An international marketplace where jobs go to the cheapest labourers has replaced nuclear confrontation…This fear is especially strong in many developed countries outside the United States where high levels of unemployment threaten national cohesion. In the United States, as in many other countries, the news horizon is tending to draw closer – from the international to the national and from the national to the local…There would be a certain irony in seeing our world turn local just as it was about to become global. (Moisy 1997: 83–4)

This hard diagnosis has been repeated by various other journalists and scholars ever since. In another *Foreign Affairs* article, titled 'The Shrinking of Foreign News', Garrick Utley (1997) argued that the major US networks stick close to home. The chief foreign correspondent for NBC News and ABC News claimed that foreign news coverage of the leading American networks had been halved over the past decade. Garrick referred to a *Tyndall Report*, showing how total foreign coverage on US network nightly news programmes had 'declined precipitously, from 3,733 minutes in 1989 to 1,838 minutes in 1996 at ABC, the leader, and from 3,351 minutes to 1,175 minutes at third-place NBC.'

A similar narrowed news agenda has been observed for US newspapers too. In a paper for the *American Society of Newspaper Editors*, the editor-in-chief Edward Seaton, claims that the decline in foreign news has even been more dramatic for newspapers:

> Time devoted to international news by network television declined from 45 percent in the 1970s to 13.5 percent in 1995. That is a 70 percent drop. Three-fourths of the drop has come since the end of the Cold War. And I am certain, given the current entertainment meltdown of U.S. network television news, the numbers are even lower today. Newspapers, which I know more about, never gave as large a percentage of their space to international news, but the decline in the amount they do allocate is even greater than television, from

10.2 percent in 1971 to something less than 2 percent today. That's a decline of more than 80 percent. (Seaton 1998)

Quite similar alarming analyses were taken up by media and communication scholars, such as Daniel Hallin (1996: 255), who found that international news in US newspapers 'has declined from 10.2 per cent of the news hole in 1971 to 2.6 per cent in 1988.' Talking about the United States too, John Tomlinson (1999: 171) stated that 'network coverage of foreign affairs has fallen by two thirds in two decades…and by 42 per cent between 1988 and 1996.' And he continued that similar trends could be observed in other developed countries such as the UK, where 'documentary output on international topics across all British terrestrial TV channels fell by 40 per cent between 1989 and 1994' (ibid: 171).

This tendency is not only confined to tabloids or widely-consumed, commercial news media, as a recent analysis of leading British quality newspapers indicates. Using 'less international news coverage as a possible indicator of tabloidization', Shelley McLachlan and Peter Golding (2000: 78–9) found that both *The Times* and *The Guardian* had shown a gradual decline. The results for *The Times* showed a continual decrease from a high of 3.7 stories per page in 1957 to a low of 0.4 per page in 1997. Following the same analysis, *The Guardian* had shown a 'general downward trend…from 2 international news stories per page in 1962 to a low of just 0.6 per page in 1992' (ibid: 79). Similar, though less alarming findings were reported in some other European countries such as Germany or France (e.g. Krüger 1997).

Besides this overall quantitative decrease in the time and number of foreign news stories, critics have also pointed to the dominance of the big international story in the news. Major news items such as Israel-Palestinian conflict, 9/11 or the Iraq invasion, tend to dominate the news, also in tabloid and wide-popular media. The 'big foreign story' syndrome might look like a corrective to the overall gradual decrease of foreign news, but finally it is not because all other foreign news items tend to be ignored. Audience research on foreign news preferences in the US (e.g. Tai & Chang 2002) indicate that the audiences only show a narrow interest in a limited category of foreign news stories, most clearly stories which drive for big dramatic stories (natural or human-made disasters, violence, wars and terrorism involving Americans, and natural disasters).

Finally, these hypotheses on the degradation of foreign news seem to have, in addition, a *qualitative* turn too. This relates to the way foreign and international news items are treated. The argument here is that in recent decades, Western news media did not only cut into the time and the amount of foreign news stories, but also that its presentation and format underwent significant changes. This can go from scheduling ever-shorter bits of foreign news stories at the end of the news programme to putting them into a carousel format with a repetitive musical tune beneath it. Also the use of the upbeat story before the foreign news carousel (i.e. announcing an up-coming story as a teaser) can be seen a 'marginalizing' technique in scheduling foreign items (Zillmann et al. 1994).

Another technique in 'softening' international news items deals with 'domestication'. This widely-researched practice refers to rendering foreign events relevant and comprehensible to domestic audiences (Gurevitch et al. 1991). Given the importance of cultural proximity as a news value, it seems to be necessary that international and foreign news stories must, more than ever, be domesticated in order to attract audience's attention.

These techniques all serve the purpose of softening the (often) hard character of foreign/international news, or to making it relevant and comprehensible to the citizens. So, it seems that not only the amount of foreign news is shrinking. Faced with increasing competition for ratings and with declining audiences for news (e.g. Bird 2000; Moisy 1997), foreign items seem to be marginalized and, as much as possible, domesticated, personalized and 'made relevant'. They are presented in a much more fragmented way than local news, often treated without any broader interpretation or context.

Questioning the paradox

Conceptual questions

The question, however, is whether these alarming analyses of this paradox on globalization and the news are legitimate, especially in Europe. As we have seen, there has been sufficient empirical evidence on the shrinking news agenda hypothesis for the US. Before going into some empirical data, it seems to be necessary, we think, to look more closely at the issue at stake. More specifically we need to taken into account wider technological and other shifts in the world of the news and the news ecology. The lament over the narrowing news agenda and the consequences for the media's role in society is powerful indeed, although there may be some weaknesses.

Before going into some empirical work, inspired by the RHACNA project, we need to go into some conceptual difficulties – mainly the one on defining foreign/international news in these times of globalization. We already referred to the new news services and the Internet in particular, which, as Stig Hjarvard (2000: 17) wrote, 'will gradually make the boundaries between national, foreign, and international news media less clear and obvious.' But more generally, we should return to theories on globalization and the recent reconfiguration of the state, the national, and the new geography of power. As such, and following Sassen (1998: 17), one can question whether 'many global economic and political processes can be seen as national or foreign, even when these processes are materialized…in national territories or when they go to a large extent through national institutional arrangements.' Given the globalizing tendencies and, in Europe, the integration process, it is questionable whether, 'we cannot simply assume that because a transaction takes place in national territory and in a national institutional setting it is ipso facto national' (ibid: 17). These overall changes make the very concept of foreign news highly questionable, let alone difficult to operationalize in concrete research.

Secondly, and more generally, we also have to look at the wider new news ecology in which we live. In an interesting article on the change of the concept of news in our advanced, late-capitalist societies, Simon Cottle (2000: 20) wrote how 'news has become an all-pervasive and an inescapable part of modern existence.' Traditional news has been transformed into a rich variety of cultural forms, from 24-hours news channels, print media, radio broadcasts to on-line technologies. In many countries a growing number of newspapers, radio and television channels, and other news providers offer new, interactive services, changing also the very nature of what is foreign news. In the US, UK and many other European countries virtually all newspapers and the vast majority of regional titles are present on the web in a digital format. The major broadcasters (e.g. BBC, France Télévision) and news agencies (e.g. Reuters) offer comprehensive Internet services. The growth of the Internet will only enhance the way people receive and use the bulk of their news information, including those on foreign societies.

Thirdly, even if we retain some strict definition of foreign and international news (no link with local and national reality), then it should be clear that most media still preserve this type of news coverage – even when it is compounded in one page, or, for television, at the end of the news in a fragmented and distracting carousel format. It shows that, in some way or another, there still is a forceful recognition of the necessity of (foreign) news for the civic ideal. Whatever the criticism on the amount and formats of foreign news stories, they have not disappeared.

This might be illustrated by the front page of the German tabloid par excellence, *Bild Zeitung* – which has often been considered one of the worst illustrations of dumbing-down tendencies in the European press. As we might see from Illustration 1, the newspaper dedicated quite some space on its front page to foreign and international news stories. Even the leading story is devoted to a major international item, i.e. the coverage of the 15th United Nations General Assembly in New York in September and October 1960. At this (often tumultuous) meeting of all UN member states, the world relations and ongoing conflicts were discussed, including the question of world security and the general East-West relations, the process of decolonization and the admission of new members, as well as more local conflicts such as the Congo crisis. The news media, from popular tabloids to more serious, highbrow newspapers, devoted much space to the debates at this historical 15th session of the General Assembly. In particular US President Eisenhower's speech on sovereignty (29 September 1960) and dramatic shoe-banging incident provoked by the Soviet leader Krushchev (12 October 1960) filled the time and space of nearly all news media in Europe and the world.

But also, on other days, the UN meeting occupied a prominent part of the news agenda, including some minor and dramatic stories. On 4 and 5 October, 1960, for instance, the front pages of most European newspapers focused upon how Krushchev and the Soviet delegation attacked Secretary-General Dag Hammarskjold, and not only the serious papers devoted ample space to the incident. This hard international political issue also openly appeared on the front of more popular papers such as *Bild Zeitung*. We may be surprised now to see that on the front pages but lots of other foreign news items appeal to the audience. In *Bild Zeitung*, these are mainly soft foreign news stories referring to France (on Brigitte Bardot) and one to Spain and Belgium (on the Spanish princess and future Belgian Queen Fabiola).

Jumping four decades further on, and taking into account *Bild*'s bad reputation, it is clear that sensationalist and human-interest national news dominates. But at the same time, we might be surprised by the relatively high amount of foreign and international news stories on 4 October (and other days) in 2000. Even on its front page, *Bild Zeitung* devoted ample space and a fixed category of short news items ('Nachrichten') for (even hard) foreign and international news items (e.g. news from the USA, Russia, the Czech Republic, Latin America).

Bild Zeitung front page on 4 10 1960.

Bild Zeitung front page on 4 10 2000.

Empirical evidence?

While this example might not be representative, we will have to get some more systematic research in order to map some more reliable changes in the output of foreign/international news. In this perspective, we can first look at the RHACNA data (see Section 2 and Appendix), which tried to grab the longitudinal changes for snapshots in the year 1960, 1980 and 2000. This longitudinal research project focused upon two days of news in the main serious/elite newspaper and the leading popular one.

What is interesting for the question of the shrinking news agenda hypothesis here is the geographical focus in the news. More specifically, we will focus upon the amount and share of non-domestic and non-national news. In Figure 1 we see that the news section, specially devoted to 'foreign news', is relatively small and tends indeed to decrease in some countries. This might be true for most countries, including the newspapers in Belgium, Finland, France, Germany, Poland and the UK.

In order to get a better, more nuanced view upon these changes, we proceeded to a more extended analysis of the situation in one EU member state, Belgium (see Peeren &

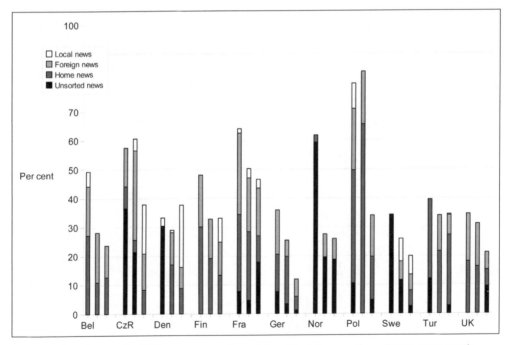

Figure 1: Share (per cent) of different news sections of the editorial news volume (1960, 1980, 2000).

Biltereyst 2002). This longitudinal research was based on a content analysis of the editorial news (no supplements, no advertising) for the years 1960, 1970, 1980, 1990 and 2000. Using the RHACNA coding scheme (see Appendix), we made a more detailed analysis of one continous and one selected week (12 days). Two newspapers were chosen: the leading socio-economic and political newspaper *De Standaard* (conservative, moderate Catholic, free-market orientation, Dutch-language, circulation of 76.000) and the leading popular newspaper *Het Laatste Nieuws* (right-wing liberal, free-market orientation, Dutch-language, circulation 287.000).

In order to be able to interpret the changes in foreign/international news output by both newspapers, it is important to draw some key features in the structural and socio-economic development of the Belgian/Flemish press. Up until the 1980s, the latter was characterized as a mid-market press (no real tabloids, no real elite quality daily newspaper); the main feature of distinction was its clear political orientation. The Belgian/Flemish press was the only politicized newspaper market, with extreme leftist, socialist, centre and right-wing newspapers.

In the 1970s and 1980s, the economic and social crisis worked only as a catalyst for a deeper process of de-politicization of the press sector. In this period, the state as well as political parties, trade unions and other ideologically-inspired social organizations withdrew from the press market, leaving open space for new forms of (capitalist) management. Besides a full-scale process of concentration, rationalization and competition, we also saw a different strategy to position the different newspapers. In the new market, dailies were differentiated no longer on an ideological axis, but more fully on the basis of cultural and socio-economic differences.

This all meant that, for instance, *De Standaard*, which was considered the flagship of the Flemish Catholic party, tried to get rid of this exclusive religious working ethos, while positioning it more fully as a quality newspaper for the political, business and intellectual elites. *Het Laatste Nieuws*, which was for nearly a century seen as a supporter of the Liberal party, moved more clearly into a more conservative populist newspaper with all characteristics of a tabloid (big headlines, stress on human interest and sensational stories, big photos, etc.).

This overall context of structural, managerial change is important in order to understand editorial and content-related choices. Looking more closely at the longitudinal content analysis for both newspapers, we see some striking similarities with the overall RHACNA results. First of all, there has been a tremendous growth in the overall editorial news output (Figure 2). For *De Standaard*, the number of editorial pages even doubled in forty years (from an average of 14.7 to 32.4 pages). Comparable to many other European newspaper markets since the Second World War, local Belgian newspapers have seen a tremendous growth in their daily news output, especially since the 1990s tendency of providing ever more supplements (which are not even included in these figures).

Looking more closely at the shrinking news agenda hypothesis, we analysed different features of what the newspaper identified as hard foreign and international news. Figures 3

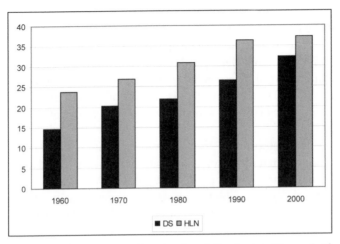

Figure 2: Average number of pages in *De Standaard and Het Laatste Nieuws* (without supplements, 1960–2000).

and 4 indicate that this hypothesis is not as clearly marked as one should have expected. For *De Standaard* we see that hard domestic news tends to be growing in the 1990s. But it clearly maintains an average of 2 to 3 pages of hard foreign news. In recent decades it even seems that foreign and international news has become a crucial feature in the play of distinction among the few quality papers in the market. A really significant shift, especially since the 1980s, in *De Standaard* has been the rocketing growth of economic news (from an average of 1 editorial page in 1960 to 8.8 pages in 2000), and to a lesser degree of culture (from 0.7 to 2.1 pages) and information on television and media (0.6 to 2.2). Hard news on internal, domestic affairs remained quite stable over the past four decades (from 3 to 3.3). This all means, of course, that the shrinking news hypothesis or the parochialism hypothesis is not confirmed in absolute figures. In relative terms we saw a decrease, of course, due to the overall growth in editorial material. Besides all this, it must be underlined that many items, not catagorized under 'foreign news', such as economics, culture and sports, often maintain foreign and international features.

The picture for the more popular newspaper, recently turned into a tabloid, is more revealing (Figure 4). Here we see indeed that the balance between hard domestic and foreign news ever more favoured the first. In four decades, we saw a weak decline in foreign news items (from 2 to 1.4 pages), although in the sample for 1990 the average news output increased due to the Gulf War. Hard domestic news, however, grew more clearly (from 1.9 to 4.8 pages). In *Het Laatste Nieuws,* local news (from 2.7 to 6.7 pages), sports (6 to 8.7) and television and media (0.6 to 3.3) were among the steady growers.

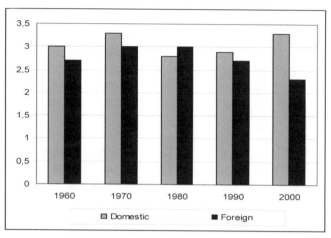

Figure 3: Average number of pages of domestic and foreign news in *De Standaard* (2 weeks, five years) (1960–2000).

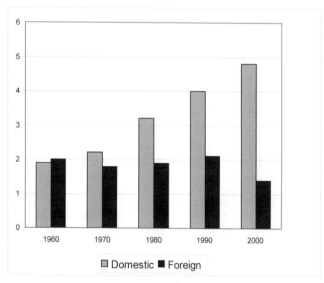

Figure 4: Average number of pages of domestic and foreign news in *Het Laatste Nieuws* (2 weeks, five years) (1960–2000).

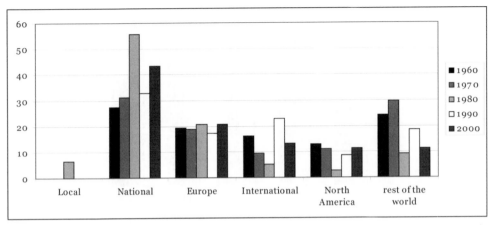

Figure 5: Geographical focus on the front page in *De Standaard* (2 weeks, five years) (1960–2000, per cent).

Quite similar tendencies can also be observed when looking more closely at the front-page stories only. Both newspapers tend to increase their national news stories, although this is more fully exploited in the tabloid (Figure 6). In *Het Laatste Nieuws* domestic news tend to significantly increase in importance, clearly to the detriment of other categories. Taking this code as an indicator of the paradox, we see that the tabloid saw its interest for non-western stories shrink.

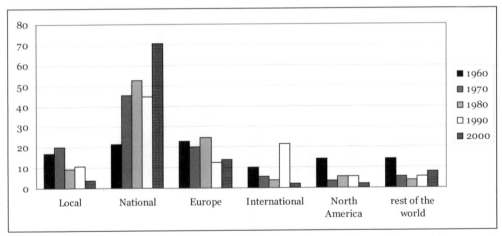

Figure 6: Geographical focus on the front page in *Het Laatste Nieuws* (2 weeks, five years) (1960–2000, per cent).

Surely, these data need to be interpreted in its contemporary political-economic context. In this Belgian case, we should, for instance, refer in 1960 to the UN General Assembly and the process of decolonization, independence and the subsequent crisis in the Congo. The sudden uprise of national news items in 1980, both in the quality and the tabloid paper, on the other hand, dealt with serious national linguistic and politico-cultural conflicts.

De Standaard 4 10 1960

Het Laatste Nieuws 4 10 1960

De Standaard 5 10 2000

Het Laatste Nieuws 5 10 2000

A final clear distinction between both newspapers dealt with the type of foreign news on the front pages (Figure 7). Here we brought some theme issues together under hard and soft/other issues. The first refers to themes such as politics, war and conflict, crime/justice, and social and educational events. The other category deals with 'softer' items such as sports, popular culture and entertainment, human interest, peculiarities and the bizarre, accidents, as well as a rest category.

Looking more closely at the proportion of hard foreign news items we clearly see a continuing majority of hard foreign news items on the *De Standaard* front page, while softer foreign news tends to dominate for the tabloid. Here human interest, sports, and popular culture and show business are most prominent. Hard political foreign news items dropped here from 37.1 to 11.8 per cent. For the quality newspaper, this political category continues to dominate (41.5 per cent in 2000), together with a growing interest in economic items (from 0 to 11.3 per cnt).

Summarizing this case study, it first seems to be important to underline that much depends upon the actual political and economic news facts themselves, of course. But overall, we need to be quite careful in concluding that the shrinking news paradox is a general tendency. In some sense, even for the tabloid case, there is no real quantitative decrease in foreign and international news items. In relative terms, there is a shrinking foreign news agenda in relation to the tremendous growth in the overall output.

Very important in all this seems to be the profile and the target group, where quality newspapers provide considerably more, and a 'harder' type of, foreign and international news. They once did and they still do. For this type of newspaper, foreign and international

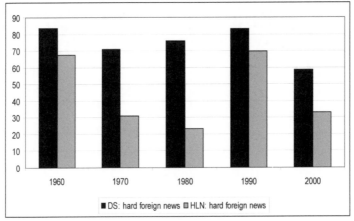

Figure 7: Proportion of foreign and international news stories on the front page in *De Standaard* and *Het Laatste Nieuws* (2 weeks, five years) (1960–2000, per cent).

news has even become a crucial competitive element in the supplemented editorial pages as well. The tabloid in the case study clearly decreased the output of harder political-economic foreign news, both in quantitative and qualitative terms. The question on the paradox needs to be reconsidered, taking into account the social-educational level and the whole process of differentiation, segmentation and targeting in the newspaper (media?) market.

Final Thoughts

This chapter does not claim that foreign and international news coverage is sufficient, good, better or worse than it was, say, forty years ago. It is clear that, notwithstanding the wider news environment, there is a clear problem with the narrowing news agenda in many of the most popular mass media. It is true that, as Elisabeth Bird (1998) claimed, 'the human interest story, especially the big, national story, is pushing out diversity of information from the news media.' It is also true that many foreign and international news items are treated without any interpretation, comment or context. We should take into account differences in audience segments in a changing news environment, where an overwhelming majority of citizens cites television as their main source of information (PEW 2008: 2).

As (news) media researchers, however, we should not become nostalgic or underestimate the emergent possibilities of the wider media and news environment. Given the centrality of news in the democratic project, we should recognize the complexities and contradictions. The new news environment and the Internet create tremendous opportunities for journalists, while particular groups of citizens actively use these sources to be better informed about what happens elsewhere. A 2008 PEW report underlined how these 'net-newsers' and news 'integrators' are mostly affluent and well-educated, illustrating the importance of economic and cultural capital. In other words, we must stay critical towards new forms of social exclusion, or towards the existing drive towards fragmentation and individualization.

Finally and on a more theoretical level, we must accept that the powerful globalization discourse is fundamentally contradictory, complex and not all-pervasive. The media's inward tendency might be an integral part of the wider process of globalization. It may even be that the paradox on the shrinking foreign and international news is an inherent part of the rapidly changing social geography of today's media, culture and society.

Acknowledgments

I would like to thank Stijn Joye and the Ghent University students who did most of the coding and analysis.

Notes

1. The distinction between foreign and international news is quite difficult to make. We define foreign news as news dealing with a process or an event with a particular dateline and with mainly national repercussions (e.g. the coverage of the *Dutroux affair* in Belgium for non-Belgian news media). International news deals with an event or a process, which might have a particular dateline, but which has a wider influence or impact (e.g. the US invasion of Iraq).
2. In this research project, coordinated by the International Press Institute (IPI) (1953), a systematic study was undertaken on a four week sample of foreign news in ten Western-allied countries (between October 1952 and January 1953). The study included a content analysis, but also interviews with journalists, foreign correspondents for newspapers and news agencies, as well as leading editors.

References

Allan, S. (1999) *News culture*, Buckingham; Open University.

Baechlin, P. & Muller-Strauss, M. (1951) *La Presse Filmée dans le Monde*, Paris: Unesco.

Biltereyst, D. (2001), 'Global news and complex citizenship: Towards an agenda for research on foreign/international news and audiences' in S. Hjarvard (ed.) *News in a globalized world*, Copenhagen: Nordicom, pp. 36–60.

Bird, E. (1998) 'News we can use: An audience perspective on the tabloidisation of news in the United States', *Communication Research*, 5: 3.

Bird, E. (2000) 'Audience demands in a murderous market: Tabloidization in U.S. television News' in C. Sparks & J. Tulloch (eds.) *Tabloid Tales,* New York: Rowan and Littlefield.

Bondebjerg, I. (2001) 'European media, cultural integration and globalisation. Reflections on the ESF-programme Changing Media – Changing Europe', *Nordicom Review*, 22: 1, pp. 53–64.

Cottle, S. (2000) 'New(s) times: Towards A "Second Wave" of News Ethnography', *Communications: The European Journal of Communication Research*, 25: 1, pp. 19–41.

Franklin, B. (1997) *Newszak and news media*, London: Arnold.

Galtung, J. & Ruge, M.H. (1965) 'The structure of foreign news', *Journal of Peace Research*, 2, pp. 64–91.

Gerbner, G. & Marvanyi, G. (1977) 'The many worlds of the world's press', *Journal of Communication*, 27: 1, pp. 52–66.

Gurevitch, M., Levy, M.R. & Roeh, I. (1991) 'The global newsroom: convergences and diversities in the globalization of television news', in P. Dahlgren & C. Sparks (eds.) *Communication and citizenship: Journalism and the public sphere*, London, Routledge.

Hagen, I. (1994) 'Expectations and consumption patterns in TV news viewing', *Media, Culture & Society*, 16: 3.

Hallin, D. (1996). 'Commercialism and professionalism in the American news media' in J. Curran & M. Gurevitch (eds.) *Mass media and society,* London: Arnold, pp. 243–64.

Harrison, J. (2006) *News,* London: Routledge.

Hester, A. (1971) 'An analysis of news flow from developed and developing nations', *Gazette*, 17, pp. 29–43.

Hjarvard, S. (2000) *News media and the globalization of the public sphere*, Copenhagen, Working Paper No. 3.

IPI (1953) *The flow of news*, Zurich: International Press Institute.

Krüger, U.M. (1997) 'Politikberichterstattung in den Fernsehnachrichten', *Media Perspektiven*, 5.

McChesney, R.W. (2004) *The problem of the media. U.S. communication politics in the twenty-first century*, New York: Monthly Review Press.

McLachlan, S. & Golding, P., (2000) 'Tabloidization in the British press: a quantitative investigation into changes within British newspapers', in C. Sparks & J. Tulloch (eds.) *Tabloid Tales: global debates over media standards*, Boulder: Rowman & Littlefield, pp. 75–89.

McNelly, J.T. (1959) 'Intermediary communicators in the international flow of news', *Journalism Quarterly*, 36, pp. 23–6.

Masmoudi, M. (1979) 'The new world information order', *Journal of Communication*, 29, pp. 172–85.

Moisy, Cl. (1997), 'Myths of the global information village', *Foreign Affairs*, 76: 3, pp. 78–87.

Östgaard, E. (1965) 'Factors influencing the flow of news', *Journal of Peace Research*, 1, pp. 39–63.

Peeren, Y. & Biltereyst, D. (2001) Nieuws *over de Wereld: Een longitudinaal onderzoek van het nieuwsaanbod in de kwaliteits- en de populaire pers*, research report 4, Gent: Communication Studies.

Peeren, Y. & Biltereyst, D. (2002) Nieuws *over de Wereld: Nieuws, mediagebruik en burgerschap*, research report 5, Gent: Communication Studies.

PEW (2008) *Audience segments in a changing news environment*, Washington: PEW.

Sampson, A. (1999) 'The crisis at the heart of our media', *British Journalism Review*, 7: 3, pp. 42–51, reprinted in Tumber (1999) pp. 201–12).

Sassen, S. (1998) 'The state and the new geography of power' in A. Calabrese & J.C. Burgelman (eds.) *Communication, citizenship, and social policy. Rethinking the limits of the Welfare State*, Lanham: Rowman & Littlefield Publishers.

Schramm, W. (1959 One *day in the world's press: Fourteen great newspapers on a day of crisis*, Stanford, CA: Stanford University Press.

Seaton, E., (1998) The *diminishing use of foreign news reporting*, May 1998, http: //asne.org/index. cfm?ID=627. Accessed 30 August 2009.

Simpson, C. (1994) *Science of coercion: Communication research and psychological warfare*, New York: Oxford University Press.

Sreberny-Mohammadi, A., Nordenstreng, K. & Stevenson, R.L. (1984) 'The world of the news study', *Journal of Communication*, 34: 1, pp. 134–38.

Sreberny-Mohammadi, A. (1991) 'The global and the local in international communications' in J. Curran & M. Gurevitch (eds.) *Mass media and society*, London: Edward Arnold, pp. 118–38.

Tai, Z. & Chang, T.-K. (2002) 'The global news and the pictures in their heads', *Gazette*, 64: 3, pp. 251–65.

Thussu, D.K. (2004) 'Media plenty and the poverty of news', in Ch. Paterson & A. Sreberny, (eds.) *International News in the 21st Century*, London: John Libbey Publishing, pp. 47–62.

Thussu, D.K. (2007) *News as entertainment: The rise of global infotainment*, London: Sage.

Tomlinson, J. (1999) *Globalization and culture*, London: Polity Press.

Tumber, H. (ed.) (1999) *News: A reader*, Oxford: Oxford University Press.

Unesco (1954) *How nations see each other*, Paris: Unesco.

Utley, G. (1997) 'The shrinking of foreign news: From broadcast to narrowcast', *Foreign Affairs*, 76: 2.

VRIND (2002) *Vlaamse regionale indicatoren*, Brussels: Ministry of the Flemish Community.

Wu, H. Denis (2000) 'Systemic determinants of international news coverage: a comparison of 38 countries', *Journal of Communication*, 50: 2, pp. 110–30.

Zillmann, D., Gibson, R., Ordman, V.L. & Aust, C.F. (1994). 'Effects of upbeat stories in broadcast news', *Journal of Broadcasting and Electronic Media*, 38.

Zipf, G. (1946) 'Some determinants of the circulation of information', American *Journal of Psychology*, 59, pp. 401–21.

Chapter 10

Fakty vs. *Wiadomości*: On Competition and Confusion in Polish
TV News

Wieslaw Godzic
Warsaw School of Social Sciences and Humanities

T his chapter is about the textual aspects of Polish television news magazines: their subject matter and agenda setting, their formal composition, and mode of address. I will try to analyse what I see as a difference between the news values preferred by broadcasters and those preferred by viewers. The main question is about how we are to understand the function of television news if it is to be a profit-oriented TV genre. It is obvious that such a study needs to be contextualized, i.e. the object of analysis must be understood in light of the historically-produced conditions of the public sphere in the young democracies of Eastern/Central Europe.

Impossible public sphere in the heart of Europe

By the public sphere we mean first of all a realm of our social life in which something approaching public opinion can be formed. Access is guaranteed to all citizens... Only when the exercise of political control is effectively subordinated to the demand that information is accessible to the public does the political public sphere win an institutionalized influence over the government through the instrument of law-making bodies. (Habermas 1984: 49)

For ordinary Poles as well as political activists, such words describe not *their* world but the so-called 'western-oriented world'. There was a time when there was no public sphere in Habermas' sense in the 'heart of Europe', as Poland has been called. Instead, from the end of the Second World War, up to the 1989 breakthrough, we can distinguish between three types of public space:

1. An *official public space* inhabited by communist/socialist parties and government-dependent institutions. All cultural, social, and even local groups of inhabitants were controlled by the Communist Party. Freely expressing one's opinion was dangerous, if not impossible. The propaganda system, as well as having an Orwellian-like control of everyday life, influenced not only people's opinions in all media, but also box-office statistics and weather forecasts!
2. Since 1976 we can talk about an *oppositional public space* in Poland. These were clandestine activities resulting in the Solidarity Movement of 1980–1981. Books printed in small illegal publishing houses and brought from abroad with no formal permission were

distributed among a number of different social groups, ranging from young university students to pensioners. Illegal VHS films and audiotape recordings of political cabarets and speeches were very popular among the majority of Poles.

3. Nevertheless, the extraordinary position of the Roman Catholic Church cannot be overestimated in the public/social sphere. The third public space in Poland was thus the *religious* one. It was very close to an oppositional sphere in content but there was a semi-legal space for it: churches or other buildings belonging to the Church.

Before 1989, the press was designed to serve as a propaganda instrument; an instrument of party control. The official newspaper of the Communist party, *Trybuna Ludu*, was established principally to achieve these goals. The daily, whose circulation in the late 1980s approached nearly 1,900,000, had dominated the market. Although it is known that its returns were high, it is difficult to give an exact estimate since there is a lack of documentation that could provide the appropriate data. Dependence on the Communist party marked the contents of not only *Trybuna Ludu* but all newspapers. It implied not only a propagandist function imposed by the Communists but in general a predominance of politics in all kinds of papers, including popular tabloids.

After 1989 the Polish newspaper market totally changed. The new political system brought freedom of speech, of the press, and of association, which meant independence and neutrality in the majority of Polish papers. In April 1990, censorship was abolished. The last issue of *Trybuna Ludu* was edited in January 1990 and it changed into the daily *Trybuna*, a paper affiliated with the post-communist party SLD, but with a smaller circulation and a more national range than its predecessor. The editorial staff of another paper, *Express Wieczorny* tried to maintain a good market position for their paper but due to stiff competition this proved exceedingly difficult, and the *Express Wieczorny* disappeared from kiosks in the 1990s.

Nowadays the most prestigious daily with the largest circulation is *Gazeta Wyborcza*, established in 1989 to support Solidarność before the parliamentary elections. The paper has gained a predominant position in the market, and maintained it until the present. *Super Express* is one of the contemporary Polish papers established in the period of enormous increase in Polish press titles after the political and economic changes. It was intended as a popular newspaper inclined to sensationalism. Surprisingly, in just a few years, partly due to some promotional campaigns, *Super Express* became the second-largest daily on the market in 1999, with a circulation just below that of *Gazeta Wyborcza*.

An examination of television's historical role in Polish society reveals the surprising finding that archival sources would seem to indicate that members of the Communist Party's ruling elite were not convinced about television's possibilities as a medium for propaganda. They were of the opinion that the press was able to exercise a greater influence, and therefore allotted television a relatively large degree of freedom of expression. This is one of the principal reasons why Poles of the older generation often have nostalgic memories of Polish television from the 60s as propagating a high level of culture and having ambitious entertainment programmes. A weekly television theatre, modelled on the British *Masterpiece Theatre*, gained a large following, with renowned Polish theatre actors presenting their work.

It was only in the 70s, during the regime of Edward Gierek, the-then first secretary of the Communist Party, that the practice of 'success propaganda,' as it was officially known, became universal. A great number of cultural programmes of a high level were done away with and for this reason the majority of accomplished performers openly resisted the Communist party. Television broadcast reports of the party congresses were unbearably boring, since no one who did not adhere to the official party doctrine was allowed to voice his opinions. The main propaganda programme on television was *Daily News*. It, too, was serious, stuffy and pompous. The newscasters gave the impression that they did not identify with what they were saying, their language was artificial and pretentious, and 'news' tended to be about 'economic visits' by Edward Gierek. When the declaration of martial law in December 1981 was reported by the *Daily News,* the main voice of state propaganda, it was selectively and with suitable emotion. Television viewers, however, learned how to interpret this segment of the news in an 'oppositional way': if it was reported that the shipyard was working normally, it certainly meant that the workers were on strike. Deep down this signified a complete breakdown of institutional communication, of the authorities and the instruments of their authority. The situation would only change when the authorities were chosen by democratic elections – but by that time completely new problems would appear.

Polish society was, and is, a society in transition since 1989 – a main feature of which seems to be a controversy over values. The battle between public and commercial values is visible in all dimensions of modern society but the media serves as the main battleground. The Polish media system is in the process of being shaped. The political elite and new governments tend to use the media to further the goals of transformation and reform. But nobody in this country-in-transition is ready to make decisions about crucial dilemmas such as the position of the media between the state and the market, i.e. their financial foundations in a competitive marketplace. Broadcasting law is still far from its final shape in the Polish Parliament and, once, a big corruption scandal came to light when more than US$17 million were offered to change the law in favour of 'some groups of politicians'. There is a common assumption that the newly-created system of media organization is closer to the power centre than to society at large.

The developments in the Polish media landscape since the 1980s cannot be properly understood unless one also considers the great importance of the emerging consumerism in the country. New consumer groups of all classes, sexes, ages, and levels of education have emerged and they have learned the consumerist vocabulary very quickly. The older generation can now express their hitherto-repressed desires, which are significant for the specificity of Polish (and possibly East European) consumer culture. In a sense they serve as 'signs of democracy' ('I can buy Pepsi, Coca- Cola, etc. so I am a free citizen') and many link consumerism, democracy and human rights. The enormous rise of the new media is of course playing a part in the establishment of such an understanding.

With the above sketch of the Polish media landscape as a background, let us now turn to the most important of all media, television, bearing in mind the enormous rate of TV-watching: almost 4 hours daily for Poles.

The risky challenge or *Fakty* against the Polish news ritual

Wiadomości ('News') is the main news programme of the Polish public/state Television Channel 1 (TVP1). Broadcast daily at 7.30 pm, *Wiadomości* was, for more than 30 years, the most influential source of news, as well as the main propaganda tool for the former communist regime. In October 1997 the new commercial station TVN launched *Fakty* ('Facts') broadcast at the same time as *Wiadomości* but changed after seven months to 7.00pm.

There was an unusual and significant event on 30 May 2002 at the Opole Song Festival. While the prizes of were being awarded on *Superjedynka* (TVP1), the presenter Tomasz Kamel introduced a 'special edition' of the TVP1 news programme. Viewers, on their TV screens at home, and the festival audience on a huge screen there, saw the popular presenters of the flagship news series, Kamil Durczok, Jolanta Pieńkowska and others, present a humorous account of riots in Opole in response to the results of the Festival, which led to the smashing up of music stores in protest. The producers of that particular news report and the main news magazine, *Wiadomości*, then appeared at the Opole scene, commenting that these were 'facts but not really true, but so it is with facts'.

The vast majority of viewers read the statement as part of the rivalry between the main public TV station and the private TVN, and in particular with their newest magazine *Fakty*. And this is how their competition saw it. On 1 June 2002 a satirical TVN programme *Ale plama!* ('What a shame!') made fun of the incident, and of the appearance of the TV presenters 'in the role of idiots' in particular. It was the commercial television channel accusing the public one of populism and of propagating lowbrow tastes; an accusation that seemed justified.

The battlefield of *Fakty* and *Wiadomości* does not end at TV news magazines; it embraces the whole sphere of information and even political commentary. This could be illustrated briefly with a few examples:

On 23 September 2003, for the first time in the history of Polish Television, TVN created and broadcast an alternative Electoral Studio after the Parliamentary Elections. The channel thus took on one of its biggest challenges – entering a sphere hitherto reserved exclusively for public television. Actually, the rivalry happened to be a battle of fairly similar shows, though not on equal terms. The critics emphasized the professionalism of the Electoral Night in TVP and criticized the chaos within the TVN programme. On the other hand, they praised TVN for a more interesting studio design – and what is probably most important within this battle is that TVN was the first station to broadcast predictions of the outcome of the elections.

TVN was also the first television company in this part of Europe to start a 24-hour news channel – TVN24. In response, public television transformed the structure of its regional programmes and created TVP3, a news and political commentary channel based on the regional divisions of public television. Another important stage in the rivalry was the live broadcast by TVN24 and TVP3 of the Komisja Śledcza, the Parliamentary Hearing Commission, on the so-called 'Rywin Gate', where the media revealed attempts at corruption and illegal affairs during proceedings on amendments of the Television and Broadcasting Act.

The two news programmes represent formats that differ in at least three ways:

Themes: *Wiadomości* presents mainly political material from the point of view of Warsaw or the 'Bermuda triangle' (Parliament – Prime Minister – President); *Fakty* mainly shows sensational news, violence, emotional appeals and populist reports.

Production: *Wiadomości* has the best equipment and network of correspondents in Poland and abroad; it is also funded by public money. The competition is here reminiscent of the battle between David and Goliath.

Symbols and Social Aspects: *Wiadomości* is heir to the propaganda from the communist period, associated with all the stereotypes and negative judgments of the former regime's television. On the other hand *Fakty* was, to begin with, regarded as a politically- and financially-independent programme. However, with time, a part of society started to look less favourably on the 'benefits' of the free market economy, regarding the 'good old times' with nostalgia.

A more thorough analysis of the rivalry between these two channels could perhaps proceed as follows:

Fakty was transmitted for the first time on 3 October 1997 at 7.30 p.m., a sacred time for all TV-viewers in Poland. By this time children were in bed and, for forty years, the grown-ups had tuned in to the *Dziennik* ('Daily News'), later called *Wieczór z Dziennikiem* ('Evening with Daily News') and finally *Wiadomości* ('News'). TVN thus challenged its much older opponent directly when they decided to launch their News at this hour. TVN reached only 60–70 per cent of all viewers, and had no tradition with which to challenge the biggest station and its flagship programme. But TVN came up with the idea that its TV newscasters should look like typical American anchormen: one of their presenters, Tomasz Lis, had studied journalism at an American university, and later worked there in this capacity. *Fakty* became a great success.

TVN clearly lacked experience. Watching *Fakty* in their first week, we can observe similarities with the satirical programme *Łapu-capu* (broadcast on the Polish edition of Canal+): the presenter and the reporter interrupted each other, a nervous reporter made linguistic mistakes, and finally she had to resort to the written script. It improved technically but from the very beginning this commercial TV news magazine seemed to represent a revolution within Polish television news.

Let us look more carefully. The lead item of the first transmission of *Fakty* on 3 October 1997 was sensational material about a yacht drifting on the high seas. The host of the programme, Tomasz Lis, using a serious tone of voice, gave a dramatic account, followed by film footage from the beach and an aerial view from a helicopter. It then returned to the newsroom so that the host could talk to the reporter on the scene. The screen was divided with the newsroom on the left and, on the right, the reporter at the scene, with the dramatic event finally filling the whole screen. This extremely rhetorical structure became dominant for years, characteristic of the station, and often imitated by others. Its rhetoric was dependent upon the strong personality of the presenter, who was not just the reader but also author of the text. From the very beginning it was meant to be a form of friendly dialogue with the viewers – not just because the studio was decorated in light colours, with a coffee mug on the desk, creating an informal feel characteristic of American news and talk shows but also because of Tomasz Lis's style of discourse.

At first *Fakty* was watched by only one percent of viewers, which was regarded as a failure by their competitor *Wiadomości*. In May 1998 the programme was moved from 7.30 to 7:00pm and after a few months the ratings increased to 10 percent (approximately 3.5 million viewers).The second day of January 2000 was an exceptionally successful day for *Fakty* as it was the first time more viewers watched the TVN news programme than that of their competitor.

If we disregard the initial technical problems of the first week, we can easily see that the viewers were presented with a new quality of television genre. If creating and filling the viewers' needs is essential to the genre, then unquestionably this was the product the viewers got and can be summarized as follows:

Defining the pattern of hierarchy between report and commentary

From the outset, *Fakty* started with a clear statement and with an anchorman as witty host and author, who controls all and does more than just report events.

Innovative language forms

Fakty hosts showed that words convey meaning, and that this meaning has its rhetorical tradition dependent on context. It is worth emphasizing that the presenters of the programme started treating words as building blocks.

The following analysis covers one week (3–8 of October):

4 October: Lis, in his conversation with President Wałęsa, drew the President's attention twice to the fact that he said, 'I think' which probably meant in this context 'I am not certain'. The president was obviously surprised by this meta-language interruption.

4 October: the presenter used more meta-language comments of this type: 'that's all about a republic, now about a monarchy' as a transition from a news item from the US to news from Spain.

5 October: Grzegorz Miecugow started the programme with a shot of boxing gloves in reference to the Polish champion, Andrzej Gołota's defeat, saying: 'It's obvious what to start with: and it was to be so beautiful...' – which is a quotation from a popular song.

10 October: Tomasz Lis began with the words: 'we'll start with a report from the battle field of the coalition building. The day was to be as any other day. Lots of speculation, little information', which shows both an ironic attitude towards the journalists' new genre and, in the second sentence, a biting remark about the Polish political scene. Thus, it is both a description of the situation and an attitude towards a way of describing it.

7 October: After years of dry 'newspeak' by political commentators, scared to death of live comments, a reporter standing in front of the Chancellery of the Prime Minister forcefully introduced a new strategy of commenting on political events which was to become popular over the next few years. TVN used short, witty remarks, which are at the same time pretty obvious, e.g: 'The government closed down with a lack of good political manners. The question arises, is there such a thing as good political manners?' This could be a question put by the man on the street or by a concerned citizen – the strength of the news magazine lies in the synergy of both these attitudes.

'Cracow always aspired to be the capital, and it is going to be one. At least for three days. Not, however, the capital of Poland, but rather, the capital of European Poetry'. This report from 4 October is an example of the balance between an official form, and light, poetic speech with an awareness of rhetorical forms. These forms are mainly riddles or puns introduced at the beginning of the item. It often functions as an introduction to a filmed report and used to build suspense.

'Instant' news: On 7 October, the third news item was the arrival from Paris of the well-known former tennis player, Wojciech Fibak. A few minutes earlier, information was given about the sportsman's problems in Paris, where he was accused of contacts with criminals. Now *Fakty* presented a short interview with Fibak, given just after his arrival at Warsaw Airport, followed by a shot from the studio showing a satisfied host saying 'Wojciech Fibak came to us straight from the Airport', and immediately started a studio interview. This gives us an idea of how *Fakty* planned to fight their main rival *Wiadomości*: TVN offers immediate action, without delays – what counts here is the news *now*.

Sensation tamed – the public point of view becomes tabloid

In the same item the interviewer asked the sportsman, with a hint of concern but at the same time with determination: 'I need to ask you: have you ever had any contacts with prostitutes?' Tomasz Lis had gone beyond traditional standards of decency, but the question he asked was not only almost already there, it was expected by the man on the street. When I tried to judge how sensational the first TV news magazines were, it seemed natural to draw a line between what is public (serious) and tabloid (sensation, lightweight). But this was very difficult because, whether it was serious or not, the mode of presentation was identical. In a transmission from Italy (5 October) concerning the Polish Pope, the analyst began with a serious tone, as the news was of a 'public' character. However, after a few banal sentences it emerged that the most interesting aspect was the Pope's meeting with a 126-year-old woman 'whose life was the basis for the Brazilian TV soap opera popular in Poland, *Isaura, the Slave Girl*.' On the same day an item about kindness to animals was treated with extreme seriousness and the animals were shown during a special Holy Mass while their owners spoke with solemnity of their relationships with their pets.

This erasure of the distinction between the serious and the trivial was also visible in the last three items of the first *Fakty* programme on 3 October. Firstly, news of a party given to celebrate the opening of TVN's headquarters was obviously a form of promotion and cannot be treated as a serious public matter, until we hear that a large amount of money was given to those suffering from a flood. The next item was a tabloid one about a dog terrorizing a whole city, with closing shots of some mongrel accompanied by the words 'this is probably the most wanted dog in Poland'. The final item concerned the boxing star, Andrzej Gołota, and his preparation for his next fight. The presentation, which combined shots of a visit to his old school and interviews with former teachers and fellow pupils, was a combination of the light and popular with a more serious and traditional treatment of the topic, which seemed to invite questions about how we create sports stars in our new, consumption-based, reality.

Public/commercial discourse about public safety

The primary objective of an analysis of the main editions of two competing news series, *Wiadomości* (TVP1, 7: 30pm) and *Fakty* (TVN, 7: 00pm) from 22 January 2001 (Monday) to 28 January 2001 (Sunday) was to distinguish themes relating to safety and then to estimate how often they appeared. The mode of presentation of the material was then compared and analysed. It was not possible to give any 'grades' or to set one scale for these two news programmes as it has been known for a long time that they differ and use different strategies of communication. Therefore I decided to look for common ground or for differences in approach to issues regarding safety.

To start with, the definition of 'safety' seems very vague, therefore I decided to group safety issues in the following way:

- PER: Personal safety, referring to life, health and property protection;
- PAT: pathological threats, referring mainly to organized criminal groups, drug addiction and alcohol problems.
- LAW: referring to the building of an awareness of the law;
- SOC: social safety, referring to such issues as unemployment or homelessness.

It was not always easy to decide to which of these categories information belonged. The decision was based on the intended message of the broadcaster. For example, news about keeping interest rates at the same level does not, by its nature, belong to any of the categories. However a commentary referring to the market and stock exchange, suggesting clearly 'that our money's safety is involved', made this qualify within SOC. Also news about president Putin's decision to reduce the number of Russian troops in Chechnya qualified as SOC, again due to the commentary suggesting that this decision should convince the viewer that his world is safe.

The comparison of the number of safety issues is not at all surprising, but it undermines the stereotypical belief that there is a clear dividing line between what is commercial and what is public.

FAKTY   WIADOMOŚCI

Total number of themes between 22–28 October 2001.

105

Total safety themes:

49 including:

	FAKTY	WIADOMOŚCI
PER	27	22
PAT	9	10
LAW	1	–
SOC	13	17

This shows a strong similarity between the two stations in treating safety issues. We could even say that *Fakty* is *more* preoccupied with safety. For *Fakty*, safety issues constitute 58 per cent of all the news during the analysed period, against 46 per cent for their competitor. But if we take into account that safety issues had a longer exposition time on public television, then we could say that both programmes were equally concerned. The emphasis was mainly on PER and during the analysed week the news referred to the trials of killers and most of all, the shocking murder of a four-year-old boy.

The second most popular category was SOC. Both programmes were preoccupied with unemployment and budget problems that could result in serious national security problems. SOC also included, on 23 January, the 'Vetting' Trials of Tomaszewski (*Fakty*), and Marian Jurczyk (*Wiadomości*).

Third in the list is PAT, drug addiction and organized crime, with an emphasis on Mafia boss trials.

What is shocking is the lack of news referring to awareness of the law – I found only one piece of information, a discussion on the death penalty, which in fact could not even be easily classified within this category.

It seems that the viewers got two symmetrical, but at the same time different, programmes. It looks as if the stereotypical approach to 'commercial' as opposed to 'public' constantly clashed with the presented material and most of all with the mode and form of presenting it. For example, on 25 February we hear the news of the apprehension of a criminal gang in the town of Mikołajki with the punch line: 'This means that in summer, the only thing to keep sailors awake at night in the capital of Mazury (Mikołajki) will be good weather and favourable winds.' Surprisingly, this was from a public-TV journalist and not so different from Tomasz Lis's statement, introducing the news of hospital troubles in the city of Końskie, 'you need to have a horse's [strong] health [a Polish idiom] to fall sick in Końskie' (Końskie means the town of horses).

To get a clearer idea of the situation, we will analyse the treatment of issues of safety on 24 January, a fairly typical day with *Fakty* including 5 safety items out of 10 and *Wiadomości*, 8 items out of 17.

1. 'The Doomsday' – by *Fakty*

On this day, *Fakty* started with political news, referring to the first public meeting of the leaders of the new political group, the Civic Platform. But then came a number of items referring to violence and everyday safety threats. Tomasz Lis spoke dramatically about the 'absolutely shocking new details of a four-year-old murdered boy in the Vistula River'; we see a concerned presenter and, in the left upper corner, the picture of a four-year-old with a headline across the screen: 'Mother – to kill!' After warning that 'scenes might be violent' we see a bag representing the boy's body being thrown into the water. This was followed by photos of the dead boy and statements from suspects. The prosecutor graphically described the crime and commented 'they did it casually, just as if throwing a kitten into the water', but implying that it was so abnormal that it sends shivers down your spine. The police spokesman had no doubts that if the mother, who was in touch with the murderers, had only asked them to spare the boy, he would still be alive. 'The last minutes of the child's life will remain a mystery', the reporter concluded. The viewer may doubt whether he needs this detail of information about the investigation and, shocked by the violent crime, would rather have this mystery left to tabloid journalism. This however, is not the end. While there is talk of 'mystery', the murderers do not seem to have hidden anything and the viewers may have serious moral doubts about whether a full and detailed account should be on the national news. The journalists, using police material, seem to act for the police, or for the court. The reporter, dressed in an elegant tie and coat (we could question whether this suits the crime scene and the theme) finished with a rhetorical remark: 'It is going to be very difficult for the court to find a scale on which to judge this case'. The presenter did not see it as a rhetorical remark, adding as a commentary: 'but maybe this is very easy'. As a shocked viewer I feel that I do not want to see a terrible crime being used as the basis for a play on words. Moreover, is he suggesting the need for the death penalty, or for lynching?

The next news item came from the Białystok Court, where Henryk Niewiadomski, the leader of the Wołomin Gang (an organized crime syndicate, located in the city of Wołomin, near Warsaw), was sentenced to seven years' imprisonment. While the news concentrated on the aggressive behaviour of the convict's family, with long shots showing the bandit's reaction, the host and the reporter concentrate on the legal nuances and the chances of an appeal. There is no attempt to discuss the history of the case or the charges. But there is no time to concentrate on this, since Lis, who specializes in rhetorical questions, asks dramatically, with reference to another item: 'Is there anything which could justify the commutation of life imprisonment for Jolanta Brzozowska's killers?' The Supreme Court has upheld the verdict, but what is interesting is that, here, the news covers the creation of the Anti-Crime Organization, which results from this lawsuit. This is one of the few socially-valuable parts of this report. 'Today is doomsday for criminals', says the presenter and informs us about the court's verdict on the murderers of a cell-phone dealer.

I am already used to this tone of voice of *Fakty* presenters, but I would rather not watch close-ups of murderers nor hear presenters say, in passing, 'as in the case of Jolanta Brzozowska…so with Małgorzata Rozumecka…' There is a huge difference between these two women: the first was killed and the second one murdered someone. Although this was stated in the commentary, the pragmatics of television communication suggests a linking of these two names. These news shows of *Fakty* are oriented towards scandal and sensation and there is nothing wrong with this; this type of journalism is unquestionably needed, and many times results in the discovery of the truth. What is worrying, though, is that there is no line drawn between the victims and the criminals. Moreover, the killers are made into TV heroes. The host's comments go too far: no longer a witty remark, but creating ambiguity and relativism in judging the situation.

2. 'The murderers were really terrified by their deeds' – *Wiadomości*

After casual observation, it would appear that *Wiadomości* does not seem to make the same mistakes. The first item refers to the Henryk Niewiadomski trial and the comments are logical, clear and short. The shots from court were equally long but the defendant's speech was reported, unlike *Fakty*. The face of the convicted was not shown, not through any legal restrictions, but perhaps communicating to the viewers that, though we should present what this man has to say, he does not deserve to be shown. This is definitely a better method than TVN's glorification of the criminal.

The second item comes from the Supreme Court and refers to it upholding the verdict of life imprisonment of Brzozowska's murderers. *Wiadomości* presents a statement of a representative of the Anti-Crime Association, a psychologist's comments, and data showing an increase in juvenile crime.

The fourth item presents details of the murder of the four-year-old boy. In contrast to *Fakty*, the viewers were not warned of the dramatic scenes, though the material was similar to TVN's. After the murderers had voiced their opinions, it seemed that the viewers were supposed to feel some sympathy for them, as the reporter commented that 'they were terrified by what they had done.'

Between cool distance and chaotic familiarity

These two approaches differ mainly in intensity rather than quality. *Fakty* aims to be shocking, intriguing and aimed at catching the viewer's attention. They have the right to do this – but I am convinced that in this case they went too far. It is not a question of good taste but a lack of ethics, as the criminal takes precedence over the victim. *Wiadomości* has arrived at 'ground zero', which is correct, pretty reliable, and gives the impression that this is the best and only mode of presentation.

In summary, it is not a question of one being better than the other. These are two different kinds of journalism, and not surprisingly the more dynamic one is presented by commercial rather than public TV. I can see elements that convince me that *Wiadomości* is approaching *Fakty's* formula rather than the other way round. The data shows that there are really no quantitative differences: the only differences are in style, which can be analysed only from very vague examples: not showing the face of the defendant but playing his voice; showing the boy's corpse twice not thrice, as *Fakty* did; shorter editorial comment. Such are all features too insignificant to fully represent the style.

The conclusion is that, while we can agree that TV viewers are generally in a safe position, since television is a witness acting in their name, different principles and strategies of communication govern the same material. *Fakty's* strategy aims at making the evil less terrifying: 'look' – they say – 'it is not dangerous, and even if it is, we are together'. Community spirit is, in this case, extremely strong and obviously TVN is looking for this community spirit. *Wiadomości* tries to distance itself from the dangers and perils of the world. The sad expression on the face of presenter is not at all buddy-like but suggests a distanced star. *Wiadomości* says: 'do not be afraid, we are protected by powerful forces, which help us all'. A strategy of individual address and personalization of communication (*Fakty*) is set against a civil and emotional approach (*Wiadomości*). We can see that the first strategy is winning but not because this is an unquestionable principle but because the implementation of the second strategy has serious faults. *Fakty* creates an entertaining discourse and entertainment show with safety issues. The perspective drawn suggests that this is an everyday, familiar situation. They seem to say: 'the bandit is one of us, well-judged by his peers.'

The division drawn above resembles Aristotle's concept of social spheres. There is a distant, inaccessible way of dealing with public matters represented by *Wiadomości*, which Aristotle called *ecclesia*. *Fakty* uses the everyday, familiar and domesticated (*oikos*). But both programmes miss *agora*: the sphere of real people communicating about public matters. In television, the ability to create *agora* depends on theme selection, mode of address and even the presenter's clothes. We all know that safety issues are a serious threat in Poland, now we should realize that the producers of informative programmes could be part of the threat.

It is obvious that we can draw a number of different conclusions from this battlefield of *Wiadomości* and *Fakty*. On the one hand, we realize that this competition is commercially inevitable. However, I believe that public TV should compete with moderation; it should never provoke, as it did during the Opole Festival. Its aim, though it speaks to the same public, should be to use a different register.

On the other hand, it is worth realizing that in this battle, public TV is not privileged just because it is 'public'. All the news programmes are similar, regardless of their financial status. This similarity is best described in *Really Bad News*, prepared by Glasgow Media Group, the basis for much work in British Cultural Studies:

> To conclude, TV is not an objective medium, in a sense that it breaks the formal responsibility for a balanced media. Our research draws us to the conclusion that broadcasting institutions are strongly hierarchical: which results in a lack of connections between them and a wide range of 'official' and 'accepted' sources. This in turn results in news favouring some ways of perceiving the world. (Goodwin 1990: 46)

Long live public-as-commercial television!

I am positive that the above analysis shows that the borderline between public and commercial is blurred, with 'public' broadcasters using commercial standards to capture the audience. In the examples given, the commercial broadcaster is constantly keeping the viewers' attention by using the reverse strategy of the 'simulated public (meaning everyone's) view'. Another implication of the material could be that the 'classical' public sphere is threatened, not by the strength of commercial influences but by the lack of a public sphere concept as such in Poland, with its specific economic and cultural circumstances. .

Nowadays a number of serious arguments are presented to justify the importance of public television to a European information society. It is believed that public television has a special function in society – civil, social and educational and thus should be financed mainly by public funds. However, statements by Polish media moguls indicate ideological populism rather than any concern with the public sphere. It seems that the Polish view of the public sphere in the media sector is peculiar to itself. Public television presents scandal without artistic merit. It represents our simple and most basic desires. What is lacking in

Poland today is a strategy that presents a real picture of people 'as they are' in a way that encourages reflection about change for the better.

What we have learned from the battle of *Fakty* vs. *Wiadomości* barely figures in the light of global controversies between public and commercial news magazines. The most influential academic works, such as the Glasgow Media Group's analysis of news coverage in the mid-1970s and John Corner's analysis of the differences between BBC and ITN coverage (Corner 1995, chapter 3) provide researchers with the tools to discuss such issues impartially. In Poland there is a general presumption by the viewers, with little awareness of the genre and its strategies and means of expression, that television, as an institution, can be regarded as 'impartial' and 'fair'. *Fakty* is seen as entertainment, even if it communicates a very serious message and *Wiadomości* as the shaper of citizens' values, even if it makes extensive use of entertaining discourse. I worry about the future of my compatriots who do not have the critical tools to participate in the contemporary media scene.

The *Wall Street Journal*, 20 November 2003, contained an article entitled 'The Model Un-Europeans,' dealing with Poland's participation in the situation in Iraq. The article had a drawing of Prime Minister Leszek Miller and ended with the following fragment: 'To build a new Iraq, and to start democratic changes in the least democratic parts of the world, will be – to quote another un-European head of government – 'the right thing to do'. On that we absolutely agree with Mr. Blair.' There would be nothing remarkable about this, if not for the fact that the author of the text was none other than, as the paper states – 'Mr. Lis, the anchorman of *Fakty*, Poland's highest-rated private television evening news show.' One could ask who Lis has in mind when he says 'we' and why he is simply taking the position that the politicians have taken until now. Has the main anchorman of Polish television attained the position of a politician since he published his sixth book entitled *What's happening with Poland?* A news anchor as politician, a politician as news anchor, public as commercial, commercial as public – that is the Polish media scene in the first years of the twenty-first century.

References

Corner, John (1995) *Television Form and Public Address*, London, New York, Melbourne, Auckland: Edward Arnold.

Goodwin, Andrew (1990) 'TV news: striking the right balance?' in A. Goodwin & G. Whannel (eds.) *Understanding Television*, London: Routledge, pp. 42–59.

Habermas, Jürgen (1984) 'The public sphere: An encyclopaedia article', *New German Critique*, Autumn, pp. 49–55.

Chapter 11

When the Elite Press Meets the Rise of Commercial Culture

Dominique Pasquier

Ecole Nationale Superieure des Télécommunications - Telecom ParisTech

C ould press coverage of culture be a good indicator of changes in cultural hierarchies and the recognition of the status of art? This is the question I would like to explore in this chapter by studying the evolution of the culture pages in a sample of different European popular and elite dailies selected from 1960, 1980 and 2000.

In all the countries studied, coverage of culture has increased a good deal, proportionally more than the increase of number of pages in the dailies, if we take into account the fact that most quality dailies have a TV/Radio supplement and many of them also have specialized supplements on entertainment and culture. As in the case of the financial sections (in which the increase is even bigger), we may relate this phenomenon to social processes (such as the general rise of the education level in western Europe over the last 40 years and the processes of urbanization) as well as to the development of television and other mass media. There is clearly a larger readership for culture and a new need for orientation as media consumers.

However, I will pay less attention here to quantitative changes than to qualitative evolutions. The way the press deals with culture has gone through obvious transformations in the topics covered, in the ways of tackling them, and in the modes of presentation. Of course, these transformations relate to general changes in the press that are not necessarily specific to culture, such as the systematization of specialized headings or the rise of visuals. Yet they also express and refer to new approaches to culture in Western societies: less reverent toward the high-brow humanist tradition and more concerned with media-linked cultural forms; less focused on cultural products and more interested in the personal characteristics of their authors. This double process of blurring frontiers between high culture and commercial art on the one hand and of the star status of cultural producers on the other has been the focus of debates in the sociology of culture during the last decade. I will examine how the press has translated in its columns these tensions around the status of high culture and the constitution of artistic values, and I will highlight the respective popular versus elite versions of those transformations.

Blurring frontiers?

The academic debates around Pierre Bourdieu's theories of cultural legitimacy after the publication of *Distinction* in 1979 offer an interesting intellectual frame to set the main questions I will address. In this book, Bourdieu's focus is on cultural capital, the relationship to cultural products and social domination. The theoretical model developed in *Distinction* relates cultural capital to the expression of tastes, and proceeds via three movements: distinction, fascination, deprivation. People with higher cultural capital have the power to classify, and rank in hierarchies, cultural products that, in turn, will consolidate their own social classification (thus, one could say that those who classify are classified by their own classifications). People within the ranks of the middle class show their cultural good will towards those classifications: they recognize their legitimacy in spite of the fact it deals with cultural goods that are out of their own cultural universe. In the lower segment of the population, people are obliged to consume symbolic goods that have been de-classified by those who elaborate the standards. Their relationship to culture is defined by constraint and lack. Their cultural universe has no autonomy.[1]

The repercussion of Bourdieu's model has been huge amongst the French academic community as well as among the larger public; later, it also had a considerable impact abroad. *Distinction* was the first of a long list of best selling books written by Bourdieu. It imposed to a great extent the idea that very rigid cultural hierarchies should be related to processes of social domination.

Some sociologists of culture have challenged Bourdieu's model, among them Olivier Donnat, a French researcher well-known for his longitudinal surveys about cultural practices in France (Donnat 1998). Donnat argues that Bourdieu's analyses are historically-dated; they describe a cultural hierarchy that indeed functioned that way up to the 1980s, but which is no longer so accurate (Donnat 1994).[2] First, he shows that Bourdieu's model cannot explain why high culture lost a large part of its prestige within the generation under 35, which is the generation that directly benefited from school democratization: how does one explain the decline of high culture in a generation that has a higher cultural capital than previous generations at the same age?

Donnat's main argument is, therefore, that high culture does not have the same status as it used to have because of the radicalization during the 80s of a process of synergy between media, advertising and culture. We witness today a hybridization of cultural universes: the proliferation of youth-culture products; the commercial promotion of high-culture products (he takes the example of compilations of classical music on CDs on the larger market during the 80s); the decline of the distinctive power of some cultural practices such as book reading; as well as the development of forms of cultural eclecticism allowing more numerous and more diversified forms of coexistence of tastes. This younger generation might now associate a taste for high culture with a taste for cultural forms that are not – or not yet – considered as legitimate culture, without feeling socially stigmatized.

Donnat's analysis thus offers a more fluid model that leaves open the possibility of blurring frontiers between high and low culture, and he identifies new forms of taste combinations that do not follow the previously dominant cultural hierarchies, and which borrow elements from a much wider range of cultural products.

Can we find traces of this mutation in the press coverage of culture? The answer is yes. Donnat is even right in dating it, since the major changes in the elite papers' coverage of culture happened after the eighties. Let us take *Le Monde* and *Le Parisien* as illustrations. In

1960 there are strong differences in the elite and popular versions of culture; twenty years later, the elite paper makes modest incursions into popular culture but still has a rather highbrow definition of the kind of cultural products that deserve to be reviewed. In 2000, the transformation is spectacular; the range of cultural products promoted is much more similar. Interestingly, it is the elite paper that changed direction the most in the inclusion and treatment of topics or modes traditionally present in the popular daily. This general trend towards what we might call a greater de-differentiation is manifested through three main evolutions.

First evolution: a change in topics, with a decline of coverage of the most elitist cultural practices in favour of commercial media. In the 60s, high culture is very present in *Le Monde* with an extensive coverage of performing arts such as concerts, ballets, opera, theatre (they even list those in the Paris area). Coverage of television, on the contrary, is minimal: there is no programme listing and the short daily column about one of the previous day's TV programmes does not hide its elitist premise. Comments are restricted to documentaries and cultural programmes, never about serials, game- or variety shows. At that same period, *Le Parisien* focuses on movies – which are extensively reviewed, and television – with a complete guide to programmes. It pays some attention to theatre plays or even books, but gives them very little space. In 1980, *Le Monde* still covers major classical music concerts and gives a complete list of theatre productions. The major changes seem to have taken place after that date: in the 2000 editions, there is no guide and very few articles about live shows in *Le Monde*; coverage of movies, TV-programme listing, and books occupy the larger space in the culture pages. *Le Parisien* reinforces its attention to TV programming and still has a lot of space dedicated to movies.

Second evolution: the quality press opened its columns more and more to minor genres and commercial culture. The coverage of books in the French elite newspaper is a good example of that trend. Book coverage went through a spectacular increase over the years: it was non-existent in the two issues of *Le Monde* selected from 1960; in 1980, it appears as a section of 7 pages inside the daily of the Thursday edition; and in 2000 it is a supplement – in fact two supplements: one about general books, the other one about paperback editions (altogether 28 pages). The 1980 articles all deal with high-culture books, either novels (a German writer and French authors published by high brow publishers such as Le Seuil and Gallimard) or essays (a full page is devoted to Deleuze and Guattari's new philosophical essay, including an article reminding of the impact of their book, *Anti Œdipus,* on French society; the other essays covered are in political science and anthropology).

In 2000, the choices are much more eclectic: the whole front page of the supplement is devoted to the re-editing of the 1950 version of *Tintin au pays de l'Or Noir*, with a large image from the album. There then follows half a page of reviews about several new books of science fiction selected by a journalist known for covering TV series, and a full page synthesis about new trends in detective novels. Next to these interesting incursions into the popular culture side of books, one may also find reviews of works by historians, as well as some by philosophers and sociologists. From literature there is a full-page review devoted to a novel by a German writer described as 'difficult to read' ('l'œuvre déroutante d'Arno Schmidt'). Interestingly, popular and higher culture books are intertwined in the supplement, with no difference in their typographic treatment. Thus, the quality paper has clearly extended its definition of 'culture', now including youth culture as well as minor genres, besides still dealing with more traditional types of literature.

We have a confirmation of the process when noting that, on the same day in 2000, the popular paper and the quality papers share several common subjects for cultural articles, among them the review of a book anthology about the Beatles. In 1980, most *Le Monde* musical articles still deal with classical music, even if we may find a small column about a rock group (but playing in a high-brow theatre). In 2000, most articles about music deal with jazz or rock/pop music, and, while there are no articles about opera or classical music, we may read a half-page article dedicated to the new success of French musical comedies. The same year, *Le Parisien* includes articles about Bob Dylan, a jazz player, a French variety singer, a musician who remixes classical music pieces into more accessible tunes, and a long review about a successful French musical, *The Ten Commandments*. Actually, music appeared as a cultural sector early on in the process of hybridization, as Richard Peterson has shown when studying 'changing highbrow taste'. And this evolution, as he notes, is notable through the press treatment of, for example, country music (Peterson & Kern 1996).[3]

Third evolution: Last but not least is the emphasis on personality in culture coverage. *Le Parisien* started to place this focus on authors rather than works as early as the 1960s. Articles about books deal with writers, articles about movies with directors or, more often, the leading actors and, in all cases, it gives personal details about their lives. One example is an article about a novelist in one edition of *Le Parisien* from the 60s, which, while giving a few insights about the book's content, discusses many details about the author: the region of France he is from; his parents' profession – winegrowers, which explains his taste and knowledge about wines; his love of long-distance travel; and includes many anecdotes. This personalized angle becomes more and more present in *Le Monde* over the years. In the 60s, cultural coverage is neutral and focused on the works. Now, there are systematic insights into the private life of the artists. In *Le Monde* from 2000, major new movies get two articles: one a review of the film, the other one an interview with the director about why he made the movie, with reference to his professional and also personal biography. This personal approach to authors correlates with another phenomenon: visualization, which I take up below.

Those three evolutions all point in the same direction: quality-press coverage of culture is closer to the popular press than it used to be in the 60s, though the popular paper did not change its angle on culture significantly, despite giving much more space to it. The changed standards came from the bottom, rather than the top, unlike the scheme described by Bourdieu. A similar reverse process has been noted and studied in a sector such as fashion. Fred Davis (1992) shows how high fashion has been borrowing more and more elements from street culture (Dior basket shoes) or from the lower-class items of clothes (Chanel jeans). We are now facing a much more complex cultural landscape where tastes and standards do not follow a linear path from the upper to the lower classes, or from urban to rural populations. There are many peripheral sources for culture, such as ethnic influences, suburban or youth subcultures. There is no longer one centre that diffuses standards of legitimacy, but rather various and crossing influences that all contribute to impose new cultural values. The evolution of *Le Monde* illustrates well this process of recombining a traditional highbrow approach to culture with accounts of culture linked to mass media or advertising.

Still, we should not overestimate the extent of this rapprochement. Some significant details show that there are nevertheless divergent conceptions of culture between the two newspapers.

- *The hit parade approach is much more present and important in the popular paper.* Bourdieu denounces it as a symptom of heteronomous (as opposite to autonomous) modes of recognition, which go in a circular movement: the more you sell, the more you will be selling. Each week, *Le Parisien* publishes the top ten book and CD sales, the top ten attended movies, and the 7 best-rated TV programmes from the week before. Those lists occupy a full page, with short vignettes about the moves up and down. *Le Monde* only publishes a hit parade for movies and, visually, it is not very compelling. The sales success of cultural products is clearly not the only, nor a major, criterion for coverage in *Le Monde*.

- *There are different cultural sectors in the two papers which are seldom reviewed in the form of articles.*

We might compare the treatment of books compared to television, for example. In *Le Parisien,* the best-seller list is often the only form of book coverage. Though placed in *Le Monde*'s main section, TV might be covered only by the listing of the programmes of the day. Even in the TV/radio supplement of *Le Monde* there are few articles about programmes themselves, but rather general articles about the media industry or specific producers. So, a cultural sector might be covered in both papers but with large differences in the paper's involvement.

- *Within a specific culture section, editorial choices of cultural products differ.*

If both papers may now cover the same books, there are nevertheless books that are only reviewed by the quality paper, such as foreign novels or books of the human- and social sciences.

- *There is a 'quality' way of talking about minor or commercial genres that is very different from the one in the popular press.*

This could be called a cultivated look, which includes cross references, historical details, international comparisons, i.e., a connoisseur's approach. The popular paper does not bother framing such productions with ambitious backgrounds.

• *Finally,* we *might note that the focus can differ when using the personification angle.*

On the same day in 2000 *Le Parisien* and *Le Monde* published articles about the movie *Crouching Tiger, Hidden Dragon*, but *Le Monde* interviews the director, Ang Lee, and *Le Parisien* the main actor, Chow Yun Fat. And more generally, *Le Monde* focuses more on the producers of culture rather than the performers.

New modes of recognition? The star system of culture

In further writings about artistic recognition, Bourdieu developed some other points that he had previously sketched in a seminal article from 1971 about the market of symbolic products. In this article he was mainly opposing a restricted cultural field of production, aimed at enlightened peers, to a large-production cultural field, where consecration is obtained by an heteronomous logic through the general audience's judgement. He acknowledged as a fact that the development of media, and especially television, has contributed to blur frontiers between the aesthetic pole and the commercial pole. In *Contre Feux* (1998 & 2001) he denounces the loss of autonomy of the cultural field and the effect of mass media upon cultural uniformization. For Bourdieu this loss of autonomy has to be understood as an effect of interdependency between fields: for example, the influence of the journalistic field on the cultural field leads media, and especially television, to privilege cultural works and producers that suit well the market's requirement (like being a good talker, able to defend one's work, or being telegenic). There is a circular reinforcement logic: cultural industries promote works and producers that are in their turn capable of promoting the media: mediagenic authors promote media shows as well as being promoted by them.

In Bourdieu's most recent analysis, therefore, larger and larger areas of culture have fallen under the influence of those heteronomous processes of consecration by the mass media. But there is still a small sector of restrictive production that escapes it, and where artists keep on seeking recognition by their peers within their specialized field. This sector is presented as an alternative, where artistic recognition by peers is opposed to commercial recognition by the media. This bi-polar structure is largely developed in *Les règles de l'art* ('The Rules of Art') (Bourdieu 1992) about the literary field. On one side we find cultural products with a short life cycle, intended for mass markets, highly promoted by media and integrating consumers' pre-existing expectations, on the other, products from the 'anti economic economy of pure art' (ibid: 202) with a slow diffusion in narrow markets. As Le Guern suggests, the Bourdieu model therefore relies on very rigid distinctions between low and high culture, visibility and notoriety, commercial and pure art, which has been submitted to various types of critiques (Le Guern 2003). Sociologists of art, for example, point to the fact that artistic values have long been constituted at the articulation of market and of cultural institutions through the cooperation of art dealers, critics, collectors, curators and auctioneers, who all work for the promotion of artistic notoriety (Moulin 1995 & 1997). Moreover, strategies of promotion mobilizing the media appear to have become more numerous since the 80s, as shown in Moulin's discussion about American avant-garde art, those 'rockers of the art whose celebrity and career were constructed on life styles' (Moulin 1997: 74). The history of art is marked by a shift from art work to signature, and the media just amplified the move by making another shift from the art work to the singular person of the author of work.

Donnat (1994) underlines the evolutions in modes of artistic recognition since the 80s when the process of integration of advertising and media in the cultural economy started growing, but he does not oppose media visibility to artistic notoriety as does Bourdieu. On one hand, he argues, the media tend to promote artists that have already acquired some notoriety among their peers. On the other hand, the processes of recognition have evolved; all artists now have to manage two modes: one in their peer's society and one linked to the media industry. And reputations acquired via the media may be converted to a capital useful in the artistic field (for example, after a successful participation in a television show, an author might get taken on by a better publishing company) We can no longer oppose internal recognition to commercial exposition, nor can we situate artists on a scale that goes linearly from 'art for art's sake' to commercial art. And we cannot, as Bourdieu does, oppose recognition to diffusion.

This move is again quite apparent in the press corpus and can be studied through the rise of the visual element in the coverage of culture. Visualization illustrates important changes in modes of promotion and artistic consecration. As we can see in Tables 1 and 2, culture is a sector where the rise of visualization has been very important between 1960 and 2000. It has more than doubled in quality papers and now covers 9 out of 10 culture stories in the popular papers. The popular papers started to have a strategy of visualizing stories in any content section early on, with, on average, nearly half the stories containing a visual in

Table 1: Quality papers: Percentage of illustrations by stories' content, 1960, 1980, 2000, all countries (five most important stories).

	1960	1980	2000
Front page	35	48	44
News (home and foreign)	33	35	59
Economy	21	44	72
Sport	41	71	82
Culture	37	53	76

Table 2: Popular Papers: Percentage of illustrations by stories' content, 1960, 1980, 2000, all countries.

	1960	1980	2000
Front page	47	48	76
News (home and foreign)	49	53	85
Economy	23	33	87
Sport	76	90	100
Culture	51	75	89

the 60s, compared to one out of three for the quality papers. Data by countries show that visualization of cultural coverage was much more present in the Scandinavian press that anywhere else at that date.

The French dailies may be taken as an example to illustrate the qualitative evolutions. Back in the 60s when visuals were not that numerous, especially in the quality paper, culture was mainly illustrated with small reproductions of posters of films or a few photographs of important performers, usually extracted from a movie or a theatrical show. In that sense it was a picture of the *work*, even if it showed a scene with actors. At that period, one may also notice a much more elaborate way of using visuals in *Le Parisien* than in *Le Monde*. In its daily page dedicated to '[t]he screen, the scene, the books, the music, the arts, the music hall, the cabarets' (sic), *Le Parisien* already uses large close-ups of actors from a movie scene (three appealing pictures of couples of actors occupies a large part of the page, among them Yves Montand and Marilyn Monroe for the release of *The Millionaire*) and there is even a small photograph of an author to illustrate a critique of his new book. By comparison, visuals in *Le Monde* are very austere: they are mainly adverts, showing a book cover or theatre and movies posters, used to break up the monotony of lengthy programme listings.

In 1980, the reviewing of books in *Le Monde* relies on new visual elements, using mainly material from the publishers' advertising for new novels (essay authors have the same kind of advertisement as before, a black and white photograph of the front cover). Advertisements for novels now contain the book cover and photographs of smiling authors. Movie poster reproductions are much bigger than before, and given more space in the programme lists. Thus, advertisers in 1980 understood the importance of visuals to sell cultural goods, though the paper itself does not. They use few visuals with the articles: at the most, drawn sketches but no photographs. However, *Le Parisien* in the same year already has a heavily-visualized approach to culture. Performers are the great winners of the operation: movies or cabaret actors, TV hosts and journalists, and singers all get more coverage than hitherto.

In the year 2000, *Le Monde*'s book supplement has many articles, accompanied by large photographs of the authors, again novelists, and there is not a single advert for books without a visual, even in the case of essays. Furthermore, we find many more photographs in other cultural sectors: a picture of the Beatles, one of a flamenco singer, as well as several pictures from movies to illustrate critical articles, and smaller pictures of TV programmes (always films) in the list page of the day. That might not sound much compared to *Le Parisien,* which now has large photographs to go with each article, but clearly the reader gets a very different impression when going through the pages of articles about books that now depend on visual effects to avoid the impression of there being too much text to read.

A short comparison with the British and Italian quality papers[4] over the same time period seems to indicate that the decline of coverage of products of high culture has been less important in those two countries than in France. In *The Times* or *Il Corriere della Sera,* 2000 editions, we find many more articles about art exhibitions, classical music concerts or ballets. But between 1980 and 2000, when culture was given a larger space in both papers, the expansion went in favour of more eclectic choices. *Il Corriere della Sera's* coverage of music combines articles about jazz or variety with reviews of operas and ballets, rather than rock festivals, and with programme guides for all the main Italian cities, as well the La Scala programme. *The Times* gives considerable space to television programmes and American commercial movies, as well as to reviews of classical concerts and ancient-art exhibitions. Moreover, the shift of focus from art works to producers, and its correlative process of an increasing visualization, especially with more photographs of performers, is very similar to the one observed in the French press. In *The Times* in 2000, articles are illustrated by pictures of movie actors (Eddy Murphy, Paul Newman) or TV serial stars, as well as photographs of classical musicians and even a reproduction of an oil portrait of an early twentieth century composer. The mediation of art by artists appears to be a general phenomenon in the European press and it is clearly not restricted to the less legitimate cultural producers. The sample of Italian and British quality papers shows that high art might get the same visual treatment as commercial culture.

The press corpus analysed here tends to show a process of popularization of the elite way of looking at culture. This process encompasses some contested issues. Some might argue that these evolutions herald the end of the independence of culture from market constraints. Others might, on the contrary, think that it opens new opportunities to counter the failure of cultural democratization of high culture for the larger public – since, as all studies show, attendance at cultural institutions such as museums or theatres is still an elite practice. Does the increase of celebrity culture mean a decline of interest in the arts? This is a question that could not be answered without a reception study that would probably show that appreciation of the personality angle and the stardom of artists varies by age, gender and social origins of the consumers. But the process itself has clearly to be related to the development of television and the magazine press in all western countries, and its correlated transformation of consumers' approach to culture. Dailies would take a risk by turning their backs on the visual culture that they have developed to appeal to their own readership: they have to actually illustrate the individuals they write about, even in the financial section. One may wonder what the use of a novelist's picture offers to the understanding of his/her book, but one could not ignore that television has developed this need for familiar faces and constructed intimacies at a distance (Meyrowitz 1994). And it is perhaps not surprising that the popular dailies made this move to the visualizing of art earlier than the qualities, as their readership is more geared to a television culture than to a written culture.

We could consider with more optimism the fact that, over the forty year period considered here, the increase of culture coverage coincides with broader conceptions of culture in the most elitist papers. It does not mean that they are trying to attract a larger readership down the social scale but rather that cultural hierarchies are less rigid than they used to be. In a way this process has been initiated by artists themselves in many sectors, especially the visual arts and music, with avant-garde movements integrating into their work influences from the media and the advertisement. This de-hierarchization process might now be resonating among the cultural consumers themselves and may signal the end of the strict opposition between pure art and commercial culture that the romantic revolution had imposed at the end of the nineteenth century.

Notes

1. This point has been much discussed by Grignon & Passeron (1989). Passeron does not contest cultural legitimacy in Bourdieu's theory but he challenges what he calls the legitimist shift in the model, which, as a consequence, forbids a sense to the cultural world of popular classes. He argues that domination works, but not all the time, and not in every case. We should study the failures of domination, he says, not in the strategies of resistance (as would Cultural studies' researchers, Passeron estimates that resistance means the acknowledgement of the principle of domination), but in those moments when what he calls a 'forgetting of domination' happens. He refers on that point to Hoggart's analysis in *The Uses of Literacy*, which shows that popular cultures don't have a mystified and subservient attitude to culture and can develop an autonomous cultural universe. Passeron's critics give interesting explanations to explain why media studies in France were so slow to produce anything in the 80s (who wants to study the hollowness of a culture?), and even slower to integrate Anglo-Saxon works about reception though at the same time Barthes, Metz and de Certeau were extremely successful exports.
2. A broader historical perspective would show that it was during the beginning of the twentieth century that rigid classifications between high art and popular art were established. Paul DiMaggio, in a seminal article, analyses the relationships between social structure, patterns of artistic consumption and production, and the ways in which artistic genres are classified (DiMaggio 1987). One may refer also to Levine's analysis of the status transformation of Shakespeare's plays in America, from a popular art form to the fare of an elite audience, during the two first decades of twentieth century (Levine 1988)
3. 'Intellectuals have long provided the grounds for an aesthetic understanding of jazz, blues, rock, and blue grass music. More recently country music has begun to be taken seriously as magazine articles in elite cultural periodicals such as *American Heritage* and books by humanist scholars begin to provide omnivores with the tools they need to develop an aesthetic understanding of country music. (Peterson and Kern 1996)
4. No comparison with the popular paper is possible since there is no equivalent of the northern European tabloid press in France or Italy.

References

Bourdieu, P. (1971) 'Le marché des biens symboliques', *L'année Sociologique,* 22, pp. 7–26.

Bourdieu, P. (1979) *La Distinction, critique sociale du jugement*, Paris: Editions de Minuit.

Bourdieu, P. (1992) *Les règles de l'art. Genèse et structuration du champ littéraire*, Paris: Le Seuil.

Bourdieu, P. (1998) *Contre-feux*, Paris: Liber – Raisons d'agir.

Bourdieu, P. (2001) *Contre-feux 2*, Paris: Liber – Raisons d'agir.

Davis, F. (1992) *Fashion, Culture, and Identity*, Chicago: The University of Chicago Press.

DiMaggio, P. (1987) 'Classification in art', *American Sociological Review*, vol 52, pp. 440–55.

Donnat, O. (1994) *Les Français face à la culture*, Paris: La Découverte.

Donnat O. (1998) *Les pratiques Culturelles des Français. Enquête 1997*, Paris: La Documentation Française.

Grignon, C. & Passeron, J.C., (1989) *Le Savant et le Popupaire. Misérabilisme et populisme en sociologie et littérature*, Paris Gallimard-Le Seuil.

Hoggart, R. (1958) *The uses of literacy: Aspects of working-class life*, Penguin Modern Classics.

Le Guern, P. (ed.) (2003) 'Les nouvelles formes de la consécration culturelle' (New forms of cultural consecration), Introduction, *Réseaux*, 21, n°117, pp. 9–44.

Levine, L.W. (1988) *Highbrow/Lowbrow: The emergence of cultural hierarchy in America*, Cambridge: Harvard University Press.

Meyrowitz, J. 1994, 'The life and death of media friends: New genres of intimacy and mourning' in R. Cathcart & S. Drucker (eds.) *American Heroes in a Media Age,* Cresskill, NJ: Hampton Press.

Moulin, R. (1995) *De la valeur de l'art*, Paris: Editions Flammarion.

Moulin, R. (1997*), L'artiste, l'institution et le marché*, Paris: Editions Flammarion.

Peterson, R. & Kern, R. (1996), 'Changing highbrow taste: from snob to omnivore', *American Sociological Review*, vol.61, pp. 900–7.

Chapter 12

The Sounds of Change: Representations of Music in European Newspapers 1960-2000

Klaus Bruhn Jensen
University of Copenhagen

Peter Larsen
University of Bergen

Introduction

If any one social field can be said to articulate and symbolize the reconfiguration of culture in Europe during the post–1945 period, it is music. For one thing, rock'n'roll, as well as other popular music forms, became constitutive elements of, and resources for, the exercise of citizenship by anti-authoritarian movements from the 1960s onwards. For another thing, classical music was in for one more round of critique and challenge, partly from within the institution of art music, reassessing its repertoire of expressive forms, partly from without as part of continuing debates about and across the high-low divide of culture as such. During the same period, both popular and art music forms were practised under economic and technological conditions that were widely perceived to entail intensified commercialization. This chapter presents an analysis of how music was represented in the newspaper press of selected European countries during the period 1960–2000. While portraying the state of the musical field during this period, newspapers have also traditionally served as a forum for the promotion of, as well as reflections on, music as a social means of communication.

Perhaps surprisingly, music remains among the least-researched aspects of the media and communication field. That is in spite of the omnipresence of music in audiovisual, electronic, and digital media, as well as in the everyday soundscapes (Schafer 1977) of home, shops, and cultural institutions. This silence of research may be due, at least in part, to the inherent difficulties of theorizing and analysing music as communication. Unfortunately, media studies have found little inspiration within traditional musicology because of its abiding emphasis on 'great works by great men.' In recent decades, a growing body of work has served to consolidate a field of popular music studies that examines music as both social practice and cultural form (for overviews, see Frith & Goodwin 1990; Middleton 1990). Since the 1980s, moreover, the 'new musicology' has helped to refocus attention on the historical and socioeconomic contexts from which music arises and engages its users (e.g. Kramer 2002; Leppert 1993; McClary 1991). Most recently, after a long period of preoccupation with visual forms of communication, research seems on the verge of including sound in general among the modalities that an inclusive field of communication studies needs to address (Bull & Back 2003; Jensen 2006).

Methodology

The present study aimed to examine three interrelated research questions:

RQ 1: How has the coverage of music been organized in relation to other types of subject matter in newspapers?

By documenting the layout and formal organization of music coverage, including the presence of photographs and other visuals, one may begin to establish a profile of how music has been conceived of by newspapers in terms of categories such as 'arts' and 'politics.'

RQ 2: To what degree have different musical traditions, particularly 'classical' and 'popular' forms, been related within the coverage, and according to which journalistic agendas?

Beyond issues of whether Bach and The Beatles might occur on the same page, this research question directs attention toward specific understandings of music as a social phenomenon, for instance, the 'stardom' of certain performers within both art and entertainment.

RQ 3: By what modes of address have readers been invited to become interested in and, perhaps, engage themselves in music as a cultural practice?

The modes of address include not only genres, such as the preview and review of concerts, but also various aspects of intertextuality and intermediality that serve to embed newspaper coverage into the wider cultural environment of which both the daily press and concert venues are a part.

The sample consists of so-called 'qualities' and 'populars' – the comparatively serious broadsheet newspapers and the more-or-less-sensational tabloids that have remained prototypes of the daily press in Northern Europe – for the years 1960, 1980, and 2000, from Denmark, Germany, and the United Kingdom (see Appendix for details). In this way, the analysis draws on the comparative framework that informs several articles in this volume, and which is accounted for elsewhere.

It should be specified from the outset that the present analysis was exploratory in nature, seeking to identify a range of expressive forms and interpretive categories by which music has been represented to the newspaper-reading public. Whereas some of these categories lend themselves to further research of the quantitative content-analytical variety (Berelson 1952; Krippendorff 2004), other findings will be of interest, for instance, for qualitative case studies of how music as a distinctive form of communication has been articulated within different media and discourse types (e.g. Wetherell, Taylor & Yates 2001). To exemplify, the very occurrence of photographs in reviews of classical music during 2000 and their previous absence suggests changing premises regarding the appropriate means of representing music; the very co-occurrence of classical and popular music in the tabloids of one country, but not

Table 1.

		Organization & layout			Music cultures			Music event & news text		Individual & system		Text / media / action		
		Supplement	Section	Mix	Visualization	High	Low	Mix	Preview	Review	Personalization	Politicization	Intertext	Intermedia	Interaction
1960															
DK	'Pop'		x	x	x	x	x	x	x	x	x	x	x	x	
	'Qual'			x	x	x	x		x	x	x		x	x	
G	'Pop'		x	x	x		x		x		x	x			
	'Qual'		x	x		x	x		x		x				
UK	'Pop'		x	x	x		x		x	x	x		x	x	
	'Qual'		x	x	x	x	x	x	x	x	x	x	x		
1980															
DK	'Pop'		x	x	x		x		x		x	x	x	x	
	'Qual'		x		x		x		x	x			x	x	
G	'Pop'		x	x	x	x	x		x		x		x		x
	'Qual'			x	x	x				x					
UK	'Pop'		x	x	x		x		x		x			x	
	'Qual'		x	x	x	x	x	x	x	x	x		x	x	
2000															
DK	'Pop'		x	x	x		x		x	x		x	x	x	
	'Qual'	x	x	x	x	x	x	x	x	x				x	
G	'Pop'		x	x	x	x	x	x	x		x	x			x
	'Qual'			x	x	x	x	x		x	x	x	x		
UK	'Pop'			x	x	x	x		x		x		x		
	'Qual'	x	x	x	x	x	x	x	x	x	x	x	x	x	x

DK: Denmark / G: Germany / UK: United Kingdom.
'Pop': popular tabloid newspaper / 'Qual': quality broadsheet newspaper.

of another country, may bear witness to different (newspaper) cultures. Thus, the primary concern of the chapter is the identification, description, and interpretation of *types* of music coverage, not the recurrence of *tokens* in any statistically representative sense.

The analysis proceeds in three steps. First, music coverage was identified and documented with reference to a range of categories:

- *Organization and layout*: the occurrence of music in a dedicated cultural supplement, in a headlined section, or mixed in with other types of coverage, as well as the presence of any visuals
- *Music cultures*: the occurrence and co-occurrence of 'high' and 'low' musical forms in either qualities or populars, perhaps within the same section or page
- *Music event and news text*: the presence of previews and/or reviews
- *Individual and system*: the 'personalization' of, e.g., performers over and above their art, and the 'politicization' of music with reference to its sources in or implications for other social institutions
- *Text, media, action*: the occurrence of intertextual features, intermedial references, and 'interactive' components such as quizzes through which readers may win concert tickets.

Second, each of these categories calls for description and elaboration with reference to the actual sample of newspapers. Special attention is given here to similarities and differences between qualities and populars in the countries examined, since these prototypes of media are likely to bear witness to changing conceptions of the cultural field and of the place of music in it. Third, selected themes, as represented in the newspapers, for example, the high-low divide and the relative emphasis on local and global musics, are placed in their cultural and historical context, and interpretations are offered of their implications for the place of music in contemporary society – as an aesthetic as well as a political phenomenon.

Findings

Organization and layout

As summarized together with other findings in Table 1, the organization of newspaper coverage of music has taken two main forms. On the one hand, music has been presented along with other cultural forms as a specific domain, whether as 'arts' or as 'entertainments'. In this regard, the sample suggests a growing segmentation of cultural coverage, so that, by 2000, most of the papers included either a headlined section or a supplement that was devoted, in part, to culture. In one country (Denmark), the quality newspaper comprised a supplement, a section, as well as culture mixed in with other coverage. Variations, however, are found in the German and British popular newspapers: In the British *Daily Mirror*, music and other cultural events appeared in 2000 as part of celebrity and television sections; in

Germany's *Bild Zeitung*, cultural coverage remained mixed in with other topics throughout the period in accordance with the 'Tivoli layout' of this paper.

On the other hand, music-related coverage has continued to appear in a variety of contexts. In Germany, both popular and quality papers in 1960 noted the arrest of a pop singer who ran down a policeman in his car and, in 2000, they similarly covered musical performances as part of the ten-year anniversary of German reunification – the quality newspaper under the heading of *Bratwurst und Barock* ('burgers and baroque'). And, not surprisingly, the economic implications, for instance, of the Napster file-sharing service and of mergers in the record and media industry in 2000 brought music into the financial pages in all three countries.

A particularly noteworthy feature of newspaper layout during the period is the growing use of visuals, especially photographs. The present sample indicates that photographs of performers, instruments, and musical events have become an integral part of coverage, and that this visualization of news came later to the qualities than to the populars. While the journalistic, technological, and marketing backgrounds to this development fall outside the scope of the present analysis, it is interesting to note that photographs thus seem to have crossed several divides of cultural journalism – between qualities and populars, and between high and low music forms – so that images of classical performers may now be considered appropriate within quality arts coverage.

A preliminary interpretation of the organization and segmentation of coverage suggests that music, and other aspects of culture, have gained a higher as well as more distinct profile within the newspapers examined, as indicated by supplements, sections, and visuals. Although the study did not aim to measure either the overall or the shifting proportions of music coverage, a review of the copies in question makes clear that more, more clearly designated, and more illustrated, coverage of music has become available to readers, if only because of the greater bulk and the growing visualization of newspapers as such during the post-1960 period. An additional research question was how this profile of music in the press relates to the wider, high and low cultural formations with which readers are aligned.

Music cultures

The familiar duality of high and low forms within modern culture (e.g. Berman 1982; Huyssen 1986; Williams 1983) finds an emphatic expression in music. As shown famously by Bourdieu ([1979]1984), musical tastes are among the most sensitive indicators of cultural orientation and social position. Nevertheless, the high-low divide does not map neatly onto the quality-popular prototypes in these newspapers.

Table 1, again, summarizes the occurrence of music of the high (classical, symphonic, operatic) and of the low (rock, jazz, folk) variety in different newspapers across the sample. In addition, the sub column entitled 'mix' serves to indicate whether these forms appear together in the same page or section.

In overview, the quality newspapers offer the more inclusive kind of coverage since, with one exception (Germany in 1980), low musical forms appear on their pages for all the years and countries examined. Moreover, it is not uncommon to encounter high and low music side by side in the qualities. In 2000, this was the case for the qualities in all three countries. In comparison, one issue each of the Danish popular *B.T.* (1960) and of the German *Bild* (2000) feature classical and pop performers on the same page. However, in most of the popular newspapers examined, classical music does not enter into their cultural universe, certainly in any elaborated form.

The implications of the occurrence and co-occurrence of these different musical forms depend importantly on the qualitative detail of how each is represented, narrated, and argued about, and the theme is addressed further in the discussion section below. What appears as inclusiveness on the part of quality newspapers might still be premised on a cultural hierarchy which, explicitly or implicitly, subordinates popular musical forms – and perhaps correspondingly silences classical music in popular newspapers.

Music event and news text

Newspapers have historically covered recent concerts and, from the twentieth century, new recordings by shifting technologies. As such, their service to readers ranges from basic listings of upcoming events to more or less elaborate assessments of, and reflections on, the art and practice of music. For present purposes, this service can be summarized briefly in terms of 'previews' and 'reviews'.

Previews, first, come in very diverse forms, and occur in both qualities and populars. To exemplify, *The Times* for 1960 included an article-length account of an arguably unconventional programme for the upcoming philharmonic season, whereas the *Daily Mirror* for the same year announced a record, to appear the next day, featuring a comedian. Further, listings of when concerts and operas take place, or when radio or television broadcasts are scheduled, have been included in both types of newspapers, although not in all countries for all the years examined.

Reviews, in comparison, appear to be given special priority in the qualities. Criticism and evaluation particularly of classical concerts and records are regular features, and a 2000 issue of the *Frankfurter Allgemeine Zeitung* even included an essay-length contribution on Beethoven by the German philosopher Peter Sloterdijk. Certainly, the popular newspapers, to varying degrees, also provide reviews and recommendations but, at least in the present sample, mostly in a short, even ultra-brief format, such as 'a lovely melody that has been around a long time and now sprouts new words' (*Daily Mirror*, 6 October 1960).

Individual and system

Two key debates concerning the current state of the public sphere have addressed, on the one hand, tendencies in the press to focus on personalities rather than issues and, on the other hand, the potential political relevance and implications of cultural practices. In the terminology of social theory, these debates reconsider the relationship between individual agency and social structure at a discursive level (Giddens 1984). In short, is culture represented as the accomplishment of geniuses and stars? And, is culture said to proceed in a realm of its own, apart from social conflict and the exercise of power?

Regarding the personalization of cultural coverage, first, diverse perspectives on the individuals producing, performing, and facilitating music have been present throughout the period examined. In 1960, the *Daily Mirror* spotted a pop singer out dancing at a bar abroad; in 1980, the same paper reviewed the fate of the (financial) winners and losers on the periphery of The Beatles phenomenon in a substantial series of articles; and, in 2000, the *Mirror* noted the passing of Rolling Stone Keith Richards' father. Second, personalization is not a feature of the popular newspapers only, even if their coverage appears more elaborate and conspicuous in this respect. In a 1960 issue of the *Frankfurter Allgemeine Zeitung*, the opera singer Maria Callas denied having married the wealthy businessman Aristotle Onassis; the 1960 *Times* introduced the life of the composer Arnold Schönberg as a refugee during the 1930s as a background to his work. In 1980, again, both of these qualities noted the jailing of the punk rock musician Johnny Rotten.

The political implications of music and sound, similarly, are developed in some, if relatively few, instances in both qualities and populars. Interestingly, a British quality and a Danish popular for 1960 both served as forum for debate, initiated by letters to the editor, on when to broadcast 'serious' music on the radio; in the British case, a response was offered by the BBC director in charge. Also in 1960, *Bild* took up the larger question of auditory environments, including a reference to music, criticizing that loudspeakers in public places frequently serve as sources of noise, not of relevant information. In later years, the politics of music was taken up with reference to topics such as the disco culture of the 1980s; a 2000 retrospective exhibition on rock music and fashion; and music exchange via the Internet.

Text, media, action

The last element of the basic analysis served to identify interrelations between newspaper coverage of music, other media representations, and media-related action. Such interrelations are sometimes associated with technological and institutional change under headings of digitalization and convergence (Slevin 2000; Van Dijk 1999). In addition, however, these interrelations should be examined as cultural categories with a historical lineage (Bolter & Grusin 1999). 'Intertextuality' was developed early on within literary theory to account for the recurrence and reformulation over time of themes and genres (Bakhtin 1981; Kristeva

1984). 'Intermediality' has been on the agenda of media research at least since McLuhan (1964). And, 'interactivity' is still being developed as a theoretical and operational concept in order to account for the nature of interchanges between humans and (computer) media, and between humans through media (for an overview, see Neuman 2008).

Intertextuality, first of all, is in evidence in several varieties. The 1960 preview of a record by a British comedian relies, for example, on the reader's background knowledge of historical figures such as General Custer (as built through popular culture) to make its points and jokes. In the same year, *The Times* assumes a different kind of background knowledge on the part of its readers when it elaborates on a performance of Arnold Schönberg's works with reference to other classical composers and pieces. In both cases, the references between texts establish a frame of reference or horizon of expectations (Jauss 1982) that lends meaning to the text at hand. Accordingly, intertextuality can serve as a means of including the reader in a community of meaning (Fish 1979); it can also exclude readers beyond the particular horizon of expectations and its associated competences.

Media, moreover, rely on each other for inspiration as well as promotion. In the case of music, a natural reference point, in addition to records, is radio and television. Programmes have been duly listed in the three countries and, to varying degrees, previewed and reviewed, such as a 1980 preview of a radio opera by a Danish quality newspaper and its comparable 2000 preview of an opera evening on one of the public-service television channels. In some cases, intermediality is commercially motivated – as when the 1960 *Mirror* presents a Top 20 courtesy of the *New Musical Express*. In other cases, advertising as such serves to direct readers to music-related media: An advertisement in the Danish 1960 popular promises a life-size portrait of a hit singer as an insert into a magazine.

Interaction, finally, has traditionally been considered an ideal of political communication, not just in the case of contemporary 'interactive' media, but as the potential involvement of citizens, facilitated by media. The media serve as resources for social action and as portals to culture. In certain instances, the involvement of readers primarily serves marketing purposes: *Bild* of 1960 advertises the possibility of ordering 20 hit songs via the newspaper; *Bild* of 2000 covers a reader and fan who was given the opportunity to meet the singer Lionel Richie in person. In other instances, detailed previews along with listings of venues or radio and television channels can be considered resources for cultural participation. In one case, the 2000 *Times* offers a 'consumer's guide' to the composer Johann Sebastian Bach, digesting much information in an informal style to the uninitiated, which might promote both enjoyment of and dialogue about his works. Whether this implies a consumerist 'dumbing-down' of classical music or a facilitation of listeners' involvement across a wider cultural field is one issue for discussion and further research.

Discussion

High and low musics

Like other arts, music is a socially- and historically-contested phenomenon. Surveys have suggested that a broadening of musical tastes could be observed in all social groups during the period studied here. Nevertheless, in one study of US developments the most striking changes took place within the cultural elite: During the sample period, traditional supporters of high art developed a taste for and openness towards certain forms of popular music (Peterson & Kern 1996). Such a shift is exemplified by the Danish quality papers, which only mentioned popular music once in 1960 but, by 1980, provided comprehensive coverage of a variety of popular forms. In comparison, such coverage was rather more modest in *The Times* throughout the sample period and almost absent from the *Frankfurter Allgemeine Zeitung,* except for a couple of short paragraphs.

Not surprisingly, in all three countries, the quality papers have offered broad coverage of classical music, primarily in the form of reviews and in-depth discussions of recent trends, but including, as well, 'early music' (Renaissance and Baroque) and twentieth-century avant-garde arts. In these same papers, however, an ongoing process of defining 'art' and 'popular' music can be witnessed. On this point, *The Times* has stood out by including jazz under the heading of 'The Arts.' Already in 1960, *The Times* carried a detailed report from the Monterey jazz festival, emphasizing the avant-garde, such as the free forms of Ornette Coleman and John Coltrane, and the Third Stream compositions by Gunther Schuller, alongside reviews of classical music from Monteverdi to Schönberg. Later years feature reviews of avant-garde drummer Sonny Murray and pianist George Shearing. Arguably, jazz, particularly avant-garde jazz, qualified as 'high' culture.

In the popular newspapers in 1960, music coverage appears quite limited overall but does refer to a relatively wide range of musical forms, although classical music and jazz are rare guests. In the Danish case, a series of short paragraphs visit a broad spectrum of popular music from operettas to George Formby. German as well as Danish populars in 1960 print stories about music and musicians from the 'lowest' part of the field: a festival for street singers (*B.T.*) and a Berlin *Schlager* singer's alcohol problem (*Bild*).

In the subsequent years of the sample, popular newspapers devote an increasing number of pages to popular music (partly in accordance with the increased number of pages in newspapers generally). At the same time, a reduction in the variety of musical forms covered is in evidence. By 1980, most material represents the international mainstream of popular music – ABBA, the Bee Gees, Diana Ross, etc. – despite some coverage of local artists in the Danish papers. Furthermore, the popular newspapers reflect an institutionalization of the field since, during the 1970s, popular music had become consolidated and specialized, with stars, a canon of 'classical' works, and fans with a highly-developed sense for the often subtle distinctions between and within genres and subgenres. Accordingly, in 1980, retrospective articles about artists like The Beatles and Bob Dylan, and about works like The Band's *Big Pink* album, could expect to address a knowledgeable readership.

Classical music and jazz, as mentioned, hardly feature in the popular newspapers; a few short paragraphs in the Danish 1960 issues are exceptions that prove the rule. Instead, when coverage of classical music is found in the German and British populars, it is not 'about' music but serves different purposes. A few lines in the 1980 *Bild* about the conductor Karlheinz Böhm, who had been forced to postpone an opera premiere due to sudden illness, resemble the story about punk rock singer Johnny Rotten's jail sentence in providing a bit of human-interest excitement. One implication is that 'high' music will be mentioned regularly when the story in question fits familiar journalistic and narrative patterns in the popular press. Another implication is that this coverage may conceive of music in metonymic terms, that is, as a 'symbol' of a larger social and cultural worldview. While the German quality paper printed the entire lecture by the philosopher Peter Sloterdijk introducing the performance of Beethoven's Ninth Symphony in the Hamburger Musikhalle on the Day of the German Unification, *Bild* sided with the audience who became annoyed 'after a 30-minute lesson in philosophy' and tried (unsuccessfully) to applaud him off the stage. The criticism seems directed less at the music or the speaker than at the embedding cultural practice and social hierarchy.

The local and the global

For a little over 100 years, technologies of sound reproduction – gramophones, radio, and current digital devices – have made music available outside a specified time and place of performance. Still, music – as composed, performed, and communicated about in newspapers and elsewhere – remains associated with particular historical periods and national origins.

Given the continued profile of music as a *live* performance, it is a matter of course that qualities and populars in all three countries mainly deal with local events. Across the high-low divide, most previews as well as reviews concern local/national concerts, orchestras, soloists, bands, etc. An interesting exception is *The Times*, which carries in-depth coverage of international events throughout the sample period. Special correspondents report from concerts and festivals in the US, Vienna, and Tunis, and provide opera reviews from Paris and Helsinki. On a more modest scale, the Danish popular paper in 2000 printed a review of a Bob Dylan concert in Hamburg.

Regarding the origins of the compositions performed, not unexpectedly, the classical repertoire under review in the various national newspapers is international, except for a review of a concert commemorating a local Danish composer. 'High' music has always been international in its orientation, if selectively so. The core repertoire was written by a relatively small group of Central European composers.

Popular music represents a different kind of 'selective internationalism.' The period 1960–2000 coincided with the globalization of the music industry and with the rise of an international youth culture which thrived, not least, on international popular music. This historical context is clearly present in the reviews of both concerts and records. Most of the coverage relates to popular music that is Anglo-American, either by origin or by inspiration.

The exceptions to this dual emphasis on the Central European classics and the Anglo-American popular mainstream are few and far between. Again, *The Times* offers something extra. In 1960, for example, it includes quite a large, almost anthropological, description of a concert in Tunisia with indigenous performers playing local music. Similarly, the Danish 2000 quality paper provides reviews of local musicians playing music from the Balkans and of a record inspired by traditional Irish folk music.

Writers and readers

The possible social uses of music, and of music criticism, are indicated by their implied readers (and listeners) (Iser 1978). The present sample suggests stability as well as change in terms of the newspapers' modes of address and textual genres.

For the period as a whole, reviews with much detail predominate in the qualities, as noted, whereas shorter previews and celebrity stories are characteristic of the populars. In both cases, the communication presupposes a specific disparity in knowledge between writer and reader, a 'gap' that the newspaper may help to close, but the process of closing it will be different in each case. While relatively little background knowledge is required for most of the popular previews, a sophisticated, even expert, knowledge will be necessary to appreciate some of the quality reviews, although most texts have been designed to be informative and explanatory. A 1960 piece in *The Times* on Schönberg's violin concerto starts with an instructive introduction to the work; in the same year, readers of the Danish quality paper are told why Schumann's third symphony is called the *Rheinische*. Furthermore, the actual wording invites readers into a specific community of meaning or knowledge (while excluding others): The Danish 1960 quality states that 'general opinion' has long since recognized a certain soloist as one of 'the greatest contemporary masters'; a *Times* reviewer in the same year complains that 'although the trio sonata has now become an accepted part of our everyday musical life,' it is seldom heard in the concert halls; and another *Times* reviewer admits that 'for most of us Schönberg's violin concerto is still novel enough to be thrilling.' Thus, the quality newspapers come to presuppose a knowledge of classical music, its history, works, composers, and performers, plus specific listening habits as well as a mastery of basic musical terminology. To be one of 'us,' 'you' – the reader – must meet certain requirements.

The shift from music coverage that is mixed in with other topics to sections and supplements, especially in the quality newspapers, is of particular interest. In a socio-cultural perspective, the mixed-in coverage in the Danish 1960 quality might suggest an ideal reader that is a classic public-sphere citizen who wants to be informed about cultural events on a par with politics and the economy – a reader for whom a critical discussion of a concert in honour of a contemporary Danish composer is as important as financial problems within the Scandinavian Airlines System or Swiss military reform. In comparison, the placement of musical matters under 'The Arts' in *The Times* already in 1960 might suggest that music is an area apart from politics and a specialty to be handled by specialists addressing readers with special interests. In any event, it is such a compartmentalization of music and other cultural forms that can be retraced in the present sample, and which should be examined further in the context of changing conceptions of both journalism and citizenship.

A final aspect of the implied reader of these newspapers is the kind of cultural agency that the texts have anticipated on the part of their historically-changing readership: What can readers know and do about music with newspapers as their resource? Despite the small sample, it is interesting to note that the reviews of classical music in the 1980 and 2000 quality papers presume much less of an exclusive community of readers. There are no more references to a generalized 'we' and hardly any examples of 'pedagogical' presentations of trivial information. Instead, the texts seem to have been written for specialists by specialists, and some of the *Frankfurter Allgemeine Zeitung* reviews even anticipate the readership of a learned journal. In an interesting analogy, reviews of popular music from 1980 and 2000 exhibit some of the same basic features as the classical reviews. The treatment of popular concerts, as well as new records, in both Danish and British newspapers is premised on subtle distinctions and includes comprehensive references to other artists within the genres in question. Journalists address readers who may be connoisseurs of classical music, of popular music, or of both.

Conclusion

This exploratory study of European newspapers has identified an increased compartmentalization as well as prioritization of music and other cultural coverage during the period 1960–2000 (RQ1). While these features may be the outcome, in part, of a professionalization and marketization of the press during this period, they also suggest changes in how the public is invited to conceive of culture as a social practice. Further research is needed on how such discursive forms of organization and expression relate to what may be an ongoing 'culturalization' of sociopolitical life, the economy, as well as of the life projects of individuals (e.g. Beck, Giddens & Lash 1994; Harvey 1989). Second, the divide between high and low (musical) cultures can be seen to persist in this sample of newspapers (RQ2). This is so even though quality papers have come to pay more attention to popular music and even if readers of qualities as well as populars are addressed, to a degree, as 'experts of pop.' Music is one of the social fields in which basic values clash and conflicts are played out, as witnessed here by the two distinctive versions of the Sloterdijk incident. Third, the newspapers' modes of address similarly suggest that the quality papers offer more substantial resources than the popular papers for cultural participation, even while the explicitly political and interactive aspects of their music coverage also remain limited (RQ3).

It should be added that the high/low distinction refers to and covers a heterogeneous socio-musical field of subgenres and tastes (Bourdieu [1979]1984; Gripsrud & Hovden 2000; Rosenlund 2000). Moreover, the distinction itself is transitory. In a historical perspective, neither the musical features nor the social functions of high and low forms of music are fixed. This is illustrated, for instance, by changing conceptions of jazz and of 'traditional' or 'folk' music. At any given time, there will be a section of the socio-musical field which is 'in some sense subaltern, but with contents that are contested and subject to historical mutation' (Middleton & Manuel 2007). Although technical and aesthetic criteria have often been invoked to define certain types of music as low or subaltern, such criteria are first and foremost expressions of preferred lifestyles and, ultimately, of social power relations. As a result, the distinction between superior and subaltern musics remains in flux (Larsen 2002).

1960–80 was a period of particular flux as the emerging youth culture contributed to significant changes in attitudes towards popular culture, including music. Several forms of music that were considered subaltern at the beginning of the period – varieties of jazz, rock, and folk music – became accepted, if not as 'high,' then as a legitimate presence within the socio-musical field. In subsequent decades newspapers have participated in the redefinition and negotiation of music as a cultural practice, as reflected in the national samples of this study.

The role of music journalism in recent history may recall the importance of music criticism at the beginning of what is commonly considered the 'classical' period of Western music. When, by the late eighteenth century, music became noticeably more 'absolute,' instrumental, and complex in its mode of communication, readers needed some basic guidance on how to listen to and appreciate this art (Goehr 1992: 236–39), which early newspapers and periodicals could offer. Music criticism has remained central to high culture and the quality press, being one element of the deliberative potential of the public sphere. In recent decades, the media have become a more inclusive cultural forum (Newcomb & Hirsch 1984) and, increasingly, a site of conflict over the definition and legitimation of specific cultural practices: 'Is this music worth spending my money, time, and identity on?' The times are still a-changing, and the beat goes on.

Appendix

The sample for the analysis reported in this article, consisted of newspapers of both the quality and the popular variety in Denmark, (West) Germany, and Great Britain. The sample was purposive, and aimed to tap the range of discursive forms by which music has been covered 1960–2000. The dates of the sample issues were ordinary weekdays, as follows:

- 1960: 4 & 6 October
- 1980: 7 & 9 October
- 2000: 3 & 5 October

(In one instance, for practical reasons the analysis referred to the 4 October 2000 issue in Germany. Since the aim was not to compare particular events across the three countries, this was considered acceptable for the purpose of an exploratory analysis.)

In Germany, *Bild Zeitung* and *Frankfurter Allgemeine Zeitung* were examined for all three years; in the United Kingdom, similarly, the (Daily) *Mirror* and *The Times* were chosen. In Denmark, newspapers were selected so as to reflect the quality and the popular respectively with the highest readership during the year in question: for 1960, *Berlingske Tidende* and *B.T.*; for 1980, *Politiken* and *Ekstra Bladet*; and for 2000, *Morgenavisen Jyllands-Posten* and *Ekstra Bladet*.

References

Bakhtin, M.M. (1981) *The dialogic imagination*, Austin, TX: University of Texas Press.

Beck, U., Giddens, A. & Lash, S. (1994) *Reflexive modernization: Politics, tradition, and aesthetics in the modern social order*, Cambridge: Polity.

Berelson, B. (1952) *Content analysis in communication research*, Glencoe, IL: The Free Press.

Berman, M. (1982) *All that is solid melts into air: The experience of modernity*, London: Verso.

Bolter, J.D. & Grusin, R. (1999) *Remediation: Understanding new media*, Cambridge, MA: MIT Press.

Bourdieu, P. ([1979]1984) *Distinction*, Cambridge, MA: Harvard University Press.

Bull, M. & Back, L. (eds.) (2003) *The auditory culture reader*, Oxford: Berg.

Fish, S. (1979) *Is there a text in this class? The authority of interpretive communities*, Cambridge, MA: Harvard University Press.

Frith, S. & Goodwin, A. (eds.) (1990) *On record*, London and New York: Routledge.

Giddens, A. (1984) *The constitution of society*, Berkeley, CA: University of California Press.

Goehr, L. (1992) *The imaginary museum of musical works: An essay in the philosophy of music*, Oxford: Clarendon.

Gripsrud, J. & Hovden, J.F. (2000) '(Re)producing a cultural elite?' In J. Gripsrud (ed.) *Sociology and aesthetics*, Kristiansand, Norway: Høyskoleforlaget.

Harvey, D. (1989) *The condition of postmodernity*, Oxford: Blackwell.

Huyssen, A. (1986) *After the great divide: Modernism, mass culture, and postmodernism*, London: Macmillan.

Iser, W. (1978) *The act of reading: A theory of aesthetic response*, Baltimore, MD: Johns Hopkins University Press.

Jauss, H.R. (1982) *Toward an aesthetic of reception*, Brighton, UK: Harvester Press.

Jensen, K.B. (2006) 'Sounding the media: An interdisciplinary review and a research agenda for digital sound studies', *Nordicom Review*, 27(2), pp. 7–33.

Kramer, L. (2002) *Musical meaning: Toward a critical history*, Berkeley, CA: University of California Press.

Krippendorff, K. (2004) *Content analysis: An introduction to its methodology* (2nd ed.), Newbury Park, CA: Sage.

Kristeva, J. (1984) *Revolution in poetic language,* New York: Columbia University Press.

Larsen, P. (2002) 'Populærmusikken og de andre musikalske genrer' (Popular music and other musical genres), in J. Gripsrud (ed.) *Populærmusikken i kulturpolitikken,* Oslo, Norway: Norsk Kulturråd.

Leppert, R. (1993) *The sight of sound: Music, representation, and the history of the body,* Berkeley, CA: University of California Press.

McClary, S. (1991) *Feminine endings: Music, gender, and sexuality*, Minneapolis, MI: University of Minnesota Press.

McLuhan, M. (1964) *Understanding media,* New York: McGraw-Hill.

Middleton, R. (1990) *Studying popular music*, Milton Keynes, UK: Open University Press.

Middleton, R. & Manuel, P. (2007) *Popular music,* http: //www.oxfordmusiconline.com. Accessed 10 January 2009.

Neuman, W. R. (2008). 'Interactivity', In W. Donsbach (ed.), *International encyclopedia of communication*, Malden, MA: Blackwell.

Newcomb, H. & Hirsch, P. (1984) 'Television as a cultural forum: Implications for research', in W.D. Rowland & B. Watkins (eds.) *Interpreting television,* Beverly Hills, CA: Sage.

Peterson, R.A., & Kern, R.M. (1996) Changing highbrow taste: From snob to omnivore, *American Sociological Review,* 61(5), pp. 900–7.

Rosenlund, L. (2000) *Social structures and change: Applying Pierre Bourdieu's approach and analytic framework,* Stavanger, Norway: Høgskolen i Stavanger.

Schafer, R.M. (1977) *The tuning of the world*, New York: Alfred A. Knopf.

Slevin, J. (2000) *The internet and society,* Cambridge: Polity Press.

Van Dijk, J. (1999) *The network society,* London: Sage.

Wetherell, M., Taylor, S. & Yates, S. (eds.) (2001) *Discourse theory and practice: A reader,* London: Sage.

Williams, R. (1983) *Keywords,* London: Fontana.

Chapter 13

Celebrity Culture and the Public Sphere: The Tabloidization of Power

Graham Murdock
Loughborough University

1889 saw the publication of a lavish book of photographic portraits entitled, *Our Celebrities*, featuring prominent statesmen, scientists, and literary figures (Hamilton and Hargreaves 2001: 49). At the beginning of 2004, Britain's main commercial television channel, ITV1, broadcast the third series of its hugely popular show, *I'm a Celebrity...Get Me Out of Here*. It featured a group of contemporary celebrities – a former royal reporter, a footballer, an athlete, a disc jockey, two popular singers, a glamour model, Jordan, and a minor aristocrat and convicted fraudster – camped out in the Queensland rain forest and subjected to a series of gruelling and humiliating physical tests. In the French programme, *Celebrity Farm*, a similar group of minor singers, models, actors and television presenters were locked in a remote farmhouse for seventy days without electricity or running water and required to tend to the animals.

These instances point to a decisive shift in the meaning of celebrity, which was first identified in a research paper published in 1944 written, by the German cultural critic, Leo Lowenthal, then in the United States. After analysing the popular biographies printed in a selection of mass market American magazines between 1901 and 1941, he concluded that attention had progressively migrated from 'idols of production' to 'idols of consumption', with 'leading names in the battle for production' – entrepreneurs, scientists, and inventors – disappearing from view to be replaced by 'the headliners of the movies, the ball parks, and the night clubs' (Lowenthal [1944]1961: 115–6). This process accelerated during the post-war years installing these new celebrities at the centre of popular mediated culture. When Graeme Turner and his colleagues analysed celebrity stories in popular magazines and news media in Australia in 1997, they found that 55 per cent focused on figures from the world of entertainment and 15.5 per cent on sports personalities. In stark contrast, only 8.5 per cent featured politicians and only 2 per cent businessmen (Turner, Bonner & Marshall 2000: 18).

Drawing on the corpus of newspapers selected for the longitudinal analysis of change reported in the preface, this paper charts the development of this structure of attention in the British tabloid press and assesses its consequences for the vitality of the political public sphere.

As Lowenthal recognized, contemporary celebrity culture is rooted in the relentless rise of a consumer society in which leisure has displaced work as the major arena for self realization, and the political struggle to universalize decent standards of living is seen as less important than selecting a personal lifestyle. Images of celebrities dramatize the roles available in the theatre of consumption by pitching the spectacular and out-of-reach against the ordinary and mundane. On Wednesday 19 November 2003, the British *Daily Mirror* carried a major story criticizing the lax security at Buckingham Palace. It recounted how one of its journalists had used bogus references to gain employment as a footman and been able to roam almost at will among the Royal apartments taking photographs clandestinely. One double-page spread showed the royal table laid for breakfast revealing that two of the richest people in the world keep their 'cereal in Tupperware boxes', eat their jam from the original screw-cap jars, and listen to the news on a cheap-looking portable radio.

Images of the rich and famous, backstage and off-duty, are central to the contemporary culture of celebrity. They are core components in a new machinery for picturing events and personalities in which shifts in photojournalism have played a key role.

The Collective Photo Album

Printed images of the famous and notable became increasingly available in Europe from the seventeenth century onwards, pinned up in public places and bought to be displayed in private homes (Braudy 1986: 267). The arrival of photography invested them with a new sense of immediacy and veracity. As Susan Sontag points out, 'nonstop imagery (television, streaming video, movies) is our surround, but when it comes to remembering, the photograph has the deeper bite' (Sontag 2003: 22). Photography fixes meaning in a peculiarly powerful way. It combines the uniqueness of the captured moment with the ability to distil the plot of a more general story. Like a campaign slogan, a sound bite, or 'a sentence extracted from a novel' (Kaufmann 1982: 195), the best remembered photographs are both unrepeatable and iconic. They are pasted into a collective photo album offering a storehouse of resonant images subject to instant recall. This assemblage draws on many sources, from advertising imagery to police photographs of crime suspects, but the most frequent deposits are made by photojournalists and newspapers editors. Whatever its past life, once an image enters the news machine it becomes part of the vernacular visual archive through which societies picture their hopes and fears.

The popular Panopticon

At the end of the eighteenth century, the English philosopher, Jeremy Bentham, drew up plans for a new type of prison which he called the Panopticon. He imagined a permanently-lit circle of cells linked to a central watchtower from where the guards could keep watch on the prisoners whenever they wished whilst remaining permanently concealed themselves. No such prison was built in Europe but its principles of looking proved irresistible to the steadily-growing number of state agencies whose expansion paralleled the rise of photography. The official pictures taken of suspects in police stations, inmates in asylums, patients in hospitals, workers in factories and pupils in schools, display the same repetitive pattern of surveillance 'the body isolated; the narrow space; the subjection to an unreturnable gaze; the scrutiny of gestures, faces and features; the clarity of illumination' (Tagg 1988: 85). The powerless had no choice but to subject themselves to the unremitting scrutiny of those in positions of authority.

In contrast, the powerful took pains to ensure that any photographs taken of them showed them in the best possible light. For over eighty years, technology colluded with these efforts at image-engineering. The first generation of cameras were bulky, and required exposure times of between three and twenty seconds. They provided the perfect conditions for the posed portrait.

Innovations in the production of likenesses coincided with advances in popular reproduction and circulation. In 1850, the American photographer Mathew Brady (later to become famous for his Civil War photographs) published the *Gallery of Illustrious Americans,* a volume of lithographic reproductions based on his National Gallery of Daguerrotypes in New York, which, as Doggett's guide to the city noted, featured 'some of the most distinguished men of this country' including the President, members of the Supreme Court and 'many other eminent persons' (Daguerreian Society 2009). Albums of portraits were still relatively expensive, however. Popular ownership of celebrity images became more accessible with the introduction of the compact and free-standing *carte de visite*. The French photographer, Disderi, recognizing the market potential of this new format, launched his *Gallerie des Contemporains* in 1860, offering subscribers a weekly celebrity image and capsule biography for two francs.

The more astute power-holders were also quick to grasp the public relations advantages of circulating engineered images on a mass basis. Abraham Lincoln, was convinced that his 1861 election victory was partly due to the widespread circulation of pocket-sized photographs of himself, printed on visiting cards and depicting him as the embodiment of the new national spirit (Rojek 2001: 126).

Emperors and monarchs had long employed portraits on coins, stamps and banknotes to project a carefully-crafted image of authority. They appeared in profile emphasizing a noble brow, a firm jaw and a resolute gaze, fixed on the far horizon. In contrast, photographic portraits generalized the more familiar style previously reserved for privately-commissioned paintings designed to be hung in domestic interiors. They pictured subjects facing the camera, inviting eye contact with the viewer. The early culture of celebrity, of which Lincoln was part, involved shifts towards both democratization and personalization. Cultural capital was progressively transferred from a hereditary class 'to self-made men and women' (Rojek 2001: 13), and the carefully-measured distance between rulers and subjects gave way to an increasing familiarity. Portraits of traditional power-holders had appeared primarily on tokens whose circulation was controlled by the state. The faces of the new elites began to feature on a proliferating range of consumer goods, from dinner plates to free picture cards in cigarette packets. They were also pictured in more informal settings. At the century's turn, the French firm of Dornac & Cie published a volume of photos showing famous people in their offices, laboratories, and domestic interiors. Entitled *Our Contemporaries at Home*, it marked a further step in domesticating fame. Increasingly, however, traditional power-holders shared the spaces provided by popular imagery with a new kind of celebrity. Lowenthal's heroes of production might have their hands on the levers of political and material power but their command over symbolic life was already uncertain. Ten years before Lincoln's electoral campaign, the impresario Phineas Barnum had used photos of Jenny Lind as an integral part of his publicity offensive promoting the Swedish soprano's American tour. It was a sensation, running to 95 concerts and generating gross revenues of $712,000. From that point on photography became an integral weapon in the armoury of publicity and promotion. With innovations in camera technology, however, control over the terms of public visibility became increasingly contested.

The rise of the indiscreet

Plate cameras reached their apogee in 1924 with the introduction of the compact Ermanox, equipped with one of the fastest lenses in the world, able to shoot indoors in normal light, and with an exposure time of only half a second. As a 1925 advertisement promised, it was 'small, easy to handle, and *not easily seen*' (quoted in Freund 1980: 119 [emphasis added]).

The German photojournalist Erich Salomon took full advantage of this new facility. Starting with candid court scenes of a Colburg murder trial (shot by concealing the camera) he moved on to photograph diplomats, politicians and businessmen as they gathered, out of sight of the public, to talk and dine. The son of a wealthy Berlin family, he would leave his camera unobtrusively in a corner, covered with a hat or hidden in a bag, and mingle with the guests, waiting for exactly the right moment to use the trigger cable he carried with him (see Gidal 1972: 16). In 1928 he gate-crashed the signing of the Kellogg-Briand Pact (an international treaty renouncing war as an instrument of national policy) and took several photos from the vacant seat of the Polish delegate. His attentions were not always welcome. While working in the salon of the French Foreign Ministry on the Quai d'Orsay, he was caught off-guard by the-then Minister, Aristide Briand who exclaimed, 'Ah, there he is, the king of the indiscreet'. The popular press dubbed him the 'Houdini of photography' after the celebrated escapologist. Salomon was at pains to distance himself from any association with entertainment or sensation, preferring to see himself as a scientific observer. He insisted on signing himself 'Dr' on all his prints and, following his early training in zoology, described his work as 'tracking down the true face of personalities' in their natural habitats and 'detailing the exact circumstances in which the photographs were taken' (Artipedia 2008). By 1931 he had enough material to publish a collection entitled *Celebrated Contemporaries in Unguarded Moments*. It included artists and composers, politicians and captains of industry. The composer Richard Strauss jostled for attention with Lloyd George and the media mogul Randolf Hearst. His ability to penetrate the backstage regions of power increased still further in 1932 when he bought a Leica.

Launched in 1924 as a spin off from the Leitz company's newsreel cameras, from which it borrowed its basic technology, its unparalleled portability, flexibility, and unobtrusiveness laid the basis for a new style of photojournalism based on rapid, unobtrusive, shooting on film. The result was a popular Panopticon, which gave the general public snatched glimpses into more and more concealed corners of power. Bentham's watchtowers were no longer perpetually dark. Their personnel were increasing subject to popular scrutiny, caught off-guard. With the introduction of flash bulbs in 1930, the range of candid photography was extended still further.

In 1936, British King Edward VIII refused to end his relationship with the divorced American socialite, Mrs Simpson, and was forced to abdicate from the throne. Two pictures appeared in the press on the day after his radio broadcast to the nation announcing his decision. The first, an officially-sanctioned shot, shows him in profile, sitting upright at his desk facing the microphone. The second, taken by a news photographer waiting outside in the darkness, captures him slumped in the back of the car driving him away from the Palace, possibly for the last time, with his head resting in his hand. The official version is carefully posed to convey dignity under pressure, the 'snatched' shot reveals a man exhausted, defeated, and close to tears.

From that point on, the terms on which powerful figures was publicly visible became the site of a continual contest between efforts to engineer a favourable image and attempts to undercut them. The proliferating apparatus of public relations, photo opportunities, and pseudo-events continually collided with the less-flattering portrayals produced by candid news photography.

Press galleries

The centre of this new style was Germany, and Salomon and the other early practitioners found their outlets in the new generation of weekly magazines that had sprung up to take advantage of photography's new flexibility as a medium for documenting and commenting on social conditions. The highly successful *Berliner Illustrirte Zeitung (BIZ)*, originally launched in 1890, led the way but soon attracted imitators, most notably, the *Munchner Illustrierte Presse*, launched in 1923. With Hitler's rise to power in 1933, and the subsequent clamp-down on the press, however, the impetus for development shifted elsewhere.

In the US, *Life* was founded in 1936 and *Look* in 1937. In 1938 *Picture Post* was launched in London, achieving a print run of 1.35 million within three months. *Match*, the forerunner of *Paris-Match* launched around the same time. The aim of these new photo-based magazines was summed up in the editorial manifesto for the first issue of the French magazine *Vu* (founded in 1928). 'Conceived in a new spirit and executed by new means, *Vu* brings the universality of life to the *eye*...pages packed with photographs translating foreign and domestic political events into images...sensationally illustrated photo-stories' (quoted in Freund 1980: 136).

By the 1920s photographs were also being widely used to illustrate stories and features in the daily newspaper press, following the trail blazed by the entrepreneurial British journalist,

Alfred Harmsworth. In 1903 he decided to launch the *Daily Mirror,* aimed specifically at women. It was a commercial disaster and in 1904 he relaunched it as a picture paper. As he later recalled: 'I filled it full of photographs to see how that would do. It did' (quoted in Edelman 1966: 6). The *Mirror* was the first daily newspaper in the world to be primarily illustrated by photographs and, from the outset, it saw the emerging culture of celebrity as both plural and fluid, with photographs of politicians continually jostling for attention with pictures of actresses, entertainers and criminals.

Others were quick to follow Harmsworth's lead. The *Mirror's* main British rival, the *Daily Sketch,* was launched in 1909. The following year, *Excelsio* was launched in Paris under the slogan 'Faire voir' ('make it visual'). The appearance of these 'sensationally illustrated' titles alarmed many editors of broadsheet dailies.

They saw their role as providing an objective first draft of history together with space for rational debate on issues of the day. Many agreed with the conservative French commentator Gustav Le Bon, who had cautioned in 1895 that the rational deliberation on which mass democracy rested was systematically undermined by the chains of emotional association detonated by visual images, submerging individual opinions in the sea of collective sentiment. Crowds, he argued, are 'only capable of thinking in images, are only to be impressed by images', and can only be appealed to by a 'startling and very clear image, freed from all accessory explanation, or merely having as accompaniment a few marvellous or mysterious facts' (Le Bon [1895]1969: 60–2). This emphasis on dramatic and involving imagery came to be seen as a defining feature of the new 'tabloid' journalism, and marked for many newsmen an unacceptable shift from rational deliberation to sensation. It was for this reason that many editors of Europe's leading daily newspapers used photographs much more sparingly than the new tabloid papers. The London *Times* introduced a picture page in 1922, but refused to run photographs on its front page, as did *Le Monde.* These prohibitions, and the 'type-minded' approach to newspapers that underpinned them (see Hunt 1971: 63), continued until well after the Second World War. The *Times,* for example, only finally discontinued its practice of filling its front page with classified advertisements in 1966. By then, however, the relations between power and visibility had already changed in important ways.

From heroes to celebrities

In his fierce polemic against the rise of staged-managed 'pseudo-events' and photo-opportunities, published in *The Image,* 1962, Daniel Boorstin draws a sharp distinction between heroes and celebrities. Whereas a hero, he argues, is someone 'who has shown greatness in some achievement...the celebrity is a person who is known for his well-knownness' (Boorstin 1963: 59–67). 'The hero created himself [sic]; the celebrity is created by the media. The hero was a big man; the celebrity is a big name...these new role models are nothing but ourselves seen in a magnifying mirror' (ibid: 70).

This shift from a culture of heroism to a culture of celebrity was cemented by the professionalization of promotion and publicity. In 1880, the French actress, Sara Bernhardt openly declared that her main reason for coming to New York was to have herself photographed by the leading portraitist, Napolean Sarony. She was paid $1,500 for the sitting, in return for which Sarony retained the reproduction rights to the images. Bernhardt went on to make the transition from stage to screen, starring in a number of early silent movies, and it was Hollywood in the 1920s and 1930s that pioneered the modern business of publicity.

As the quotation that heads the website of the Garis PR and Media Group points out, in today's entertainment business, 'you're nowhere unless you've got a publicist, and your publicist is nowhere unless he can glom onto a celebrity who uses his services' (Garis PR & Media Group 2009). This symbiotic relation between celebrity and the management of visibility was the key building block for the star system that dominated American sports and entertainment in the years after the First World War. As Richard Schickel has persuasively argued: 'What happened in this period was that the public ceased to insist that there be an obvious correlation between achievement and fame. It was no longer necessary…to perform real-life heroic acts', it was possible to achieve visibility 'in the realms of play-spectator sports, acting…and almost immediately to become a celebrity' known principally for being well-known (Schickel 1973: 7–8).

The rise of television from the mid-1960s onwards played a central role in this redefinition of celebrity. The exponential rise in set ownership and the arrival of the evening's viewing as the dominant leisure activity domesticated public figures in an unprecedented way. It brought them into the intimacy of the sitting room and showed them in close-up. They became, at once, more accessible and more vulnerable, a potential demonstrated to devastating effect in John Freeman's *Face to Face* interviews for the BBC in the late 1950s, when his relentless questioning reduced the comedian Tony Hancock to tears and almost forced the famously tetchy television presenter, Gilbert Harding, to admit his homosexuality at a time when the topic was still unmentionable in public.

This new intimacy was increasingly stage-managed by a new class of cultural go-betweens. The programme hosts, presenters, news readers, weather men and women, and characters in soap operas and comedy series, linked domestic space to the world behind the screen. Where stars kept a certain distance, shielded by body guards and security fences, the imagined space for these new 'media friends' was at the viewer's side 'hanging out together, riding in a car, sharing an adventure' (Meyrowitz 1994: 64).

Television, even in the public service forms that dominated Europe until the 1980s (see Gripsrud, this volume), was also, from the outset, a powerful shop window for the newly-emerging consumer styles. By offering 'a free look at the contents of other people's lives, on demand' (Marling 1994: 5), news film of celebrities, studio sets, and the domestic interiors featured in popular dramas, gave viewers access to a wide range of available market choices and cemented their social associations. Television also had major impacts on the previously-dominant entertainment medium of cinema. Press attention progressively migrated from the big to the small screen while the medium's domestic intimacy altered fans' relations to stars.

Writing at the end of the 1950s, the French sociologist Edgar Morin detected a shift in the image of stardom, away from 'certain divine attributes (proud inaccessible solitude, an unmatched destiny)' and towards 'more familiar attributes (domestic preoccupations, a taste for fried potatoes, love of children)' (Morin 1960: 63). This growing fascination with the backstage regions of stars' lives extended to their personal failures and flaws. Robert Harrison, owner of the highly successful erotic magazines *Wink* and *Flirt*, saw the business potential of this shift and launched *Hollywood Confidential* in 1952 under the slogan 'The Lid is Off'. This, in turn, opened up a market for the more aggressive candid photography, featured in Fellini's 1960 film, *La Dolce Vita*, in which stars' and celebrities' every waking moment, private or public, clothed or naked, was open to scrutiny by the photographer Paparazzo. Although the account is disputed, a number of sources claim that Fellini named his character after a particularly annoying type of mosquito, constantly circling looking for an opportunity to bite, or the warning buzz of the paparazzi's preferred mode of transport, the Lambretta scooter. Whatever the origins of the name, there is general agreement that the character is closely modelled on Tazio Secchiaroli, a Rome-based photographer who specialized in engineering incidents with celebrities, surprising them with a sudden flash image and photographing the ensuing attempt to run or evade being photographed. Fellini's depiction of this more confrontational style struck a chord and its proponents were rapidly dubbed paparazzi, after Secchiaroli's film persona. His own career, however, moved from paparazzo to publicist. In 1964 he became the personal photographer to one of Italy's best-known film actresses, Sophia Loren, and drew on his experience of candid photography to construct a distinctive brand image of the star as earthy and eminently approachable.

Francesco Alberoni, writing in 1962, saw the intensified manipulation of public imagery creating an inverse relation between visibility and power, pointing out that, whilst the 'doings and ways of life' of stars and celebrities generate 'considerable and sometimes even a maximum degree of interest', their 'institutional power is very limited' (Alberoni [1962]1972: 75). In contrast, the key holders of material power, particularly captains of industry, remained largely invisible and, unless they were involved in a scandal, able to control the terms on which they were photographed through the judicious deployment of public relations and image-management. The result, as Leo Lowenthal had argued earlier, was a steady hollowing-out of the culture of democracy as the large issues in the political and economic realm were buried under a flood of material encouraging readers and viewers to immerse themselves 'in the pleasures and discomforts of the great' as played out in the spheres of consumption and domestic life (Lowenthal 1961: 135–6).

Politicians found themselves caught in the crossfire, pushed to reveal more and more about their off-stage personalities and private tastes. The more volatile voting became, the more they were tugged towards the construction of image rather than the performance of conviction, and the more democratic politics was subsumed into celebrity culture. In the process, as Lowenthal had observed, the Hollywood actress 'Greer Garson and Mahatma

Ghandi meet on common ground: the one "likes potatoes and stew" ...the other's "evening meal is simple – a few dates, a little rice, goat's milk'" (ibid: 123).

I want to explore these shifts by looking in more detail at the portrayal of stars, celebrities, politicians, and corporate leaders in popular photojournalism from 1960 to 2000. I will focus particularly on the two major British daily tabloid titles: the *Daily Mirror*, the first paper in the world to base its appeal primarily around its use of photographs, and *The Sun*, owned for most of this period by one of the leading media moguls, Rupert Murdoch, and the most successful daily tabloid in the world.

The stars down to earth: Bardot in bandages, Jordan in tears

By 1960, the countries of Western Europe were moving from the years of post-war reconstruction and austerity towards a mass-consumer society based on rising real incomes. As a consequence, the ideals of collective provision embodied in the institutions of the welfare state were increasingly rubbing up against a new ethos of individualism, which saw the freedom to carve out a personal life style as a sovereign right. This spirit found its most public forms of expression in the proliferating cultures of youth created by the first generation to be born after the War. American popular culture offered readily-available models for this project – James Dean, Elvis Presley, Marilyn Monroe – but the marked asymmetries in the power relations between the US and the countries of Europe produced ambivalence rather than simple admiration and imitation, together with a strong desire for home-grown models of stylish independence and rebellion. Brigitte Bardot met this demand perfectly.

In 1959, France's leading feminist, Simone de Beauvoir, wrote a short book celebrating Bardot's taboo-breaking projection of female sexual autonomy and her refusal to comply with male sexual fantasies. 'Bardot's face' she argues 'has the forthright presence of reality. It is a stumbling-block to lewd fantasies and ethereal dreams...She corners [men] and forces them to be honest with themselves' (de Beauvoir 1962: 34). At the same time, she notes how this challenge has been diffused by publicity presenting BB as 'a lost, pathetic child who needs a guide and protector' (ibid: 22). On Tuesday 4 October 1960, three quarters of the *Daily Mirror*'s front page was taken up by a photograph of Bardot, wearing dark glasses, her hand held up to her face, her bandaged lower arm clearly visible, leaving the French clinic where she had been taken after being found unconscious with cuts to her wrists. The copy, under the headline, 'EXIT THE SAD STAR', points up the stark contrast between screen image and lived reality: 'She is rich. Famous. A star. But cinema "sex kitten" Brigitte Bardot is sick.' Although the photo was unflattering, it was not 'stolen'. Bardot's producer, who was with her, had told photographers that they could take pictures on condition that they did not follow her when she left – a pledge that they kept. The same picture made the front pages of the major tabloid newspapers across Europe, including the German *Bild Zeitung* and the French *Le Parisien*. More surprisingly, it was the only photograph on the front page of the British *Daily Herald* that day.

The *Herald* was a paper solidly rooted in the British Labour Movement. Launched as a strike sheet in 1910, when employers had responded to the London printers' demand for a 48-hour week by locking them out, it had been taken over by the Trades Union Congress (the umbrella body for the union movement) in 1922. By 1960, however, it was in terminal decline, with a rapidly-ageing readership that was proving deeply unattractive to advertisers eager to take maximum advantage of the new consumerism and the emerging youth market. The photograph of Bardot, in the centre of the page, was a concession to the new climate, but it was not enough. In 1964 the TUC sold its 49 per cent shareholding to the major commercial press conglomerate IPC, who re-launched it as *The Sun*. Five years later it was bought by Rupert Murdoch who retained the title, converted it from a broadsheet to a tabloid and immediately launched a bitter circulation war with the *Daily Mirror* (Koss 1990: 1093).

The *Mirror's* daily circulation had reached a peak of over 5.2 million after Labour's election victory in 1966 but, by the time Murdoch acquired *The Sun*, it was already in decline. Like the *Daily Herald* before it, 'the newer, younger generation were gradually disentangling themselves' from both the paper and the party. 'It was a badge they no longer wanted to wear' (Greenslade 2003: 7) and, from the outset, *The Sun* was more in tune with the rising emphasis on materialism and hedonism.

The new *Sun* took the *Mirror's* highly-visual tabloid presentational style a stage further, printing large photos in the centre and at the top of the front page and deploying a range of other hooks for the eye, from variable column widths to white-on-black headlines. The *Mirror's* editor, Hugh Cudlipp, responded by trading on its reputation for campaigning journalism whilst reaching out to a younger readership immersed in the new celebrity culture. As he candidly admitted: 'We barked for the under-dog when he wasn't getting a square deal, but we also groomed him, threw sticks, gave him bones, took him "walkies", and kept him happy with a variety of diets' (Cudlipp 1976: 402). Celebrity stories became a major staple in this dietary mix.

By 1980 both titles were deploying them as major weapons in their battle for readers. Their front pages for Tuesday 7 October both featured prominent items, illustrated with large portrait photographs, announcing that the actress Hattie Jacques had been found dead from a heart attack. Although Jacques had originally made her name in films, only later moving over to television situation comedies, it is as a 'TV funny lady' that the *Mirror* describes her. Television's pivotal role in constructing the new celebrity culture is further signified by the only other front-page photograph that day. Running across the top of the page, promoting a feature on the inside pages, it shows one the best-known television presenters of the time, Angela Rippon, off-duty and dressed informally in sweater and headscarf. It is almost twice as large as the photo of Hattie Jacques. Two days later, the paper's front page is again dominated by a major trailer for an inside story about a television celebrity, the comedy-actor-turned-Hollywood-star Dudley Moore, famous for being both a talented pianist and short in stature. The image, a head-and-shoulders shot of his latest consort, a Californian beauty queen and nightclub singer Susan Anton, shows a young blonde woman tossing back her hair and smiling into the lens. It is captioned: 'SUSAN: Blonde, beautiful and big.' The inside double-page spread is affectionate but acerbic. It ends: 'They finish their coffee and wander off hand in hand, his lost in hers, she leading the gnome superstar. A lovely couple. Or a lovely one and a half.'

By 2000, tabloid coverage had been incorporated into celebrity culture in an even more thoroughgoing way. *The Sun's* front page for Thursday 5 October is dominated by a story about another 'blonde, beautiful and big' personality: the glamour model Katie Price, known as Jordan, who had regularly featured in the paper's famous Page 3 slot, reserved for photographs of topless, well-endowed young women. The story occupies two-thirds of the page. Half of this space is taken up with a photograph of Jordan in a pink bikini. The other half runs a yellow-on-black headline: 'JORDAN: I split with Dane because of Posh' and an inset portrait of the other parties to the dispute. The inside story recounts how Jordan decided to leave her singer boyfriend because of his obsession with Victoria Beckham, a member of the highly successful Spice Girls pop group and nicknamed 'Posh', dwelling on the fact that: 'The 36D blonde...fought back tears as she...admitted that she had hoped they could still work out their problems when they had their final row.' The protagonists are ideal types of the new celebrity culture: a model known only for the size of her breasts, a minor male singer whose brief career was already on the decline, and a female pop star who later became famous for marrying the world's most famous footballer, David Beckham. They belong to what Alberoni identified as 'the fringe' surrounding the more durable inner circle of celebrities. As he notes, they tend to enter and leave 'in a rather fleeting manner' (Alberoni 1972: 85). They are the perfect icons for an age of fast food and channel-surfing.

In contrast, *The Mirror's* front page for the same day is taken up almost entirely by an image of a politician, the Shadow Home Secretary Ann Widdecombe, but, as we shall see later, the way it is constructed points to the political sphere's progressive incorporation into celebrity culture.

Political trials: Gaitskell defeated, Hailsham alone, Doris doped

In 1960 the Labour Party was deeply split over the issue of unilateral nuclear disarmament, with the rank-and-file, supported by the major trade unions, in favour of Britain relinquishing its independent 'deterrent', and the party leader, Hugh Gaitskell, adamantly opposed. Matters came to a head during the defence debate at the Party's annual conference. Gaitskell lost the vote but the *Herald's* edition of Thursday 6 October presented his speech from the podium as a heroic act of conviction and defiance. The front page was dominated by a large photo of him in full rhetorical flight, his right hand raised to shoulder height, fingers spread as if holding back, or quietening, a mob. Under the banner headline 'GREAT GAITSKELL', the lead report drew explicit parallels with Britain's war-time defiance of overwhelming odds, claiming that 'Out of defeat Mr. Hugh Gaitskell has snatched victory – a Dunkirk-type victory.' These connotations were reinforced in the second report, which employed one of Winston Churchill's most famous phrases, hailing the speech as 'Gaitskell's finest hour' in which 'He turned what looked like an exultant triumph for his enemies into the hollowest of paper victories.' Directly to the right of the Gaitskell picture, however, is a photo of two young lovers who had given themselves up after eloping to get married. She is wearing a fashionable coat with a fur collar. He is dressed in a stylish jacket and bootlace tie. They are the ghosts at the celebration, images of a young audience that neither Gaitskell nor the *Herald* could effectively address. The right hand corner of the page carried an advertisement for the 'New Ferguson Golden Glide' television set, housed in a 'superbly styled, super-slim cabinet' and allowing viewers to switch more easily between the BBC's public service channel and the new commercial stations. It caught perfectly the country's move towards a more consumerist culture.

Television also accelerated the personalization of politics. By allowing viewers to see elected representatives close-up, studio interviews fuelled demands 'not just that they be competent at ruling, but that they be authentic human beings as well' (Marquand 2004: 84). On 7 October 1980 the *Daily Mirror* carried a feature article on Lord Hailsham, one of the most unpopular politicians of the post-war years. It was a masterly stage-managed exercise in humanization, depicting him as devastated by his wife's sudden death and left with only his pet dog for company. It opens:

Lord Hailsham of Saint Marylebone, Lord High Chancellor of Great Britain, sits alone in a lofty oak-panelled room overlooking the Thames, nursing a little dog…He loves his work, now more than ever before. It has become his whole life. For his personal, private life was shattered when his wife Mary was killed in a riding accident.

This narrative is anchored by a photograph, taking up a quarter of the page, showing Hailsham, dressed in a formal suit, staring dolefully into the lens and stroking 'the Jack Russell terrier, a gift from his wife many years ago.' It is captioned: 'A MAN ALONE: Lord Hailsham with his dog and his memories.' At first sight it seems odd for a Labour-supporting paper to extend such sympathy to a bastion of the Tory establishment, but the *Mirror* is also a tabloid trading in human interest and this story fitted the format perfectly, with a tag-line worthy of a popular condolence card: 'Grief is the price you pay for love.' The techniques of image management were also being applied more rigorously to the presentation of public political performances.

The 1983 election saw the Labour Party's share of the vote fall to its lowest level since 1918 and entrenched the Conservatives, led by Mrs Thatcher, even more firmly in power. The search began for a Labour leader who could restore the party's fortunes. The *Mirror* threw its weight behind this project. The front page for Tuesday 2 October 1990 was dominated by a celebrity story recounting the bitter dispute between an American soap opera star and her film producer husband over custody of their daughter. But the inside pages carried a double page spread headlined: 'The Young Guns Go for it', reporting the barnstorming performances at the party's annual conference given by three rising stars. It carried two photographs: one, a stock photo opportunity, showed the wife of the then party leader, Neil

Kinnock, opening a new kitchen in a primary school surrounded by children; the other showed a head and shoulders shot of the then employment spokesman, Tony Blair, speaking from the podium, his arm outstretched, his hand open. Behind him, on a black background, the word 'Future' fills the frame.

This image is similar to the earlier photos of Gaitskell speaking. However, the accompanying comment from the *Mirror's* columnist, Alastair Campbell, pointedly reminds his readers of the careful attention to image behind the performance, describing Tony Blair as 'he of the Dallas teeth'. Projecting a positive image on television news had displaced Gaitskell's concern with rhetorical effect. Tony Blair went on to lead the party to a landslide election victory in 1997, and Campbell took on the job of managing his media relations, becoming famous for his attention to image and 'spin'. Both men had grasped that contemporary elections 'are frequently a duel between two photographs' in which 'the candidate tries to find the right picture, the snap which encapsulates his campaign' and 'his opponent hopes for the emergence of the wrong picture, the snap they didn't want on the poster' (Lawson 2004: 21).

The *Mirror*'s double page spread of Thursday 5 October 2000, on the Conservative Party's annual conference, vividly demonstrated this struggle in action. Continuing the tradition of catching power-holders in an off-guard moment, it printed two very unflattering pictures of delegates slumped in their chairs asleep, surrounded by empty bottles and glasses. The message: that party members care more for their own comforts than the public interest and do not deserve to be elected, was underlined by the punning caption: 'PARTY MAN: Delegate is out for the count.' But the full force of the paper's ridicule is reserved for the Shadow Home Secretary, Ann Widdecombe, nick-named 'Doris' because of her supposed resemblance to Boris Karloff, famous for his film portrayal of Frankenstein's monster in the 1931 film.

In a move that drew on the tradition of polemically-altered images pioneered by the socialist photomontage artists of the 1930s, the front page spread attacking her proposal to introduce spot fines for the possession of cannabis is almost entirely taken up with a digitally-engineered image of a cannabis cigarette being smoked, with her face substituted for the ash at the end. It is captioned 'Doris the Dope'. This wording does two things. Firstly, by playing with the double meaning of 'dope' as slang for both cannabis and naivety, it invites readers to dismiss her proposal as hopelessly unworkable. Secondly, by using her given name it moves her from political culture to celebrity culture since, as Clive Scott has noted, whereas 'television personalities, in the tabloids, have an almost exclusively first-name status, with politicians, the opposite is true' (Scott 1999: 112). Widdecombe later did become a television personality when she volunteered to take part in the prime-time programme, *Celebrity Fit Club,* which followed her attempts to lose weight.

Business for pleasure: Captains of consumption

The last three decades have witnessed an unprecedented consolidation of corporate power. Waves of mergers and acquisitions have concentrated economic control in fewer and fewer hands. A revivified neo-liberalism insistently promotes the merits of market forms of organization and celebrates risk-taking and entrepreneurship as the prime motors of prosperity. Yet, in the world of the tabloids, business becomes news only rarely and, when it does, it is likely to be placed in the context of consumption. Attacks on corporate greed and consumption are waged on behalf of consumers rather than citizens or workers. The proliferating pull-out sections devoted to personal finance focus on saving for spending rather than wages or salaries. When business leaders are featured they are more likely to be drawn from the ranks of entrepreneurs working in the cultural and leisure industries. Lowenthal's heroes of production have become heroes of consumption, furnishing opportunities for style and pleasure.

On 3 October 2000, the *Daily Mirror* carried an obituary for Fred Pontin, one of the pioneers of seaside holiday camps in the post-war era. Alongside pictures of a smiling Pontin and holidaymakers enjoying themselves, the text hailed his 'cheap family holidays' for bringing 'joy to millions'. Towards the end of his career, he went on to launch one of the first firms to offer cheap package tours to Mediterranean resorts. The key figure in the development of low cost airfares, Richard Branson, was featured two days later in *The Sun,* in an advertisement promoting his new range of cheap mortgages. Alongside a portrait of Branson, looking decisive but sympathetic, the text points out that the money saved is money released for consumption, an argument enthusiastically endorsed by a satisfied customer, shown holding a copy of the contract and smiling. As she explains, the favourable lending terms 'meant that we could transform the kitchen, add another two bedrooms and build a conservatory'. She is described as a 'Stock Exchange manager' a job that confirms her financial expertise.

The public sphere in the age of celebrity

In 1962 Jurgen Habermas published his enormously influential history of the transformation of those major arenas of debate on matters of state – from spontaneous conversations to public meetings and news media – that together made up what he called the political public sphere. He saw very clearly that these spaces had been increasingly commandeered by consumerism, but insisted that 'the outcome of the struggle' between critical discourse and publicity 'merely staged for manipulative purposes remains open' (Habermas [1962]1991: 235). He has recently returned to this argument in a context where a range of new social movements have pushed traditional political parties to add previously-neglected issues, such as environmental degradation, corporate responsibility and global inequality, to the core agenda for debate and action. Responding to this unexpected development, he now sees the public sphere primarily as a 'warning system' that ferrets out and identifies emerging or neglected problems and dramatizes them 'in such a way that they are taken up and dealt with by parliamentary complexes' (Habermas 1996: 358–9). Struggles over the commercial planting of genetically-engineered crops in Europe provide a good example of this process at work (see Murdock 2004).

At the same time, the rise of celebrity culture charted in this chapter provides a powerful counterforce to this revivification of the public sphere. Firstly, as Alberoni, noted it establishes an inverse relation between visibility and material power. The new heroes of consumption are continuously in the public eye, the major holders of economic power – landowners, bankers, key investors, corporate executives – remain relatively invisible and, with the major exception of frauds and scandals, mostly able to control the terms on which they appear. In an age when corporate power is more central than ever to political decision-making, this erosion of scrutiny seriously disables informed debate on the exercise of power. Secondly, as the market in voter loyalties has become increasing volatile, politicians have had to devote more and more time to building and marketing brand identities. In the process, they have been pulled inexorably onto the terrain of a celebrity culture in which image is more important than accomplishment. The result is a hollowing-out of political debate.

This process has been accelerated by the progressive visualization of popular culture, in which critical reflection is continually undercut by the dominant styles of tabloid representation. Most photographs in tabloid newspapers are closely shot or cropped. There is little or no contextual field of vision. This has the effect of discouraging readers from extrapolating to 'wider issues or questions' and invites them to become 'absorbed by the circumstantial, the seductive detail' that anchors the accompanying story (Scott 1999: 107). Connotation displaces informed argument as the starting point for political reasoning. They see more but understand less.

Immersion and disengagement

As we noted earlier, on 5 October 2000 *The Sun* front page detailed the latest ructions in the romantic life of the glamour model Jordan. Her career was at a low ebb. As a commentator noted later: 'Whenever she went out clubbing, which was often, she'd be papped. Then the pictures would be recycled until her life was reduced to nights of drunken stumblings' (Hattenstone 2008: 27). In an effort to renew her career, in 2004 she agreed to take part in the 'reality' television show, *I'm a Celebrity, Get Me out of Here*, with which we started this paper. It was a turning point. She was very publicly courted by another contestant, Peter Andre, a singer some way past his peak, and was taken on by his management team, who set about remoulding her. She was reinvented under her real name Katie Price. She kept her persona as Jordan but married Andre, became a mother and was launched on a concerted programme of brand-extension. She secured her own reality television show, *Katie and Peter*, centred on family life with her husband and children, promoted three volumes of highly-successful ghost-written autobiography (the first selling more than one million copies) and put her name to a series of best-selling novels written by Rebecca Farnsworth based on her taped ideas. Her official website invites visitors to 'feel free to look around' and take time to familiarize themselves with the full range of her activities.

The concerted merchandizing around Katie Price exemplifies both the increasing ubiquity of celebrity culture and the proliferating opportunities for engagement that it offers. As recent British research has shown very clearly, this invitation to immersion has serious consequences for the vitality of the public sphere. Extensive evidence, drawn from a national survey, personal diaries and interviews, revealed a consistent pattern in which 'those who particularly follow celebrity culture are the least engaged in politics and the least likely to use their social networks to involve themselves in action or discussion about public-type issues' (Couldry and Markham 2007: 403). The greater the immersion in celebrity culture the greater the disengagement from political issues affecting the public interest.

Against the current background of economic crisis, rising unemployment and house repossessions and the return of austerity across the capitalist world, the struggle between the imagery of a consumer-centred celebrity culture and the ideal of a public sphere committed to deliberating on the common good still remains open for now, but for how much longer is a question that merits sustained investigation and debate.

References

Alberoni, Francesco ([1962]1972) 'The powerless "elite": Theory and sociological research on the phenomenon of stars', in Denis McQuail (ed.) *Sociology of mass communications,* Harmondsworth: Penguin Books, pp. 75–98.

Artipedia (2008) *Jeu de Paume presents Erich Salomon: The king of the indiscreet,* http: //artipedia. org/artsnews/exhibitions/2008/11/17/jeu-de-paume-presents-erich-salomon-the-king-of-the-indiscreet/. Accessed 26 August 2009.

Beauvoir, Simone de (1962) *Brigitte Bardot and the Lolita syndrome,* London: The New English Library.

Boorstin, D. (1963) *The image,* London: Harmondsworth: Penguin Books.

Braudy, Leo (1986) *The frenzy of renown: Fame and its discontents,* Oxford: Oxford University Press.

Couldry, Nick & Markham, Tim (2007) 'Celebrity culture and public connection: Bridge or chasm?' *International Journal of Cultural Studies,* Vol 10: 4, pp. 403–21.

Cudlipp, Hugh (1976) *Walking on the water,* London: The Bodley Head.

Daguerreian Society (2009) http: //www.daguerre.org/. Accessed 10 February 2009.

Edelman, Maurice (1966) *The Mirror: A political history,* London: Hamish Hamilton.

Freund, Gisele (1980) *Photography and society,* London: Gordon Fraser.

Garis PR & Media Group (2009) *About Us* http: //www.nationalpublicist.com/id3.html. Accessed 25 August 2009.

Gidal, Tim N. (1972) *Modern photojournalism: Origin and evolution, 1910–1933,* New York: Collier Books.

Greenslade, Roy (2003) 'Happy birthday?' *The Guardian: Media,* 3 November, pp. 6–7.

Habermas, Jurgen ([1962]1991) *The structural transformation of the public sphere: An inquiry into a category of bourgeois society,* Cambridge, Mass: MIT Press.

Habermas, Jurgen (1996) *Between facts and norms: Contributions to a discourse theory of law and democracy,* Cambridge, Mass: MIT Press.

Hamilton, Peter & Roger Hargreaves (2001) *The beautiful and the damned: The creation of identity in nineteenth century photography*, Aldershot: Lund Humphries.

Hattenstone, Simon (2008) 'Who wants to be a billionaire? The making of Katie Price', *The Guardian Weekend*, 22 March, pp. 19–30.

Hunt, Allen (1971) 'Design', in Ken Baynes, Tom Hopkinson, Allen Hunt & Derrick Knight, *Scoop, scandal and strife: A study of photography in newspapers*, London: Lund Humphries, pp. 59–70.

Kaufman, J.C.A. (1982) 'Photographs and history', in T.F. Burrows, S. Armitage & W.E.Tydeman (eds.) *Reading into photography: Selected essays, 1959–1980*, Alberquerque: University of New Mexico Press, pp. 193–200.

Koss, Stephen (1990) *The rise and fall of the political press in Britain*, London: Fontana Press.

Lawson, Mark (2004) 'Bring out your dead', *The Guardian*, 24 April, p. 21.

Le Bon, Gustave [1895] (1969) *The crowd: A study of the popular mind*, New York: Ballantine Books.

Lowenthal, Leo ([1944]1961) 'The triumph of mass idols', in Leo Lowenthal *Literature, popular culture, and society*, Palo Alto: Pacific Books, pp. 109–40.

Marquand, David (2004) *The decline of the public*, Cambridge: Polity Press.

Marling, Karal Ann (1994) *As seen on TV: The visual culture of everyday life in the 1950s*, Cambridge, Mass: Harvard University Press.

Meyrowitz, Joshua (1994) 'The life and death of media friends: New genres of intimacy and mourning', in Susan J. Drucker & Robert S. Cathcart (eds.) *American Heroes in a Media Age*, Cresskill NJ: Hampton Press, pp. 62–81.

Morin, Edgar (1960) *The stars: An account of the star-system in motion pictures*, London: John Calder.

Murdock, Graham (2004) 'Popular representation and post-normal science: The struggle over genetically modified foods', in Sandra Braman (ed.) *Biotechnology and communication: The meta-technologies of information*, Mahwah, NJ: Lawrence Erlbaum Associates, pp. 227–260.

Rojek, Chris (2001) *Celebrity*, London: Reaktion Books.

Schickel, Richard (1973) *His picture in the papers: A speculation on celebrity in America based on the life of Douglas Fairbanks, Sr.*, New York: Charterhouse.

Scott. Clive (1999) *The spoken image: Photography and language*, London: Reaktion Books.

Sontag, Susan (2003) *Regarding the pain of others*, New York: Farrar, Straus and Giroux.

Tagg, John (1988) *The burden of representation: Essays on photographies and histories*, London: Macmillan Education.

Turner, Graeme, Bonner, Frances & Marshal P. David (2000) *Fame games: The production of celebrity in Australia*, Cambridge: University Press.

Appendices

Appendix 1

Four Decades of European Newspapers: Background and Method

Åsa Nilsson & Lennart Weibull
University of Gothenburg

Measuring newspaper contents

The aim of the study is to grasp some general trends in newspaper content in Europe between the years of 1960 and 2000. Hence the title: *A Rudimentary Historical and Comparative Newspaper Analysis, Europe 1960–2000 (RHACNA)*. Twelve countries have participated in the study: Belgium, Czech Republic, Denmark, Finland, France, Germany, Italy, Norway, Poland, Sweden, Turkey, and the UK. The selected number of newspaper titles as well as the number of newspaper issues is limited and the content analysis is principally related to the newspapers' content profile – in terms of volume priority of various editorial sections.

The project has been carried out in cooperation with media researchers in the individual countries. They have selected the newspapers according to the given definitions and provided data on the relevant newspapers. Also the coding of the newspapers has been carried out nationally, however following the common guidelines and under supervision of the coordinating group at the University of Gothenburg.

Selection of newspapers titles

The selection of newspapers has not been based on individual newspaper titles but of the leading newspapers in each country. *Leading* is defined by circulation. However, the type of paper holding the top circulation position might vary considerably between countries. Thus, in order to provide a better basis for comparisons across nations, two different types of papers were chosen from each country: one representing the quality press and one representing the popular press.

The distinction between quality and popular press follows a British tradition – a tradition which is typical also for many other European countries, but not for all. The categories 'quality' and 'popular' are not always mutually exclusive; and the distinction fitted quite poorly in some countries participating in the study (during the whole time period or some part of it), e.g. Czech Republic, France, Italy and Turkey. In these cases, the participating countries have been asked to select the *relatively* most appropriate quality and popular paper respectively. For instance, in Turkey in 1960, the two leading papers *Hürriyet* and *Milliyet* were both classified as prestigious, but would in 1980 both be best described as popular. A similar development can be said to characterize the Czech leading papers chosen for the study, *(Rudé) Právo* and *(Mladá Fronta) DNES*. However, focusing on the relative differences within these countries, *Hürriyet* and *(Rudé) Právo* have, throughout the analysis, been defined as prestigious whereas the other two have been defined as popular. In France and Italy, the distinction between quality and popular papers is, throughout the time period, comparably weak when used on the leading papers; the selected 'popular' papers, *Le Parisien* and *Il Messaggero*, do not differ greatly from *Le Monde* and *Il Corriere della Sera*, at least not when comparing with the British press housing the *The Times* and *The Sun*.

Basing the selection of newspapers on circulation figures at each point of the year implies that the newspapers titles are not necessarily the same throughout the time period (even though this often is the case). The basic idea of the study is to trace the character of the leading paper at each point of time rather than to characterize the changes of certain newspaper titles. However, for the UK, for reasons of access to archives, *The Times* has been chosen throughout the period of analysis, despite the fact that it had not the biggest circulation in 1980.[1] The newspaper titles included for each year/group are presented in Tables A1a and A1b in the Appendix.

Selection of newspaper issues

Three years during the forty-year period have been selected as points of references: 1960, 1980, and 2000. Six of the countries participating in the project expanded their study by also covering the years 1970 and 1990; these countries are Belgium, Czech Republic, Finland, Norway, Sweden, and the UK (the latter only with regard to the popular press).[2] From each selected year, one week of newspaper issues only has been covered by the analysis – the first week of October (Monday–Sunday).[3] The more detailed analysis of newspaper contents is furthermore limited to mainly two days within each week: Tuesday and Thursday. However, all issues during the week were considered when it comes to supplements; and also notes were made of the kinds of section themes occurring in other than the Tuesday and Thursday issues.

Selection of newspaper content

The main purpose of the content analysis has been to briefly characterize the newspapers' content profile by their volume priority of editorial sections. The content analysis is broadly divided into four parts: (1) measurement of volume, including: a) newspaper volume in total; b) volume of various newspaper sections; and c) volume and theme of supplements; (2) listing of other thematic sections (any day of the week) other than those covered by the measure of volume; (3) measurements of story contents in various sections, and of advertising theme in biggest adverts; and (4) a rough measure of visualization in the newspaper, including: (a) counting of all editorial illustrations in the main issue;[4] and (b) marking the occurrence of visuals accompanying the analysed stories (cf. 3).

The newspaper measurement has covered more aspects of the contents than are shown in the analyses presented in this book. For example, the front pages have been analysed both in terms of layout and contents. For coding details, see the code form in Appendix 2.

The main point of departure for the content analysis has been the newspaper sections. The selected sections are Home news; Foreign news; Local news; Economy/Business; Culture; Entertainment/Popular culture; Sports; Health; Consumer material; Leisure material; Family pages; TV/radio; Editorial/opinion/commentary; Debate; Letters to the Editor. Also the volume of general news pages (unsorted news without any headline as to their theme or geographic orientation) was coded, as well as the total volume of any other sections. The volume of each section is measured by the exactitude of 1/4 of a page. Occurring adverts are not included in the volume of any editorial section, but measured separately. Sections smaller than one-eighth of a page are not included.[5]

In the measurements of story content, both aspects of content profile and visualization were considered. In all, four different variables were used in the analysis: 1) geographical focus; 2) main theme/topic; 3) main angle in terms of issues/institutions vs. individuals; and 4) occurrence of illustrations. With regard to economy/business stories, main theme was replaced by main perspective in terms of owners/managers vs. labour relations/trade unions. Not all aspects were applied to all section stories (see code form). When it comes to the selection of stories, the criterion used in the analysis has been the size of the article; thus the Nth biggest stories were selected from each section. In cases of identical volume, the first appearing story was selected. When it comes to home news and foreign news stories, the biggest/first appearing stories were chosen disregarding the kind of section they appeared in: home news section, foreign news section, home and foreign news section in combination or general news section whether organized under a headline or not.[6] Following this procedure, a number of 20 home news stories and 10 foreign news stories were selected. As to other sections, the number of stories has been Economy/Business: 3 stories; Culture: 5; Entertainment/Popular culture: 3; Sports: 3; Editorial/Opinion/Commentary: 2; Debate: 2; and Letters to the Editor: 2.

The validity of the analysis

Given the simplified design of the study; what can be said on the basis of a few days' newspaper content? Obviously, great caution is called for when interpreting the data. However, the focus of the study is set on volume changes and broad content profile, and the indicators used for that kind of analysis are not too dependent on weekly or seasonal changes but reflect potential long-term alterations. The way in which a newspaper gathers and presents its content under various headlines, as well as the share of advertising, are quite stable aspects of newspaper content (cf. Nilsson et al. 2001).

A second validity problem is related to reliability of the measurement. It is almost unavoidable that a comparative undertaking of this kind, based on measurements carried out in individual countries with limited contacts, might involve coding misunderstandings. The Swedish research group at the Department of Journalism and Mass Communication, University of Gothenburg has been in charge of supervision and has attempted to correct failures. Furthermore, only material that has been analysed in the same way has been used in the analyses presented here. This is also the reason why not all countries are included concerning all variables (see above).

Finally, it has to be pointed out that our focus on two weekday issues means that the described tendencies first of all reflect a weekday newspaper, the product of 'weekday journalism', aimed at a weekday reading audience. In order to widen the analysis somewhat we refer also to other occurring themes in sections from the other days of the week, themes that might be included in the newspaper precisely on a weekly basis. The classification of supplements is part of this extension of the analysis in order to be able to say more of one week's newspaper contents from a reader's perspective.

Notes

1. *The Guardian* had by then a bigger circulation, but the difference was small (*The Times*: 316'; *The Guardian* 379') (Seymour-Ure, 1996)
2. The newspaper titles included in this additional analysis covering the years 1970 and 1990 are for most countries the same as the ones selected for 1960, 1980 and 2000 (see Table A1a and A1b); however, for three countries, the titles of the popular newspapers have varied over the years and should thus be listed: Norway 1970 and 1990: *Verdens Gang*; Sweden 1970 and 1990: *Expressen*; UK 1970: *Daily Mirror*; 1990: *The Sun*.
3. The weeks cover the following dates: 1960: 3–9 October; 1970: 5–11 October; 1980: 6–12 October; 1990: 1–7 October; 2000: 2–8 October (the Nth biggest stories (2, 3 or 5) are selected).
4. A reduced national basis for analysis: Finland, Italy, Norway, Sweden, and the UK (the latter only regarding the quality paper).
5. If measurements are correct, the volume of all sections (including the volume of unsorted news, or a 'general news section') plus the volume of advertisements plus that of the front-page should equal the total number of pages. In some cases, i.e. countries, the deviation was considered too big (Belgium; Italy; Turkey); and these countries were for that reason left out of the part of the analysis dealing with the volume relationship between editorial contents and advertisements.
6. The original code form was modified somewhat in this regard; in the original version the selection of news stories was made on the basis of existing types of news section, following the general selection procedure used in the analysis. However, this led to too big a variance in the basis for comparisons between countries, newspapers and years, for which reason the coding was revised to the extent it was possible to adapt to the fact that the analysis included newspapers with different editorial profiles. The countries included in this part of the analysis are Finland, Italy, Norway, Poland, Sweden, Turkey, and the UK (only the prestige paper/*The Times*). In the revision of the coding, Turkey did not include the variable measuring the more detailed geographic focus of stories.

References

Nilsson, Åsa, Severinsson, Ronny, Wadbring, Ingela & Weibull, Lennart (2001) *Trender och traditioner i svensk morgonpress 1987–1999*, Dept. of Journalism and Mass Communication, University of Gothenburg

Seymour-Ure, C. (1996) *The British press and broadcasting since 1945*, Basil Blackwell.

Basic characteristics of selected leading newspapers

Table A1a: Publication city, main geographical ambition, main page format, frequency, and publication time of European quality newspapers 1960, 1980, 2000.

Country	Year	Newspaper	Publication city	Main geographical ambition	Main page format	Frequency	Main publication time
Belgium	1960	De Standaard	Capital	National	Broadsheet	6	Morning
	1980	De Standaard	Capital	National	Broadsheet	6	Morning
	2000	De Standaard	Capital	National	Broadsheet	6	Morning
Czech	1960	Rudé Právo	Capital	National	Broadsheet	6	Morning
Republic	1980	Rudé Právo	Capital	National	Broadsheet	6	Morning
	2000	Právo	Capital	National	Tabloid	6	Morning
Denmark	1960	Berlingske Tidende	Capital	National	Broadsheet	7	Morning
	1980	Politiken	Capital	National	Broadsheet	7	Morning
	2000	Morgenavisen Jyllandsposten	Other city	National	Broadsheet	7	Morning
Finland	1960	Helsingin Sanomat	Capital	National	Broadsheet	7	Morning
	1980	Helsingin Sanomat	Capital	National	Broadsheet	7	Morning
	2000	Helsingin Sanomat	Capital	National	Broadsheet	7	Morning
France	1960	Le Monde	Capital	National	Broadsheet	6	Noon/afternoon
	1980	Le Monde	Capital	National	Broadsheet	6	Noon/afternoon
	2000	Le Monde	Capital	National	Berliner	6	Noon/afternoon
Germany	1960	Frankfurter Allgemeine Zeitung	Other city	National	Broadsheet	6	Morning
	1980	Frankfurter Allgemeine Zeitung	Other city	National	Broadsheet	6	Morning
	2000	Frankfurter Allgemeine Zeitung	Other city	National	Broadsheet	6	Morning
Italy	1960	Il Corriere della Sera	Other city	Regional	Broadsheet	6	Morning
	1980	Il Corriere della Sera	Other city	National	Broadsheet	6	Morning
	2000	Il Corriere della Sera	Other city	National	Broadsheet	7	Morning
Norway	1960	Aftenposten	Capital	National	Broadsheet	6	Morning
	1980	Aftenposten	Capital	National	Broadsheet	6	Morning
	2000	Aftenposten	Capital	National	Broadsheet	7	Morning
Poland	1960	Trybuna Ludu	Capital	National	Broadsheet	6	Morning
	1980	Trybuna Ludu	Capital	National	Broadsheet	6	Morning
	2000	Gazeta Wyborcza	Capital	National	Tabloid	6	Morning
Sweden	1960	Dagens Nyheter	Capital	National	Broadsheet	7	Morning
	1980	Dagens Nyheter	Capital	National	Broadsheet	7	Morning
	2000	Dagens Nyheter	Capital	National	Broadsheet	7	Morning
Turkey	1960	Hürriyet	Other city	National	Broadsheet	7	Morning
	1980	Hürriyet	Other city	National	Broadsheet	7	Morning
	2000	Hürriyet	Other city	National	Broadsheet	7	Morning
United	1960	The Times	Capital	National	Broadsheet	6	Morning
Kingdom	1980	The Times	Capital	National	Broadsheet	6	Morning
	2000	The Times	Capital	National	Broadsheet	6	Morning

Table A1b: Publication city, main geographical ambition, main page format, frequency, and publication time of European popular newspapers 1960, 1980, 2000.

Country	Year	Newspaper	Publication city	Main geographical ambition	Main page format	Frequency format	Main publication time
Belgium	1960	Het Laatste Nieuws	Capital	National	Broadsheet	6	Morning
	1980	Het Laatste Nieuws	Capital	National	Broadsheet	6	Morning
	2000	Het Laatste Nieuws	Capital	National	Broadsheet	6	Morning
Czech Republic	1960	Mladá Fronta DNES	Capital	National	Berliner	6	Morning
	1980	Mladá Fronta DNES	Capital	National	Berliner	6	Morning
	2000	Mladá Fronta DNES	Capital	National	Tabloid	6	Morning
Denmark	1960	B.T.	Capital	National	Tabloid	6	Noon
	1980	Ekstrabladet	Capital	National	Tabloid	6	Noon
	2000	Ekstrabladet	Capital	National	Tabloid	7	Morning/noon
Finland	1960	Ilta-Sanomat	Capital	National	Tabloid	6	Noon/afternoon/ evening
	1980	Ilta-Sanomat	Capital	National	Tabloid	6	Noon/afternoon/ evening
	2000	Ilta-Sanomat	Capital	National	Tabloid	6	Noon/afternoon/ evening
France	1960	Le Parisien	Capital	National	Berliner	6	Morning
	1980	Le Parisien	Capital	National	Berliner	6	Morning
	2000	Le Parisien	Capital	National	Berliner	6	Morning
Germany	1960	Bild-Zeitung	Other city	National	Broadsheet	6	Morning
	1980	Bild-Zeitung	Other city	National	Broadsheet	6	Morning
	2000	Bild-Zeitung	Other city	National	Broadsheet	6	Morning
Italy	1960	Il Messaggero	Capital	National	Broadsheet	6	*
	1980	Il Messaggero	Capital	National	Broadsheet	6	*
	2000	Il Messaggero	Capital	National	Broadsheet	7	Morning
Norway	1960	Dagbladet	Capital	National	Broadsheet	6	Noon/afternoon/ evening
	1980	Verdens Gang	Capital	National	Tabloid	6	Morning
	2000	Verdens Gang	Capital	National	Tabloid	7	Morning
Poland	1960	Express Wieczorny	Capital	National	Broadsheet	6	Noon/afternoon/ evening
	1980	Express Wieczorny	Capital	National	Broadsheet	6	Noon/afternoon/ evening
	2000	Super Express	Capital	National	Tabloid	6	Morning
Sweden	1960	Expressen	Capital	National	Tabloid	7	Noon/afternoon/ evening
	1980	Expressen	Capital	National	Tabloid	7	Noon/afternoon
	2000	Aftonbladet	Capital	National	Tabloid	7	Noon/afternoon
Turkey	1960	Milliyet	Other city	National	Broadsheet	7	Morning
	1980	Milliyet	Other city	National	Broadsheet	7	Morning
	2000	Milliyet	Other city	National	Broadsheet	7	Morning
United Kingdom	1960	Daily Mirror	Capital	National	Tabloid	6	Morning
	1980	The Sun	Capital	National	Tabloid	6	Morning
	2000	The Sun	Capital	National	Tabloid	6	Morning

Note: * Missing data.

Appendix 2

RHACNA: Code Form

I   Identification & Background Data

Country	(name)
Newspaper	(title)
Year	(1960; 1970; 1980; 1990; 2000)
Periodicity (no. of issues per week)	1–7
Circulation	(per 1000 issues)

Political leaning

1   Right-wing
2   Liberal
3   Socialist
4   Independent
9   Other

Main distribution form

1   Subscription
2   Single copies sale

Page format

1   Broad sheet
2   Berliner (approx. 2/3 of broad sheet)
3   Tabloid
9   Other

Newspaper profile

1   Prestige
2   Popular

Main geographical ambition

1   National
2   Local

Market situation

1   Monopoly
2   Competition

Publication time

1   Morning
2   Afternoon/evening

Publication city

1   Capital
2   Other city

National penetration: Share of circulation outside city of publication

(per cent)

Price: Annual subscription	(local currency)
Price: Single copy	(local currency)

II   Newspaper Contents: Day 1 (Tuesday)

Volume
Total number of pages (supplements excluded)   (pages)

Front page
Five top stories – by measure of volume and order (1st biggest, etc.) – are identified and scored in terms of different aspects of their contents.

1st–5th story: **Geographical focus**

1 Local/regional
2 National
3 Europe
4 Russia (European part included)
5 North America (US and Canada)
6 South America
7 Africa
8 Middle East
9 Asia
10 Australia/New Zealand/Oceania
11 International (i.e. focus on international relations, not on any specific country)
15 Not applicable (i.e. no country specific focus at all)

1st–5th story: **Main angle**

1 Issues/institutions
2 Persons/individuals
3 Other/not applicable

1st–5th story: **Illustration**

1 Photograph in black and white
2 Photograph in colour
3 Other illustration (e g. drawing, graphics)
4 Both photo and other illustration
9 No illustration

1st–5th story: **Main theme**

1 Accidents or disaster
2 Crime
3 Politics
4 Economy
5 Sports
6 High culture
7 Popular culture/show-biz/celebrities
8 Human interest
9 Peculiar/bizarre incidents/people
99 Other theme

Editorial sections/departments

Identify and, if existing with editorial heading, estimate the volume of each section/departments below, by ¼ pages (adverts excluded). Round the estimation to nearest quarter figure. Sections of less than 1/8 of a page are not included. 'General news' refers to unsorted news with no informative headline as to its national or international focus. The sum of all sections (including General news, Other editorial sections and Advertisements) should equal total number of pages minus one (the front page).

   Top stories – by measure of volume and order (1st biggest, etc.) – are identified in certain sections and scored in terms of different aspects of their contents. Use code 0 consistently for 'no section'. *Note:* The top 10 home news stories and the top 5 foreign news stories are chosen disregarding in which section they are found (including no specific section).

General news (headlined section or not)   (pages)

Main geographic focus of general news contents   1   Home news
                                                       2   Foreign news
                                                       9   Other/mix
                                                       0   Not applicable (no general news)

Home news   (pages)

Foreign news   (pages)

Home news stories
1st–10th Home news story: **Geographical focus**
1st–10th Home news story: **Main angle**
1st–10th Home news story: **Illustration**
1st–10th Home news story: **Main theme**

Foreign news stories
1st–5th Foreign news story: **Geographical focus**
1st–5th Foreign news story: **Main angle**
1st–5th Foreign news story: **Illustration**
1st–5th Foreign news story: **Main theme**

Local news   (pages)

Economy/business (stock exchange listings included)   (pages)
1st–3rd story: **Geographical focus**
1st–3rd story: **Main angle**
1st–3rd story: **Illustration**
1st–3rd story: **Main perspective**   1   Owners/managers
                                                       2   Labour relations/trade unions
                                                       9   Not applicable

Culture   (pages)
1st–5th story: **Geographical focus**
1st–5th story: **Main angle**
1st–5th story: **Illustration**
1st–5th story: **Main topic**

   1 Literature
   2 Visual arts
   3 Theatre, dance/ballet
   4 Cinema
   5 Classical music
   6 Popular music
   7 Television
   8 Radio
   9 Other media
  99 Not applicable

Entertainment / Popular culture   (pages)
1st–3rd story: **Geographical focus**
1st–3rd story: **Main angle**
1st–3rd story: **Illustration**
1st–3rd story: **Main topic**

Sports (listings of game results, lottery etc. included)   (pages)
1st–3rd story: **Geographical focus**
1st–3rd story: **Main angle**
1st–3rd story: **Illustration**

Health   (pages)

Consumer material (e g. travel, motor, fashion etc.)   (pages in total)

Leisure material   (pages)
(departments. including e g. cross words, horoscope, competitions, comic strips)

Family pages (social news, anniversaries etc.)   (pages)

TV/radio   (pages)

Editorial/opinion/commentary   (pages)
1st–2nd story: **Geographical focus**
1st–2nd story: **Main angle**
1st–2nd story: **Illustration**

Debate   (pages)
1st–2nd story: **Geographical focus**
1st–2nd story: **Main angle**
1st–2nd story: **Illustration**

Letters to the Editor	(pages)
1st–2nd story: **Geographical focus**	
1st–2nd story: **Main angle**	
1st–2nd story: **Illustration**	

Other Editorial Sections	(pages in total)

Advertising (including classifieds) (pages)

1st–7th biggest advert: **Theme**

1 Consumer products (e g. coffee, beers and general supermarket goods)
2 Fashion/clothing
3 Household goods (e g. furniture)
4 Media technology (e g. TV sets, video, mobile phones)
5 Capital products (e g. cars)
6 Services (e g. banks, insurances)
9 Other

Visuals
Total number of visuals in editorial sections (supplements excluded)

III Newspaper Contents: Day 2 (Thursday)

Repeat Day 1

IV Additional Editorial Sections – Any Day of the Week

Other occurring editorial sections in main edition (in any issue of the week)

E g. Feature; Weather; Housing/property/real estate; Auto/traffic; Environment; Health/medical; Travel; Media; Computer/high tech/IT; Education, Science; Law; Religion/philosophy; Consumer; Cooking/Food; Fashion; Children's/Youth's Pages (addressed to children/young people); Senior citizens' page (addressed to elderly); Women's Pages (addressed to women)

LIST: ....

V Supplements

Number of weekly supplements throughout the week

Supplement 1–7: Main theme

1	TV/radio
2	Entertainment
3	Leisure/week-end reading
4	Sports
5	Housing/property/real estate
6	Auto
7	Computer/high tech/IT
8	Travel
9	Fashion/clothing
10	Media
11	Science
12	Education
13	Law
14	Religion/philosophy
15	Environment
16	Health/medicine
17	Cooking/food
18	Consumer advice
19	Family
20	Feature portrait
21	Children/youth (addressed to…)
22	Senior (addressed to…)
23	Women
99	Other theme, LIST: ………………

Supplement 1–7: Day of publication

Supplement 1–7: Number of pages

Supplement 1–7: Page format

Editorial sections in supplement; LIST: …….

Other than weekly supplements; LIST main theme: …….

Index